£4
10/10

Brian Taylor was born in Darlington. After attending London, Göttingen, and Durham universities, he travelled widely in Europe. On his return to England he taught for ten years and then, in 1969, went to Canada. For the past fifteen years he has taught in rural Alberta, where he lives with his wife and three sons.

Born and raised in western Canada, Larry Harris was educated at the University of Alberta and the London School of Economics, and has travelled to more than sixty countries. For the past seventeen years he has taught in the Arctic and in rural Alberta. He is married with three sons.

After the events recounted in this book, Hans Nütt worked for British Intelligence until 1948, when it became clear that the Russians knew his identity. He continued 'on the boat' in West Germany until 1953, when he emigrated to Canada. He now lives in Edmonton, Alberta, and is the only member of the Canadian Legion to have originally fought for the Germans during the war.

HANS NÜTT WITH LARRY HARRIS AND BRIAN TAYLOR

Escape to Honour

The gripping true story of Hans Nütt, a young
German who escaped from the Nazis to join
the French Resistance and work as a British spy

GRAFTON BOOKS

A Division of the Collins Publishing Group

LONDON GLASGOW
TORONTO SYDNEY AUCKLAND

Grafton Books
A Division of the Collins Publishing Group
8 Grafton Street, London W1X 3LA

Published by Grafton Books 1987

First published in Great Britain by
Robert Hale Ltd 1985

Copyright © Larry Harris and Brian Taylor 1984

ISBN 0-586-07002-8

Printed and bound in Great Britain by
Collins, Glasgow

Set in Times

*Dedicated to free men everywhere
who refuse to bow to tyranny*

This book was written from the recollections of Hans Nütt about thirty-five years after the events described. Except for some inevitable errors in minor details, it is all true. A few names and descriptions have been altered to protect certain individuals.

Contents

Foreword

On June 23, 1933, my father shot himself. The alternative
the Nazis gave him was imprisonment in a concentration
camp. I was not yet eleven years old, but now I knew
what Hitler and his Nazis were capable of.

Adolf Hitler had become Chancellor of Germany on
January 30. He moved swiftly to consolidate his power.
On February 24 he claimed the Communists were plotting
to overthrow him and ordered a Nazi raid on Communist
Party headquarters. On the twenty-eighth, the govern-
ments of all the Länder (provinces) were dissolved and
replaced by Nazi Gauleiters with dictatorial powers.

Trade unions ceased to exist in anything but name on
May 2. Their officers were beaten and sent to concen-
tration camps. Hitler's next step was to ban the Socialist
Party on June 22. And finally, three weeks after my
father's death, Hitler proclaimed the Nazi Party was
Germany's only political party.

In less than six months, every vestige of democracy
disappeared from Germany.

PART ONE
Escape

1

At about four-thirty in the afternoon a squall of snow blew in rapidly from the north. The bitterly cold wind, driving the snow all around us, gave me my chance to escape.

I had just dropped my two railroad ties and was trotting back towards the pile for another load when I noticed the guard there climb down and take shelter on the south side of the pile, leaving a blind area beyond the stack of railroad ties which he could not see. The other guards huddled in their shelters; the Scharführer, or head guard, was somewhere behind me, near the line of rail cars.

With sudden clarity I realized that this was my opportunity. With a little luck I could cover the hundred yards to the hedge before the other guards noticed and started firing. My decision was made in a split second. I knew the work in the Strafgruppe would kill me just as surely as if I had been sentenced to death by firing squad. I had to escape, I had to. Without further thought I kicked off my wooden shoes and sprinted for the hedge.

My only thought was to run. I was beyond fear, oblivious to the stinging pellets of snow or the bone-chilling wind or the hard ground bruising and cutting my feet.

A hundred yards to the hedge. No shots. No shouts of alarm yet.

Run, Hans, run! I ran like hell. Better to die an almost free man than a degraded prisoner in a concentration camp.

Run! No looking back. No thoughts. Run!

Fifty yards to the hedge. Twenty. Silence except for my rasping breath. Still no shooting.

The hedge close now. Willows, four or five feet high. Run!

A desperate plunge into the leafless branches that spring at me, trying to hold me back. A push and I am through the hedge.

They must have noticed. Some guard must be raising his pistol. Work must have stopped, the prisoners watching, the guards alert now, the Scharführer screaming orders.

I kept on running, panting, fear drumming in my brain. Run. Run to live. Keep moving. Run.

Shots. Remembering my infantry basic training of a couple of years ago, I began to run an irregular pattern as the firing began. Bullets whined past. Some hit the ground near me.

I was beyond logical thought. I felt no fear of being hit. My wish to be alive and free had been translated into a single, simple command in my brain: Run! Run!

There were many shots, but I realized after a few seconds that they were poor marksmen with Mauser rifles and Lüger 9 mm pistols. In any case, the pistols were designed for close combat, not long-range shooting. But if they had taken better aim with their rifles, my escape would have ended then in a snow-flecked field of frozen mud.

Run! Zigzag.

No sensation of my body at all. No feeling of exhaustion. Everything was emotion, and the emotion said, 'Flee!'

Shots. Zigzag. Run. Flee. Shots.

I stumbled making a turn, recovered quickly, and ran

on. No desire to rest. One thought only: get away, escape the guards, be free of the SS.

I glanced back over my shoulder. Three figures in the murk, but one was clearly the Scharführer. He would show no mercy; there was no giving up now. He was mean, brutal, sadistic; he would kill me immediately. I ran faster, imagining his stocky figure behind me, the dark hair plastered back with sweat and sleet, the brutal features animated by his desire to maim and kill and enjoy the sufferings of others.

Run! Zigzag.

A ditch ahead, full of water. Drainage ditch, ten or twelve feet wide. I jumped but didn't clear it. Bone-chilling water up to my chin. Half stumbling, half swimming, I reached the far side, pulled myself clear, rolled over and over to avoid presenting a slow-moving target, scrambled to my feet, ran.

Rational thought began to return. That ditch, I couldn't see SS men in their heavy uniforms and polished boots jumping into that water. A surge of hope, the ditch will halt them, frustrate them. Keep running and you are free; you will have a head start on them.

Grass underfoot now. Easier on the feet but slippery. Run joyfully. Glance over your shoulder.

The Scharführer and the two guards jumped into the ditch.

I almost stopped running in disbelief. They didn't hesitate, just plunged in and pressed on through the water, holding their pistols above their heads. They must have discarded their cumbersome rifles along the way.

A few seconds to run straight ahead in safety without zigzagging. Renewed fear, a new surge of adrenalin. Then zigzagging again, conscious now of the feel of the grass under my feet, cold, slippery, moist. The snow stinging on my face and chest, the wind icy yet welcome because I am so hot from running.

Why did they keep up the chase? Would the Scharführer and the guards be punished for allowing a prisoner to escape? Perhaps guard duty at Börgermoor-Emsland K-Lager was an easy job for an SS man. Perhaps, if they didn't catch me, they would be transferred to the Eastern Front. To Stalingrad perhaps, where according to the camp rumours, a terrible and bloody battle was in progress.

Eastern Front, Eastern Front. My feet pounded out the rhythm. Emotion overtook me again for a while. Fear speeded my steps. Fear and hate, because I now had an added motive to escape: get the Scharführer to the Russian Front to die in the snow at Stalingrad. A small revenge for my brother Willy's death in Russia.

Another ditch. Again the shock of the icy water. Out the other side into another grass field. Run, zigzag, don't slacken the pace.

Only an occasional shot now. They intend to wear me down, run me into the ground until I lie exhausted at their feet. Then the Scharführer's boot, mud on its polished leather, turning me over so I can see him smile as he raises his pistol and . . .

I needed no encouragement to run. I was beyond pain, beyond exhaustion. Field after field. Grass fields, ploughed fields, acres of bare earth. I kept running, my pursuers kept after me. Water-filled ditches, hedges to plunge through, unheeding.

A rhythm established. The pace a little slower now perhaps, but glances over my shoulder told me the distance was widening between my three pursuers and me. I had to keep going, to widen the distance until they could no longer see me and would finally give up.

As I ran I began to think. My chance to escape had arisen by pure chance, not according to any plan. Now it was time to make a plan, to make sure that I stayed free. I continued running at a steady pace, taking time to glance around me.

The snow, which had turned to sleet, then to rain, had stopped. The sky was a murky mass which melded into the mists of that unending flat plain. There were no forests in which to hide, but the sky was steadily growing darker, the hedges in the distance becoming less distinct. It would soon be completely dark and the Strafgruppe, the punishment group, would have to be escorted back to camp. My pursuers would realize this; perhaps they would give up and return to the work party to make sure no other prisoners took advantage of the darkness to escape.

But they came on steadily.

Thank God they don't have dogs, I told myself, for then I would not stand a chance. In any case they can't follow me too long. There will come a time when they will have to give up and return. I had to make sure my will to escape was greater than their will to catch me. My life depended on my escape; if captured I would be shot immediately. Certainly their future would be affected by the success or failure of their pursuit, but not as directly or immediately as mine.

My chest began to ache, my legs felt wobbly, no longer part of me. I willed myself to keep running, to plunge through each hedge and suppress the desire to stop for a breather. It was no longer necessary to run in a zigzag because they were too far behind to have any chance of hitting me. They were aware of that and no longer bothered to fire, saving their bullets for a time when I would be close enough to present a reasonable target.

It was almost completely dark now. How long had I

been running? From the growing darkness I guessed it must be after eight o'clock. I had been running for almost four hours, by my reckoning. I tried to remember if I had ever run for that long before. Never, and certainly never at such sustained speed. My body, weakened by imprisonment and poor food which had reduced my weight by about sixty pounds, wanted to quit, told me to lie down and rest, to hide behind a hedge and hope they would fail to see me. But my brain said 'Run,' and only will-power kept me moving – a shambling, gaunt skeleton, barefoot in a concentration camp uniform.

As I ran, I wondered if I had crossed from Germany into Holland. I tried to calculate. The place where we were working was some ten miles west of the Börgermoor-Emsland camp and so was close to the Dutch border. I had run for about four hours, but at what speed? At six miles per hour I would have covered some twenty-four miles. That meant I had to be in Holland now.

Twenty-four miles? I couldn't believe it. That was almost the distance of a marathon, and I had run that distance cross-country in bare feet. I was prepared to run as far again if necessary. I went over my calculations again. There seemed to be no mistake. There also seemed to be no end to the succession of fields, hedges, and ditches.

My pursuers were now at least a quarter of a mile behind me but showed no signs of giving up. They were darker figures against a dark-grey background, only just visible. I hoped I was becoming harder for them to see.

I plodded on, propelled solely by will-power, my heart hammering at every step, until I was sure it had to burst. Let it burst if necessary; better to die an almost free man than be a prisoner again, if only for the few seconds it took the Scharführer to raise his gun.

I seemed to be a creature of mind and will only, unaware of my body. My mind began to recite refrains in time to the pumping of my legs. 'Almost free, almost free, almost free.' 'In Holland now, in Holland now.' 'Soon be dark.' 'Soon be free.' 'Head west, head west.' Near euphoria, for the first time in months I experienced hope, the hope of being free of the diabolical machine that my homeland had become under the Nazis. What did it matter now that I was a bag of bones, a moving skeleton with bursting heart and aching limbs? I was out of Germany and on my way to freedom.

Ahead of me, a shape different from the others loomed up in the growing darkness. At first I thought it was just a clump of trees, a small wood, but as I drew nearer I saw it was a brick farmhouse and outbuildings surrounded by a high hedge. They were the first buildings, the first sign of human settlement, I had seen since my escape. I headed slightly to the left to pass them.

A glance over my shoulder confirmed that the Scharführer and the two guards were still in sight, so I knew I was still visible to them. I had to act now in such a way that my pursuers would be left in doubt whether I had continued running or had stopped to hide at the farm. I skirted the hedge around and behind the farm buildings. I was now out of sight of the three SS men.

I knew I had to hide somewhere on the farm. In spite of the exaltation of escaping, my legs would not carry me much farther; I had to rest. The farm might offer hiding places, and I must choose one quickly.

I cut back through the hedge and looked around. Brick house, barn attached, all doors closed against the cold night, a couple of tool sheds, and a large, open hay shed with a tin roof three-quarters full of straw bales. The shed filled with straw seemed the best bet. All the other places were too small and even a cursory search would reveal my hiding place.

Bending low in case anybody was watching, I scurried over to the hay barn. I pulled some bales of straw out until I had made a hole big enough to hide in. Reaching out from my hiding place I pulled the bales I had pushed away back into place. I could look out through a small gap between them. To make sure I couldn't be seen easily, I pulled a few handfuls of straw loose and filled most of the gap with them, so that I had only a narrow slit to see through.

It was warm in the straw bales, almost suffocatingly hot. I felt the steam rising from my body and tried to control my rasping, panting breath. I was terrified that the steam rising from my overheated body or the harsh sound of my breathing would give me away. I began to regret taking shelter; it would have been better to keep on running, leaving my pursuers to waste time searching the farm and its outbuildings.

But it was too late now. I heard the boots of the three SS men scraping on the cobblestone yard as they arrived at the farm.

I forced myself to breathe quietly, to inhale silently and to expel the breath over five seconds, counting silently to discipline my desire to suck fresh air into my aching lungs. My whole body trembled, but from exertion, not fear. I was calm about my future now; either I would escape safely or I would die an almost free man, but not a prisoner, not an abject and dishonoured slave of dictators and their minions.

For several minutes nothing happened. Then I heard the SS men ordering the farmer and his family out into the yard. I craned my neck to see better. There were two men in their late thirties or early forties. I could not tell which one was the owner; the other one would probably be his brother. The woman, about the same age as the men, would be the farmer's wife. Two teenage boys, lanky and gawky, completed the group. They were all dressed in everyday working clothes.

It was almost dark, yet I could see the look of terror on their faces as the SS men lined them up against the wall of their home. They probably thought they were about to be shot. The guards stood facing them, their pistols at the ready. The Scharführer looked at each of them intently for a second before speaking.

'Where is he? Where is our prisoner?'

'We don't understand. What prisoner?' one of the men said. He looked at the others. They shook their heads.

Then I realized that the man had answered in Dutch. The Scharführer asked his questions in German, but the answers were given in Dutch. I experienced a tremendous feeling of elation. I really had escaped from Germany and I felt that my luck would hold.

'Are you sure? No prisoner in the trousers with yellow stripes?'

'No, sir. We haven't seen him.'

'Any strangers at all?

'No, sir. I swear it.'

'You realize what will happen to you if we find him here?'

Somebody must have nodded, for I didn't hear the answer, if any.

'You will be shot immediately, you know that.'

'I swear it, there has been nobody.'

'This man we are seeking is an enemy of the Great German Reich. We must catch him.' He turned to one of his subordinates. 'You, keep an eye on these people.' To the other, 'You, come with me, we'll search the house.'

They were gone no more than five minutes, but it seemed like an eternity. When they emerged, the Scharführer was cursing. He placed his hands on his hips and looked around. 'Back in the kitchen!' he ordered. 'Sit down and don't move!'

The Dutch family moved silently back into their home. The Scharführer looked around the yard. 'You two, search those sheds. Don't neglect any hiding place. If you find him, shoot him at once!' He pulled his own gun from the holster on his belt. 'I'll look around the yard.'

Pistol in hand, he paced around the farmyard. Time after time his gaze returned to the hay shed with its piled bales of straw. I could have sworn he was looking straight at me, toying with me as if he knew exactly where I was, and challenging me to make a run for it.

I tried to breathe silently, but nothing could quell the terrible pounding of my heart. One of my leg muscles went into cramp and I gritted my teeth, terrified of moving for fear of betraying my position.

The Scharführer passed out of sight to the left, but I could hear him rooting around in the straw. I heard him muttering angrily to himself and knew he was in an even uglier mood than usual. I willed myself to remain motionless and held my breath, half closing my eyes for fear they would betray me to him. My heart pounded so loudly that I was certain the Scharführer must hear it. He moved a few bales at first, then contented himself with poking his hand in between the bales. I shrank as far back as I could in my hiding place. Silence for a second. Then a rustle as his hand pushed into my hiding place. I could have reached out and shaken hands with him. I saw the dirt on his fingers from the chase through mud and ditches before he withdrew his hand. Through the gap he left I saw his eyes glinting with fury before he turned and moved further along the stack.

A couple of minutes later the other SS men reported they had found nothing. The three of them were standing only ten feet away from me, just beyond the range of my peephole. The whole search of the farm had taken about twenty minutes.

'The bastard must have gone straight past here without stopping,' the Scharführer said, thinking aloud. 'Never mind, he won't be free long. They never are.'

Their boots scraped on the cobblestones. The Scharführer yelled angrily in the kitchen door, 'Remember, if you harbour enemies of the Reich, you will be shot.'

I waited for five minutes, making myself count up to three hundred before I moved.

My first act as a free man was to drop my trousers and void my dysentery-riddled bowels to ease the pain in my abdomen. I had been scared of doing it before then because I was convinced the smell would give me away.

A few feet further along the stack I burrowed out a new resting place and flopped down wearily into the soft straw. My limbs ached, my bowels felt tangled with the dysentery, my stomach rumbled and growled with hunger, and my feet were on fire from running so long without shoes. But I was happy. I had escaped from the camp at Börgermoor-Emsland; I was a free man and I could now make my own decisions. I fell into a watchful, half-sleeping state.

Some sixty minutes later I awoke, smelly, and itching from the lice bites. My stomach cried out with hunger, but I had a greater need than food.

Lying on my bunk in the camp, when planning what to do if I escaped, I had soon recognized that a change of clothing was essential. The yellow stripes on my trousers

were meant to be conspicuous and identify the wearer as
a prisoner. I looked down at them. In spite of the mud
they had picked up during my flight, the yellow stripes
still stood out, even in the near-darkness of the farmyard.

I could do nothing about my hair except get a cap to
wear until I could get a decent haircut, but my trousers
had to be changed. I crept stealthily around the sheds in
the farmyard. There were rakes, spades, hoes, horse
harness, parts of bicycles, anything but the pile of old
clothes I had hoped to find. There was nothing for it; I
would have to risk approaching the house.

Looking around me carefully, I crept over to the wall
of the house and edged towards the uncurtained kitchen
window. I risked a glance inside.

The five members of the family were sitting around the
kitchen table, talking. A poor household, I realized at
once. The table was plain deal but well scrubbed. An
electric-light bulb, unshaded, hung from a cord in the
centre of the ceiling and barely served to illuminate
the room, which was some twelve or fifteen feet square.
The cupboards were also plain and unpainted, the floor
was of earthenware tile. I asked myself what right I had
to inflict myself on this family and cause them further
misery, but my desperation was greater than any moral
scruples. I moved away from the window and rapped at
the door.

Silence for a moment. Then, 'Come in.'

I pushed back the door and entered.

All five of them looked up inquiringly. Their
expressions turned immediately to terror.

'Oh, God have mercy on us!' wailed the woman.

The rest sat silently but their dismay was obvious. The
woman clasped and unclasped her hands; the rest of the

family was shaking with fear. They did not have to be told who I was.

'Clothes. I need clothes.' I was unintentionally brusque, being just as nervous as they were, but my voice must have sounded full of violence.

'No, we can't give you anything,' said one of the men, his voice quivering with fear.

'I must have different clothes.'

'I'm sorry. We can't give you any.'

The woman clasped her hands in supplication. 'Please, please leave our property. Please leave. If the SS come back we'll all be shot.' She looked ready to break down completely.

I felt sorry for them but my position was desperate. 'Can you spare me any food?'

The woman went to the corner of the room and came back with a bowl of still-warm milk. 'Here, drink this. I'll make you some sandwiches.'

I drank the milk down greedily, noisily. The sandwiches had cold meat in them. I devoured them sitting at the table while the family cowered beside me in silence. It was the best meal I had eaten in months and I tore at the dark bread and the meat. I must have looked like a crazy wild animal to the family and must have smelled even worse.

Nobody spoke while I drank a second bowl of milk. They were right to be afraid; I understood their position. There was no doubt at all the SS would shoot them if they were caught helping me. I glanced at the children. Both boys were shaking worse that the three adults. They were terrified and close to tears. Except for the woman, nobody spoke, but their eyes followed all my movements. I could read in their eyes the single terrified question, 'When will he leave?'

If they had wanted they could have overpowered me
easily and handed me back to the SS, but they chose not
to. Perhaps they hated the SS more than they feared my
presence, or perhaps they were too overcome by shock to
think rationally. Whatever their reason, they did nothing
to detain me.

'Thank you very much.' I stood up from the table. 'I'll
go now.' The woman made an unsuccessful attempt to
smile; from the others came an audible sigh of relief in
unison.

Outside, the sky was clear and frosty. The cold earth
bit my bare feet, but I hardly felt it. I experienced a
powerful surge of emotion. I was free, even though my
choices were limited. I felt I had a name again, an
identity. I was Hans Nütt once more, not number 810. I
had eaten meat like a free man again. For the moment it
hardly seemed to matter that I was still dressed in the
prison uniform with glaring yellow stripes on the trousers,
or that I had no shoes, or that my outlandish haircut
immediately identified me as an escapee. None of that
was important; being free was all that mattered, and I
resolved to stay free and find a place where a man could
live honourably.

I looked at the stars. The knowledge of navigation I
had gained on the *Wega* gave me my direction. I headed
due west, away from the concentration camp, away from
my homeland.

The natural temptation to try to reach home and visit my
mother and my brother was great, but I put it aside. I
ordered myself to keep going west. I had thought of this
in camp while waiting for a chance to escape. I knew the
first act of the Gestapo would be to interrogate my family
and friends and watch for me in the area of my home.

From what I had read and heard, about ninety per cent of escapees and deserters were recaptured at the homes of friends and relatives. My mother and my brother Alfred would soon know I had escaped because the local Gestapo would be sniffing around as soon as they received the news I had run for it. I prayed my mother would understand that if she heard nothing I was still at large. It might be years before I could contact her again.

I pushed through the tall hedge surrounding the farm and set off once more across fields and ditches and through the occasional hedge. I walked at a steady pace, not running, because I felt confident the family at the farm would say nothing. If the news ever got out that they had helped me in any way, they knew the SS would take them and shoot them. I thought that perhaps I had been stupid to gamble with my life like that, but I had been desperate and it had paid off. It was hard not to whistle and sing as I walked.

For about three hours I kept heading due west at a steady pace. I was soon completely soaked again from crossing the drainage ditches. My sodden clothes clung to me in the frosty air but there was no way of drying them. The countryside was an endless succession of fields, meadows and ditches; my feet grew sore, then numb from the cold. I had to make frequent stops because of the diarrhoea from my dysentery. Yet, in spite of everything, the optimism I had felt earlier when I left the farm never left me.

I was only a few yards away from a high hedge before I realized that I had come upon another farm. Everything was in total darkness. I stopped and held my breath, listening. I was afraid of setting a dog barking, but all was still. Cautiously, I pushed through the hedge.

If I had not been sure of my navigation, I would have

sworn I had walked in a circle and returned to the first farm. In the darkness it appeared to be a complete replica. There were the same trees for shelter, the brick farmhouse, the same small sheds, and the large hay shed. I crept over to the shed and started to tunnel into the bales. A soft clucking noise broke the silence and I froze before I realized that a hen was sitting in the straw. I reached out, stroked her, and slid my hand under her warm chest. My groping hand found two eggs. Gently I eased them out, cracked the shells, and poured the raw eggs down my throat. In my half-starved condition it was a feast, and I went to sleep contentedly in the straw, oblivious of my soaking clothes, which soon began to steam and reek.

2

That morning in June 1933 my mother helped me dress quickly. My two older brothers, Willy and Alfred, were already waiting downstairs.

'Boys, you will have to be brave. Your father is dead and we are on our own now.' She held me tight, but I saw their faces and started weeping again. 'There, Hansi, Hansi, calm down,' she crooned, then looked at Willy and Alfred. 'You boys will have to be strong and help me.'

They nodded, too full of grief to say a word.

'You must also be careful,' she continued. 'Your father died because he was against the Nazis, and now people will be watching us. We must be careful what we say and what we do. Do you understand?'

Alfred and Willy mumbled, 'Yes, Mutti', and I nodded too, even though I was not completely sure what she meant. My father was dead because of the Nazis, but the rest was beyond my comprehension. I could not understand why anybody would want my father dead.

Hermann Nütt had been a coppersmith in his younger days, and we lived in Hamburg then before moving to our village near by where he had inherited some land and a house. As a member of the Socialist Party of Germany my father took part in what he always called 'The Revolution of 1918', the period at the very end of the First World War when it was apparent the war was lost. Troops and sailors mutinied, and the government of the Reich was handed over to the Social Democrat deputies. They were the men who signed the Armistice. They also became the victims of those who could not accept that Germany had lost the war.

The myth created by the Nazis and other nationalists was that Germany had never been defeated on the battlefield. They said her troops had fought gallantly under inspired military leadership and would eventually have won an overwhelming victory had it not been for the gang of 'traitors' who took over the government and surrendered to the enemy. The myth explained why Social Democrats were pursued with such vehemence by the Nazis and why, fifteen years later, my father was to take a gun and shoot himself rather than be taken to a concentration camp.

My father loved the sea and we spent many hours walking on the shore and on the banks of the Elbe estuary. We watched the ships come and go from the busy port of Hamburg. I saw the wind ruffle his sandy, thinning hair around the collar of the old white fisherman's sweater he always wore on our hikes. I saw his straight jaw and the deeper blue of his eyes when he laughed and threw food for the gulls.

From him I gained my enduring love for the sea and my ambition to be a ship's captain, an ambition later events would make impossible.

'You'll have to spend a year on a ship like that,' he told me one day, pointing at a four-masted windjammer gliding majestically down the estuary, bound for romantic places like Australia or South America.

'Why, Vati?' I asked, thrilled at the idea of climbing the tall masts and unfurling acres of canvas.

'If you want to be a ship's captain, you have to go to

navigation school, and they'll only accept men who've spent a year on a sailing ship.'

Except for my father's prominence in the Socialist Party, we were like the majority of the families in the area. I had a happy, normal childhood. I played soccer with the other boys, fished in the streams and rivers, helped a little with the farmwork and the garden, and collected stamps, butterflies, and coins.

We did not seem to be hurt too badly by the Depression. If we were in difficult circumstances, then so was everybody else. My family found the five marks a month to send us three brothers to modest boarding schools, and we were never short of food, although we had to be careful with our clothes.

My parents were strict but just, and tried to bring us up in the traditional values of honesty and loyalty and love of our country. We were Lutherans and attended church regularly. Many times I wanted to skip Sunday school and have an afternoon free wandering through the fields or playing with other boys whose parents were not as strict as mine. But I dared not play truant. Every Sunday afternoon, on my return from Sunday School, I had to show my parents proof of my attendance.

Religious instruction at school was also compulsory and occupied the first hour of every school day. Many times I envied the two boys in my class who were excused; one was a Roman Catholic, the other a Jew. I wish I were a Catholic or a Jew, I often thought to myself, then I could be free.

I was no different from my friends, or so I thought. Only the Nazis made people different. We all played with Herbert Rosenberg, not aware that he was to be different because he was Jewish. Herbert, so brilliant at mathematics that his Nazi maths teacher couldn't bring himself to despise him because of his race.

I remember few details of the rise to power of the Nazis. My father spent an increasing amount of time away from home. He was a full-time party organizer, having given up farming a couple of years previously, and had to attend numerous meetings. I suppose he was under growing pressure from the Nazis and their Sturmabteilung, the Brownshirts, but he said nothing of it to us boys. For months before his death in 1933, he did not sleep well; even a boy of my age could detect the strain and anxiety on his face. At night he often came home late after meetings, and several times I noticed him talking seriously to my mother in tones too low for us boys to hear.

But I did hear talk of Konzertlager (concert camps), and knew they were not places where people went to play violins and make music together. People were so terrified that they could not bring themselves to say their real title of Konzentrationslager – concentration camps. My father knew their real purpose, and when the Nazi thugs visited him and made it clear he was on the list to be sent away, he knew he would be worse than dead in a concentration camp. Also, he could not live with the thought of being tortured into betraying his friends

The atmosphere at school became harsher. My teachers were mostly former army officers who had been given a short course in teaching methods. This course taught them little, for they employed the same disciplinary methods as in the military. Because of this strict regime, I never felt free or happy at school with its atmosphere of perpetual fear. Canings and beatings were the standard response to any breach of discipline.

On Saturdays we had normal lessons, the same classes as on the other five schooldays. There was only one way out, as we found when one of the teachers addressed us at the end of a history lesson.

'If you want to get away from your studies on Saturdays, you must join the Hitler Youth. Then you are free.' He turned on his heel as if he were still on the parade ground and marched stiffly from the classroom. I couldn't tell if he was encouraging us or not.

I had been a Pfadfinder, or Boy Scout, until the Nazis closed down that movement and substituted the Hitlerjugend, or Hitler Youth. Now I was faced with a choice: sit in a classroom and study French verbs and German history or be outside in the fresh air hiking and camping and doing all those things a boy delights in. My friends turned to each other.

'I'm joining. I sure as hell don't want to go to school on Saturdays.'

'Me too. Anything to get outside.'

'You bet. I don't want to spend any more time with old Hugenberg than is absolutely necessary. You'd be crazy to do that.'

'What about you, Nütt?'

'I'll think about it,' I replied, knowing already that I would never join anything tainted with the name of Hitler.

The next Saturday morning I found I was not alone. A little under half my class had decided not to join the Hitler Youth. Some, I knew, did not relish the exertion; others were like me perhaps and wanted to avoid involvement in a Nazi organization. I am positive nobody joined out of a sense of loyalty to the Führer. The lure of hiking and camping rather than any ideological reasons drew them to the Hitler Youth. And not many schoolboys could resist the temptation to be free of their books for the day. I do not know how successful the Nazi propaganda in

the youth movement was, although I am sure that the
Nazis used the Hitler Youth to prepare boys to be future
soldiers for Germany. But none of us thought of that at
the time.

There was no way of knowing each other's reasons.
We had learned to be careful. There were many things
we kept quiet about and did not discuss, even with our
friends. Nobody knew who might be in league with the
Nazis and reporting on a circle of acquaintances. My
mother had repeatedly warned us to be careful and I
began to understand her reasons better as events
unfolded.

My father had known he was on the Nazi blacklist and
all of us in the family now felt that we were being
watched. Only a few months after his death, we were
harshly reminded. Although the Nazis had banned any
political parties except their own NSDAP (National
Socialist German Worker's Party), this did not mean
political activity came to an abrupt halt. My eldest brother
Willy had attended secret meetings of the Social Demo-
cratic Party ever since the decree of June 22. On his way
home from a meeting he was stopped by several of
Hitler's Brownshirts and beaten up so severely that he
nearly died. It did not pay to be a known opponent of the
Nazis.

Not being a member of the Hitler Youth, I had to
remain at my studies every Saturday. I worked hard and
made rapid progress, particularly in foreign languages. I
became reasonably fluent in English, Dutch, and French
as well as in Danish, the language of my ancestors in
Schleswig-Holstein before it became a part of Germany
in 1866. I was not to know how vital the knowledge of
these other languages would prove later; I merely thought
they would be useful when I became a sailor.

I already wanted to meet people of other nationalities and find out about their way of life. I read whatever books, magazines, and newspapers I could obtain and wondered whether what I read and heard was true. Dr Goebbels was in charge of propaganda and he did an efficient job. All the media slanted their news to support the Nazi party line. I tried to warn myself that what I read or heard was saturated with Nazi propaganda, but it nevertheless came as a shock to me later to find out how much was not true.

Except for holidays with my family, the boarding school was my home for six years, until, in the summer of 1938, at the age of fifteen, I left to become a ship's boy on a sailing ship, the first step towards achieving my ambition.

During those six years Hitler's Nazi Party strengthened its hold on Germany and set in train the events that would lead to the Second World War. I dared talk about the events of that time only with members of my immediate family when I was on holiday from the boarding school. We heard with terrified fascination of the 'Night of the Long Knives' when Hitler murdered Brownshirt leaders who threatened his leadership. About four hundred people were murdered that night; we were never told the exact number.

That was only the beginning. The SS, fanatically loyal to Hitler, was strengthened under the leadership of Heinrich Himmler, and the black uniforms became a familiar sight in the streets of Germany. The German Army was also brought under Nazi control, and every soldier swore an oath of personal loyalty to the Führer when he became President as well as Chancellor upon von Hindenburg's death on August 2, 1934. Hitler was now not only head of state but more ominously, Supreme Commander of the German Armed Forces.

Soon afterwards Germany began rearming openly. In 1935 the official existence of the Luftwaffe was announced. In 1936 the Rhineland was reoccupied by German troops in direct contravention of the Treaty of Versailles. Hitler was gambling that France and Britain would take no military countermeasures against him. He was correct in his assumption, and the world missed a chance to be rid of the Nazi gangsters.

There were also events closer to home whose effects we noted at first hand.

We had been accustomed to seeing the occasional gypsy caravan rumble through our village, to have gypsy fortune-tellers knock at the door. Now they called no more. We heard they had been rounded up, and we did not have to be told what had happened to them. We concealed our horror and tried to lead normal lives.

Other people disappeared too. We saw no more beggars or cripples; the harmless insane who had never needed to be put in an institution were now taken away. Families with a history of epilepsy, insanity, or other inherited diseases received orders to report at a certain hospital at a given time. They were sterilized to help in the purification of the Führer's master race.

I remember Herr Krüger, one of our neighbours, telling me he would jump out of a window or hang himself if they sent for him. There was a history of epilepsy generations back in his family, and he was terrified that this 'crime' would come to light.

We feared too for the Jews we knew. In spite of Nazi exhortations to boycott Jewish businesses, my mother continued to shop at Rosenberg's clothing store, but some of our neighbours were frightened into shopping elsewhere. Herbert Rosenberg, my classmate, was deprived of his German citizenship in September 1935. Jews were no longer permitted to be German citizens and were forbidden to enter into 'mixed marriages'.

It was no wonder my anti-Nazi feelings grew, but, like many others, I deluded myself that the nightmare would soon be over. Besides, I kept asking myself, what could a ship's boy not yet sixteen do about it all? There seemed to be no effective opposition to Hitler and the Nazis. The Führer kept holding plebiscites and elections and winning ninety-nine per cent of the popular vote.

So it was with mixed feelings that I left home in the fall of 1938 to join the sailing ship *Wega* as a cabin boy. On board her decks I would be able for a while to leave the growing problems of Germany behind me and throw myself into a brief and exciting period as a sailor.

On board ship I felt free for the first time since my father's death. I had escaped the growing paranoia of the German people as the Nazis strengthened their hold on every aspect of daily life, and I gradually lost my fear that the Gestapo would come for me in the middle of the night or that a gang of SS bullies would beat me up.

When the *Wega* reached port at Frederikshavn near the northern tip of Denmark, I could scarcely contain my excitement as I looked forward expectantly to making my first landfall in a foreign port. Impatiently I prepared and served supper. The crew seemed to take their time about eating, prolonging my torture of anticipation, but at last they had all finished, and I cleared the galley faster than ever.

Once on shore, I wandered the streets of the small port, happy to be on foreign soil. The people in the streets seemed jovial and relaxed, very different from the now tense and mistrustful Germans. Even the air felt different, and I strolled along revelling in my sense of freedom.

In a café, drinking a beer, I got into conversation with some Danish teenagers. They were patient with my efforts to speak Danish, which language I hadn't practised for some time, and we managed to understand each other well enough. They were refreshingly candid in their opinions, completely unafraid to speak their minds. Again I made the comparison with life in Germany and envied these young Danes.

I have often wondered why I did not take one of the many chances I had to leave Germany during that year by jumping ship in a free port. Taking that step would have meant abandoning my family as well as my homeland – and Germany was still the homeland I loved. I felt German through and through and, in so far as I understood politics at all, I must have shared the view of those to whom Hitler and his gang were a temporary aberration. Whatever the reasons, I made no attempt to flee, a decision that I would bitterly regret later.

My life now fell into a routine as our ship criss-crossed the Baltic and the North Sea. We called at ports in Sweden, Norway, Belgium, Denmark, Holland, France, England, and Scotland. In every port I met free people unafraid to speak their minds. Yet my happiness was often clouded by news of world events. It became more apparent that Germany was preparing its forces for a fight. In a letter from home I learned that my two older brothers had been drafted into the army for infantry training. War was creeping closer, and I wondered what my role in it would be.

I had little opportunity to gauge the feelings of people in Germany, for we had only one call at a German port all year. The *Wega* was laid up for a few days for repairs, and I was allowed to go home for three days. I found my mother apprehensive about the turn events were taking. I could not blame her. She had already lost her husband, her two older sons were now in the army, and her remaining child was fast approaching military age. But she tried to hide these worries from me, forcing herself to adopt an air of cheerfulness, and spoiled me by cooking all my favourite dishes and generally fussing around her 'sea captain son'. While I was home I talked with some of my former school friends. They were all reluctant to express any opinions of a political nature, seeming cautious and fearful.

It was with an air of relief that I boarded the train for Hamburg to rejoin the *Wega* and experience once more the freedom of the open sea. I felt the sea could unleash no greater violence or destruction than that which threatened my homeland at the hands of the Nazis. But my respite was short-lived. At the beginning of August 1939, when I was not yet seventeen, our ship was recalled to Hamburg.

The port was crowded when we arrived. It appeared to me that all German merchant vessels had been ordered back to their home ports. To my dismay, I was paid off and the discharge was entered in my book. The captain told me I might be recalled to the *Wega* but he doubted it. I didn't need to ask his reasons; they were apparent to anyone who read the newspapers or listened to the radio.

3

August 1939 was a month of almost unbearable tension. Everybody talked of war. The radio carried more propaganda and martial music than before, as Dr Goebbels worked to prepare our minds for the struggle ahead. My mother broke with her custom and kept the radio on all day. She appeared calm, yet she must have been under terrible strain knowing that two of her three sons were in the infantry and would certainly be involved in any conflict.

Throughout that month, Germany repeatedly provoked Poland. Time after time, military detachments were sent across the frontier to attack such places as customs posts in the hope of forcing the Poles to retaliate, thus giving Germany an excuse to claim aggression and start a full-scale war.

In the first half of this month of tension, my brother Alfred came home on a short leave, and we had the last real laugh that we would enjoy for years. The day before his return to his regiment, the two of us went to the local inn for a few drinks, silently fearing that we might never see each other again.

The atmosphere was not improved by the arrival of an SS man in full uniform. He sat at a table near us, careful to keep his back straight and his chin thrust forward. He must have sensed our distaste for him, for he leaned over toward us and called out loudly, 'A toast to Germany!'

Alfred and I raised our glasses and murmured, 'To Germany!', in our hearts toasting the Germany my father believed in and not the home of the master race so dear to our drinking companion.

The SS man smiled and moved to our table. Alfred glanced at me and shrugged, his glance warning me not to do anything to cause trouble. People at the other tables turned away, and most soon made excuses to leave, while the SS man ordered round after round of drinks.

Eventually the three of us were the only customers left. The SS man's face was flushed and sweating, and kept running his finger round inside his collar with its lightning-bolt insignia. Alfred winked. I grinned back. Our 'protector' was too drunk to notice. Alfred winked at me again and got up, under the pretext of going to the toilet. But I noticed that he went in the other direction and left the inn, to reappear a few minutes later, still smiling broadly.

Our SS man, now unable to stand unassisted, kept trying to sing snatches of the Nazi 'Horst Wessel Song', but by this time he was too drunk to remember the words.

'Time for some fresh air, old comrade,' Alfred said to him jovially.

The SS man tried to rise. Alfred put an arm around his shoulders, I took the other side, and we helped him outside, where we propped him against the wall of the inn.

'Lets's just straighten out your uniform,' Alfred suggested. 'Can't have a member of the SS appear untidy in public, can we?'

''S right.'

Alfred grinned as he pulled a shoe brush and a can of black shoe polish from his jacket pocket. He began by tidying the SS man's uniform a little, then opened the can of polish.

Making laudatory comments about the beautiful black SS uniform, he started to apply the shoe polish to the SS man's hands and face. I held his head up straight, while Alfred made sure every square inch of exposed skin was covered. The SS man giggled the whole time. Although I had downed quite a few drinks, I was apprehensive, as we were in broad view of anybody passing by. But Alfred worked on steadily and methodically, until finally our SS man, black from head to toe, staggered away down the village street, singing snatches of his Nazi marching song: '. . . with firm step and sure . . .' Alfred and I doubled up with hysterical laughter, then locked arms and walked home.

Many people in the village must have known what we had done, but nobody reported us, and we were never punished for our prank. Alfred went back to his regiment, and the march toward war continued.

I was at the house of an old friend of the family on September 1 when the news broke. Just before noon the music program on the radio halted abruptly, and a special news bulletin told us Poland had been invaded.

There was silence for a few moments, while we digested what we had just heard. I thought of Willy and Alfred involved in the invasion; they were both in the same division. I prayed they would survive. Among other people I found a feeling of apprehensive excitement; the waiting was over; now matters would be solved by action – one way or the other.

Two days later, on September 3, 1939, Great Britain declared war on Germany, followed a few hours later by France.

'A war on two fronts,' some said and shook their heads.

'The Führer will cope, you'll see,' said the more optimistic.

Rationing began with the outbreak of war. The distribution of bread, butter, and meat was strictly controlled. There was enough bread, but meat was soon in short supply. Clothing coupons were issued, and new footwear was almost unobtainable. Soap too became very valuable, and what was on sale was gritty with pumice-stone.

There was discontent among those who had opposed Hitler, but its expression was muted by fear of the SS and the Gestapo. People were now forced to work longer hours, and income tax, already high, was increased. A blackout was imposed for fear of air raids.

But the Führer's early successes made the majority of people take an optimistic view at first. During only five crowded months in 1940, German forces invaded and conquered Denmark, Norway, Holland, Belgium, and Luxembourg. In only three weeks in June, France was brought to her knees and forced to surrender. It seemed that Adolf Hitler's armies were invincible.

My brothers fought in Holland and France and survived. Then without warning, they were transferred back to Poland in the fall of 1940. One day I was talking to a Polish worker on a nearby farm. He showed me a letter from home and said his family were astonished by the huge numbers of German troops in the area, more even than during the Battle of Poland.

'My God,' I said, 'there has to be a reason for this. Why are they shipping so many German troops to Poland?'

The Pole looked at me and rubbed his nose. 'Can't you guess?'

'Russia?'

'Sure, Hitler is going to attack Russia.'

I was aghast. 'He wouldn't be so stupid.'

The Pole grinned again, maliciously. 'He's a greater soldier than Napoleon, isn't he? That's what everyone says.'

To me, the situation was nothing to grin about. Attacks on Russia could never succeed for long. There would always be early successes while the Russians fell back into the limitless expanses of their country, but then, when their enemies over-stretched their lines of communication, the Russians would descend on them in massive hordes. It had happened to Napoleon, and I could see it happening again. I didn't care if Hitler was defeated, but I had two brothers in Poland, part of the invasion force. I thought of Napoleon's retreat from Moscow and prayed that Willy and Alfred could somehow escape the debacle I felt was inevitable.

A few days later I received my call-up papers. My year's experience on the sailing ship had been taken into account and, a month before my eighteenth birthday, on October 1, 1940, I became a member of the German Navy.

I expected and hoped to be sent immediately on board a ship, any ship, but I was disappointed. For the first eight weeks I marched with the other seamen up and down the parade square. Left turn, right turn, halt, march, form fours, until Seemann Hans Nütt knew as much about drill as did his brothers in Poland. Marching drill was followed by combat training. I learned the mysteries of the rifle, the bayonet, and the hand grenade so thoroughly that I began to wonder if this was not all a deception and I would wake up one morning to find my seaman's uniform replaced by the infantryman's field-grey battledress.

But in January 1941 I was at last assigned to a ship. With a light heart I joined an armed merchant cruiser, formerly of the Hamburg–South America line. The ship lay at anchor at Gdynia and was crowded with sailors and infantry soldiers. I saw this as another indication that some military action was contemplated in the East.

After only a few days I was transferred ashore for a special course on submarine detection, using a form of asdic or sonar, and then was transferred yet again, this time to the battleship *Schleswig-Holstein*. I was to spend six months on this huge vessel.

The captain of the *Schleswig-Holstein* was a Kapitän IIC. Under him was a Korvettenkapitän and a score of Kapitän-Leutnants, Oberleutnants, and Leutnants, every one of them imbued with the strict traditions of the German Navy. This group of stern and immaculately uniformed officers never mentioned politics. It was well known that the old officer class of all the German Armed Forces spoke of Hitler in a mocking tone as 'the Corporal', a reference to the rank the Führer had held in the First World War. The officer class as a whole detested the idea of Hitler as Supreme Commander of the Armed Forces, but, in spite of their resentment, they were careful to refrain from openly criticizing him. They tried to convince themselves that, as officers, they were above politics; there was no Nazi salute in the armed forces until after the attempted assassination of Hitler on July 20, 1944.

There was little discussion of politics by either officers or crew, the majority of whom did not appear to be Nazis or to show any great enthusiasm for our beloved Führer. For myself, I did not feel an excess of patriotic fervour and simply could not see Germany winning the war, because of the severe lack of vital supplies, especially ammunition and food. Germany was short of resources compared with the British Empire, not to mention Russia, which, we knew, would soon be our foe.

The fear I felt was that experienced by the great majority of the German population. We looked to the east and were afraid. We knew we would have to fight the Russian hordes some day, and silently we asked the terrifying question, 'What if the Russians win and we are invaded by the Soviets?' This fear was never allayed by Nazi propaganda; in fact, it was intensified by the effect of BBC broadcasts and the leaflets dropped on German cities. People know that what they were receiving was Allied propaganda, but they could see the facts on which the propaganda was based, and were inclined to believe them.

What the war involved was brought home to me dramatically and sickeningly when I had been on the *Schleswig-Holstein* only a few weeks. We docked at Kiel early in the morning after a fast run from Gdynia. The city looked beautiful in the morning sunshine and, with my shipmates, I looked forward to a shore pass for the next few evenings. But as we docked close to the battle-ship *Gneisenau,* we noticed recent air-raid damage in the area. Wisps of smoke rose from newly extinguished fires, and I smelt smoke in the air.

'All right, fall in, you lot. Don't stand around gawking.' The leading seaman in charge of our squad was usually firm but friendly. This morning there was an unaccustomed hard edge to his voice. We waited impatiently for further instructions, speculating on the possibilities. Any job would be better than painting, we thought.

We were wrong. Our squad and several others were marched briskly ashore under the command of a Leut-nant, along several of the quays until we approached the enormous bulk of the *Gneisenau*. On deck, we were lined up for the Leutnant to speak to us.

'Men,' he began, 'there was an air-raid here last night. Most of the bombers were beaten off by our air defences. Unfortunately some got through, and the *Gneisenau* sustained a hit in the bows.' He paused and looked at us hard. He was only a few years older than me. 'One bomb pierced the armour plating and exploded below decks. We have the task of cleaning up the mess. It will not be pleasant work.'

I glanced around. There was little sign of damage. Far forward, near the bow, shipyard workers were working with acetylene torches in small groups, doing something to the deck plating. There was a heavy, oily smell in the air which I did not associate with acetylene torches.

We were ordered below and started to move forward through a succession of enormously thick steel bulkheads, bending our heads to get through some of the low doorways. The strange smell grew steadily stronger; it seemed to be a mixture of bunker oil and cooking oil. We began to see patches of scorched paint on the steel walls.

I shall never forget the scene of horror when the Leutnant ordered us into the forward compartment. The bomb had exploded below the deck where there were oil bunkers next to some crew's quarters. The oil had burned and boiled, flooding into the crew's quarters and killing them all. Our job was to remove the remains of over a hundred sailors deep-fried in boiling oil. Each corpse was only three feet long. That scene was more awful than any spectre in my worst nightmares.

'My God, I'm glad that's over,' one of my shipmates gasped as we left the bow compartments, retching after finishing our grisly duty.

I nodded, afraid to speak for fear of my voice rising into screams of horror.

We were led back to our ship and ordered into the showers after dumping our reeking work uniforms into large metal tubs. Nobody tried to hurry us out as we soaped ourselves repeatedly, trying to wash away the stench of the charnel-house on the *Gneisenau*.

When we left the showers and dried ourselves, we found a brand new uniform waiting for each man. We were a silent, older group as we made our way back to our mess deck. Most of us could eat no lunch that day. In the afternoon we were given rigorous physical training, ordered to run around and around the deck until we felt ready to drop, then forced through a series of violent exercises. I believe it was a deliberate plan to tire us out, so that we would be able to get to sleep that night.

Aching in every muscle, I set up my hammock as soon as the table and benches were hoisted away after supper. I soon fell asleep, but during the night the dreams came. I was on the *Gneisenau* again, carrying out the cooked and terribly shrivelled bodies of fellow sailors. Several times I woke up wondering if I had screamed in my sleep, but all was quiet around me. That morning's events were never mentioned again, although I suspect that many of my crewmates had similar nightmares for several weeks afterward. We were all conscious that the same fate might await us on board the *Schleswig-Holstein*.

In mid-June, while we cruised on blockade duty in the Oresund beween Denmark and Sweden, all shore leave was cancelled and we were put on full alert. It was obvious that something big was happening, and our speculation was heightened. On June 22, 1941, we listened to the ship's loudspeakers as Dr Goebbels spoke on the radio to announce the invasion of Russia, which had begun at four that morning. He pleaded the now familiar excuse of border violations by the Russians, but few of us believed him.

The news of the Russian campaign broke the tension we all felt. It had long been known that Germany would have to fight Russia sooner or later. Now it was happening, and we felt relief at the finality. At the same time our fears of what fighting Russia entailed were renewed. I wondered what part my brothers were playing in the invasion and said a silent prayer on their behalf.

A few days after the invasion of Russia, we were stood down from full alert and resumed normal duties. One afternoon, our training and duties were interrupted by an announcement over the loudspeakers, 'All crew members are to change into dress uniform and parade on deck at 1445.' General parades were rare but not unknown; we wondered about the reason for this one – probably a pep talk to boost morale.

It was stifling in the sun on the steel deck where we stood to attention in our ranks. The air was still, the ribbons on our sailor caps hung limp, there was no swell and the *Schleswig-Holstein* lay motionless on the smooth sea. It was not the sort of day to think of killing and death, but that did not deter the admiral of the Baltic Fleet whom the captain introduced to us. From where I stood, he was a distant figure, but no doubt he was very imposing in his admiral's uniform. His voice echoed through the loudspeakers.

'Sailors of the Baltic Fleet,' he began, 'you all know that if Germany is to survive, then we must win this war. At this moment our troops are busy smashing Soviet Russia, and soon our enemies in the East will be crushed.'

I said another silent prayer for my brothers on the Eastern Front.

'But' he continued, his voice lower and more dramatic, 'Germany has other enemies who must be defeated. We shall starve these enemies into submission; we shall cut off their vital sea links. In carrying out this work, our submarines have already won many glorious victories.'

He went on to recount the exploits of various U-boat heroes, then concluded, 'Men, the Führer needs more volunteers for submarines. Tomorrow, every one of you will take a medical examination for the submarine service.'

If he said any more, I was not listening. I was overcome by a desire to laugh at the admiral's definition of 'volunteer'.

The fear hit a few hours later.

The next day I would have to take a medical examination to see if I was fit for submarine duty. Only those men who were superbly fit were accepted, but with the exercise and good food in the Navy, I had no doubt that I would be found fit enough. Like most other sailors, I had a dread of submarines, a fear of being trapped underwater and unable to escape. It was illogical to fear submarines more than my battle station at Steering Station Number One, where I was as effectively sealed underwater as in a submarine. But my terror, if irrational, was intense.

Obviously I would have to fail the medical examination, but how? The doctors would not be easy to fool and would not be satisfied with any fairy tale I could tell them. The only thing that would ensure the success of my plan was some physical weakness.

I was in the canteen sipping coffee when the idea came to me. I put my mug down and looked at it. Coffee! If you drank enough coffee, your heartbeat became irregular. Who wanted a sailor with a weak heart on a submarine? I gulped down my coffee and got another mugful.

That evening I sat in the canteen, downing one cup of coffee after another and chainsmoking cigarettes. Previously I had smoked only an occasional cigarette, but that night I forced myself to get through as much of my tobacco ration as possible. When it was time to go to my hammock, I felt light-headed and unsteady, but hopeful that my heart had been temporarily affected.

Of course I was unable to sleep that night, except in brief snatches while I dreamed I was on board a submarine that was being depth-charged. The slim hull rocked and rattled with a succession of explosions, and I woke each time sweating, with my heart beating wildly.

In the morning I felt terrible; my head was pounding, and my mouth tasted like the bottom of a Dutch canal. I looked at the steaming jug of coffee on the mess table and almost vomited, but I forced myself to take three or four cupfuls and to smoke another few cigarettes.

'Nervous, Nütt?' one of my messmates asked. I just growled at him.

There was an air of tension about the ship that morning. Except for the few who were keen to volunteer for the 'swimming coffins', as we called the U-boats, most of us looked forward with dread to the medical examination.

At last my group was called, and we lined up outside the examining room. My turn came, and the doctor's assistant called me in. The staff doctor, a tall man in his fifties, dressed in a Kapitän's uniform, sat at a desk making notes on a card. Finally he looked up.

'Well,' he barked, 'and what is wrong with you?' Then he grinned. 'Everybody I've seen this morning has some condition, affliction, disease, or problem that they've not reported before. So, what's wrong with you?'

'Doctor there's nothing wrong with me except that I

have a feeling of great anxiety and a funny sensation around here.' I put a hand on my breastbone.

'Hmmph. Hands on hips. Now, bend your knees ten times.'

He took his stethoscope and listened to my heart. 'Stretch out your arm, spread your fingers.'

The doctor turned to his assistant, 'We'd better send this man ashore to hospital for an electrocardiogram. Arrange it, will you?'

So far my plan was working. Later that day, I was told to be ready to go ashore at 0845 the next morning. At every opportunity I tried to drink as much coffee and smoke as many cigarettes as possible.

The next morning a motor boat made a special trip to put me ashore at Dragør, to catch the bus to Copenhagen. I got off about a mile before the hospital and ran all the way. On arrival at the Naval Hospital I handed my envelope to a nurse and was soon lying down with numerous wires attached to my chest.

'Anything wrong?' I asked the nurse when the examination was over.

'Your doctor will tell you everything.'

'The doctor here?'

'No, the staff doctor on your ship.' She handed me a large buff envelope. 'Give this to your doctor. Now you can go back to your ship.'

Back on board the *Schleswig-Holstein* I went immediately to the sick bay. After a short wait, I was ushered in to the doctor. He opened the envelope, studied its contents, pursed his lips, looked at me, then read it again. He laid the papers on his desk, then got up and put a fatherly hand on my arm. 'Now I don't want you to worry. Don't worry at all. Just take it easy.'

'What's wrong doctor?' I wasn't acting now; I was

beginning to worry that they really had discovered something serious.

'There's nothing wrong, but you should take it easy. I don't want you doing any physical exertion. No more heavy duty or exercises.' He made a note on a pad on his desk. 'Just remember, take things easy. You are free to go.'

I should have been happy that I had avoided submarine duty, but I could not help worrying. Suppose the examination had revealed a real heart weakness that I never suspected, that previous medical tests had not revealed?

Next day, while my shipmates ran around the deck, I was ordered to sit on deck and read. I began to wish I was able to join them.

Later that day I was called back to the doctor's office.

'Nütt, you are not suited for submarines. In fact you are not even fit for Fleet duty. We will have to transfer you to a shore base where you will do only light work. Dismiss!'

4

The Kapitän-Leutnant in charge of the office in Kiel to which I was transferred was a former officer on the *Graf Spee*. In December 1939 the *Graf Spee* had been involved in the Battle of the River Plate against three British ships. The *Graf Spee* was finally scuttled off Montevideo, and her commander, Kapitän Hans Langsdorff, committed suicide after carrying out his orders to destroy his ship. The crew of the *Graf Spee* were interned, as Uruguay was a neutral country, but several members, including my new commanding officer, escaped and fled to Spain and then home to Germany.

About thirty years old, with very short hair, the Kapitän-Leutnant was a muscular man who always held himself perfectly straight. He was an ardent Nazi and very strict. Every order had to be obeyed promptly; the office ran under the same discipline as a ship at battle stations.

Although I still wore uniform, my duties under him were more of a civilian nature. I was, in fact, an office boy in the large brick building that was a branch of Fleet Headquarters. There were twenty or so others who worked with me in the large office. Next door to our general office was a large radio room where enemy wavelengths were monitored. There was also a staff of decoders which included some civilians.

My duties were undemanding. I relayed messages which came over the teletype from Berlin; I prepared travel warrants for sailors of the Baltic Fleet and stamped them;

I handled supply requisitions and helped prepare air-raid reports. In other words, I fought the paper war. Yet, being in Kiel, the target of many RAF bombing raids, I was under attack far more than I had ever been on board the *Schleswig-Holstein*.

The barracks where I lived were close by the office. We had more room than on board ship but were in larger dormitories. There were some forty men in my room, and we slept in bunks in tiers of three. Navy discipline was still in effect, and our area had to be kept spotless. In these barracks I made the first real friend I had had since I was a small child.

Tall, slim, and blond, Franz Siemat looked like the ideal Aryan specimen. A Rhinelander from Cologne, he was always ready to laugh and enjoy a joke. His bunk was in the next tier to mine, and although he worked in another department, we rapidly became good friends. We would often go on the town together, and, with his Aryan good looks, there was never any shortage of girls to date. But as I soon found out, there was a serious side to his nature.

'What do you think of this bloody war?' he asked me one evening, as we sat in a bar waiting for our dates to turn up.

'Well, I'm worried a little,' I hedged. One could never know who might be an informer, a Gestapo agent, and so I had to be careful about revealing my thoughts to anybody. For that reason I had been a loner all through school, during my time on the *Wega*, and on the *Schleswig-Holstein*. I had always felt there was nobody I could trust.

Franz laughed. 'You're not giving anything away are you?'

'What do you mean?'

He laughed again and leaned forward. 'Who's the Gestapo agent in this bar?' he whispered in a mock-conspiratorial tone. 'I think it's that man over there in the other corner.'

I looked over at the table in the corner. The man sitting there looked morosely into his glass of beer, his thoughts far away. In his sixties, he appeared the ideal German Bürger, a small businessman probably. His clothes were old but well pressed. His shoes had seen better days but were highly polished. He did not look anything other than a typical German who had lost so much because of the war.

I turned back to Franz. 'Perhaps, with your leading questions, it's you who's the Gestapo agent.'

Franz's cornflower-blue eyes clouded, his fists clenched and his handsome face contorted. He half rose from the table, rocking our glasses of beer. 'Don't ever say that again, d'you hear?'

I could see that his anger was genuine, not assumed. 'All right, Franz, just settle down, will you? You might say something you don't want overheard.'

We sat in silence, sipping our beer. Further conversation ended when our dates arrived, and we went together to the cinema to watch a film, uninterrupted for once by an air-raid warning.

In my bunk that night I lay awake thinking. For the first time in years I experienced the aching loneliness of being without any close friend. My family were the only people I could talk to freely and, being away from home, I felt more and more isolated. Was I the only anti-Nazi around? Did I want Germay to lose the war because of what the Nazis had done to my father? Because the SS had beaten up my brother?

In my heart I knew my reasons were more than personal

ones. Far more. A system which made people fearful of
their neighbours, which imprisoned or killed people for
their political views, which persecuted Jews, which terror-
ized its own countrymen, such a system was inherently
evil. There was a story everyone had heard of a boy who
had informed on his parents for anti-Nazi expressions
at home, resulting in his parents' being arrested and
imprisoned. No, I knew I was anti-Nazi for justifiable
reasons.

Franz seemed to be leading me on. Yet his flash of
anger had been genuine; I couldn't doubt that. He too
might be anti-Nazi and, like me, tired of perpetually
hiding his feelings, longing to know he was not alone in
his views. He too might be watching every word he
said, afraid of being found out in the crime of thinking
differently from the gangsters who controlled our
homeland.

But it could still be a trap. Suppose Franz's anger had
been assumed? Suppose I had been mistaken in believing
it genuine? Suppose he was a Gestapo agent trying to
lead me on? I had no doubt that my records, which
followed me from posting to posting, contained some
reference to my anti-Nazi background. A red mark in the
corner of the paper? Some code number? It didn't matter.
Given my family background, I was certain to be marked
down as a security risk.

Suppose. Perhaps. Suppose that . . . Eventually I fell
into a troubled sleep in which Franz appeared as a
Gestapo agent trying to trap me. Defeatist talk. Traitor
to the Reich. Saboteur. 'Hans Nütt, you have been found
guilty of . . . Guilty of . . . Guilty.'

It was several days before Franz and I had evening
passes together again. I wasn't sure what I would say if
he started talking in the same vein. I was beginning to

feel paranoid, and more conscious than ever of being alone. I longed to be at home with my mother where I could talk freely, but I knew I could not expect leave for another few months, perhaps longer.

My state of mind was not improved when another sailor in the barracks handed me a booklet. 'Have you seen this?' he asked.

I sat down on my bunk and glanced through it. Although written in German, the booklet was of British origin and had been dropped from an airplane. There were all kinds of hints in the booklets: how to fake an illness, how to sabotage the war effort by dropping sand in machines, how to ruin the potato crop.

'Very interesting' I said non-committally, dropping the booklet back on my room-mate's bunk.

'Yeah,' he replied, not even looking up from the magazine he was reading.

Another trap? Another trick by the Gestapo, an attempt to get me to commit myself? Probably not, probably it was all quite innocent, with no ulterior motive. But you couldn't be sure. That was the terrible and frightening aspect of life in Germany at that time. To all the fears and restrictions of wartime in any country had been added the dimension of distrust. Who was an agent of the Gestapo? There was never an answer to that question.

'You don't trust me, Hans, do you?'

We were walking back to the barracks after accompanying our dates home. I didn't want to talk about politics. The memory of Gerda's lips and the way she pressed her body against mine was more important just then than any talk of politics.

'Hans, did you hear me? I said you don't trust me, do you?'

'About what?' I replied warily, shifting my thoughts from Gerda's firm breasts, which she had allowed me to fondle that night.

'What if I told you I was a Communist?'

'It wouldn't bother me any,' I heard myself say.

'Hans, do you realize what you've just said? I tell you I'm a Communist, a dreaded enemy of the Reich, whom you should turn in to the Gestapo without delay, and you say it doesn't bother you. Seemann Hans Nütt,' he said, with mock solemnity, 'I should have you arrested for gross dereliction of duty, for being . . .'

'Cut it out, Franz' I said irritably, my mind now fully on the present topic. 'You're trying to tell me you're anti-Nazi, right?'

'Right.'

'Why?'

'Because I think you are too.'

'And if I am?' Cautious, non-committal

'Well, are you?'

'You didn't answer my question, Ziemat.'

'What question?'

'What is it to you if I'm anti-Nazi or not?'

'It's important to me.'

'But why, Franz?'

'Because I'll know I'm not the only one who isn't under the spell of the mad corporal.'

I let the reference to Hitler pass. If he was a Gestapo man, he could use that omission as evidence against me later. But it didn't seem to matter any more. 'All right. Yes. I'm anti-Nazi. My whole family is. My father's dead. The Nazis made sure of that in 1933. Anything else you want to know?' I spoke irritably, angrily, almost defiantly. If Franz was what he said he was, I had nothing to fear. If not . . . well, I was tired of dissembling.

'It's true, then. I had a feeling about you. Look, Hans, I'm not trying to inveigle you into any plot or anything. Honestly I'm just sick of this war, sick of the Nazis, sick of everything.'

This conversation was the beginning of a close friendship between us. I learned that Franz Ziemat had belonged to an underground Communist youth organization before being called into the Navy. With my family's Social Democrat background, I had no love of the Communists, but that no longer seemed important. Franz was an anti-Nazi and this common bond between us was what mattered.

After that night we did not talk very much about politics, but it was pleasant and reassuring to know that we could be open with each other. We both wanted the war over with and a return to a free Germany without the Nazis, but there was never any talk of us doing anything to sabotage the war effort. We were young and healthy and there was a large surplus of pretty girls, on whom a uniform seemed to have an aphrodisiac effect. In fact, we were living in a dream world, afraid to face the true reality of the war.

My work in the office continued normally except for the inevitable interruptions caused by air-raids. The news from the Russian Front remained optimistic as units of the German Armed Forces pushed steadily eastwards. A few of the transfers and travel warrants I processed dealt with Navy men who were being transferred to Russia to join units of the army. I guessed that these were men who had fallen foul of their officers, and who were being banished expeditiously and effectively. Perhaps it was also a way of getting rid of sailors suspected of being anti-Nazis, for I soon noticed that these men were being transferred to the most dangerous sectors of the front to perform what were regarded as suicide tasks. I tried not to think about what might happen to the owners of these names. I never saw them; I only handled pieces of paper and teletype messages.

Until August.

'Ziemat, Franz Wilhelm, No. 8435217.'

I stared at the teletype message. The first name I had recognized among the thousands I had processed and it was that of my best, my only friend.

I glanced around. Nobody seemed to have noticed my discomfiture. I took the teletype message from Berlin and began the requisite paper work. Surely there was some mistake? Perhaps this was not the Franz Siemat I knew; after all it could not be that uncommon a name.

A swift check in the files removed any doubt. It was my Franz Ziemat the teletype referred to. Like most of the other transfers, this one had been ordered in good time. There was a preparation time of nine days before Franz would have to leave. I continued work as normal for the rest of the day, labelling envelopes, stamping documents, filing papers, but my mind was elsewhere.

'I've got to talk to you. It's urgent,' I whispered to Franz in the barracks after supper.

He nodded. We met outside the barracks after passing the routine inspection and set off walking. I insisted we stay outside in the open; there was a risk of being overheard in a bar or café.

'Himmelfahrtskommando!' he exclaimed when I told him the news.

'That's right. There's no mistake. I checked.'

'God! It's a death sentence!'

I nodded glumly. 'Himmelfahrtskommando' or 'trip-to-heaven squad' was the nickname given to the groups who were employed removing Russian mines. The work was extremely dangerous, and few men survived more than three or four weeks before being blown to bits. It was an assignment generally given to those whom the forces wanted to get rid of.

'I suppose they could call me a hero dying for the Fatherland instead of making me an enemy of the Reich. The statistics will be better on both sides of the ledger,' he said cynically.

'I'm sorry,' I muttered. There seemed nothing else to say. We walked on in silence.

'I'm not going,' he said finally.

'What?'

'I'm not going. That's all there is to it.'

'But the orders . . !'

'To hell with the orders! I'm simply not going.'

'What will you do then?'

'I don't know yet. Give me time to think.'

We wandered aimlessly for a while. At Franz's suggestion we stopped in at a bar and drank a couple of beers. We didn't talk, and when he gave the signal we paid and left, and resumed walking.

'Just me?' he asked a few minutes later.

'What do you mean, "Just me"?'

'Was I the only one to be transferred there?'

'No, of course not. We get lots of transfers every day. Let me think, there were . . . two, yes, two other transfers today to the Himmelfahrtskommando.'

'Hmm. D'you remember who they were?'

'I'm not sure.'

'Think, man, think.'

I racked my brains. The only name that concerned me in the teletype message from Berlin had been Ziemat.

'Please, Hans, try and remember.'

'There was a Madowa.'

'Willi Madowa?'

'Yes, I think that's it. Do you know him?'

'Yes. What about the other one?'

'Ziemat . . . Madowa . . . Beitzmann?'

'Are you sure? Could it have been Boschmann?'

'Yes! That's it! That was the name. Boschmann. I think his first name was Karl.'

'Yes, it is. I know him too.'

I had never met Willi Madowa or Karl Boschmann, although Franz seemed to know them well.

'So, it's us three,' he muttered. 'Madowa, Boschmann, and me. Well, I'm not going.'

'So what are you going to do? You can't just say you're not going. That won't work, you know that.'

'I know, I know. I've got to have a plan, got to get away somewhere safe. One thing is certain, I'm not going to the Eastern Front. I'll work something out.'

We walked back to the barracks without talking, after arranging to meet the next evening. In the office next morning I glanced through the papers on my desk. It was correct; Franz and his two friends were all to be transferred to what amounted to certain death. The day seemed as if it would never end, and the heat of summer made the air oppressive. It had never bothered me before.

'Hans, will you help me?'

'Help you, how?'

'I've got a plan, and it might work. In fact, if we're careful it will work. But I need your help.'

'I'll help.' My decision was made on the spot, even though I did not yet know what Franz wanted me to do. I had thought about it a great deal at work that day. In my mind I knew I had no choice but to help Franz if I could.

The easy days of being a silent anti-Nazi were at an end. This was a matter of conscience, and it was clear what I must do. I did not feel at all brave; in fact I was terrified. But I felt I had to help.

'What do you want me to do?'

'We'll need papers. Official papers for the three of us. I've talked to Boschmann and Madowa and they're coming with me.'

'Where to?'

'Turkey. We'll be safe there. We'll have to go via Greece and we'll need papers, travel warrants, orders, etc. That's where you come in. Can you do it? Get the necessary papers, I mean?'

I thought for a few moments. Nobody would notice if I prepared a number of false travel documents. As long as I got on with my routine work nobody bothered me. I could easily prepare the necessary papers and use an official stamp on them. The rubber stamps were everywhere on every desk, and nobody gave them much thought. 'It can be done,' I said finally. 'The only problem is a Leutnant's signature that some of the papers will need, but I can forge that quite easily. Yes, I can do it'

'You will?'

'Yes, I'll do it. What we must do is work out your route, and make a list of the papers you'll need. Then I'll get to work on it.'

Franz breathed a sigh of relief. 'I hoped you'd say that. There's one other thing. If I'm caught, I'll never reveal anything of this.'

'I hope not. But remember, the Gestapo can make people talk.'

'They'll never get anything out of me. I promise.'

'Nor me. If I'm asked, I'll flatly deny any involvement. And one other thing,' I added.

'Yes.'

'Those two others, Madowa and Boschmann. I don't want to meet them. There's less risk that way.'

'I agree. They know nothing. I haven't told them who you are, so you have nothing to fear from them.'

'Okay. I'll get on with the false papers tomorrow. It may take a couple of days, depending on how busy I am with other work, but I promise to have them ready for you by Friday, and you'll have papers that will fool anybody.'

I was not as confident as I sounded. All it would take would be one telephone call by a suspicious officer somewhere between Kiel and Istanbul, and the whole scheme would collapse. It was my job to make the faked orders sound as plausible as I could.

By Thursday evening I had all the papers prepared. It was not difficult to fit the forgeries in with my normal duties. I tried to think of every possibility that could arise and prepared three sets of papers, properly stamped and signed, for every contingency. Each evening, I took the papers I had made that day and hid them in my locker. By the time I had finished, there were enough orders and warrants to fill a briefcase. For good measure I included a number of blank forms and four rubber stamps I was sure would not be missed.

Franz laughed when I handed them to him. 'Good heavens. There's enough papers here to divert a whole army corps.'

'Just about. I hope they do the trick.'

'Me too. The others asked me to thank you.'

'You didn't tell them who I am?'

''Course not. They think I got them from a girl.'

We both laughed.

The following Wednesday, Franz and his two compan-
panions left, ostensibly for the Eastern Front and a

Himmelfahrtskommando. A few days later I received the news that my eldest brother, Willy, had been killed on the Russian Front. In my grief I cursed the Nazis. Because of Hitler and his gang, our family had now lost two members to violent deaths. I wondered if my mother, my brother Alfred, and I would survive this insanity of destruction. Perhaps I had saved three men from the madness.

The other workers in our office know of my bereavement and I hoped they ascribed any absent-mindedness on my part to the loss I had suffered. With each day that passed I began to feel more confident that Franz and his two companions had escaped safely. I mentally traced their progress: Kiel to Hamburg, Hanover, Stuttgart, Munich, Vienna, and Graz; then through Jugoslavia and Greece to freedom in Turkey, along the route we had worked out together. With every passing day I settled back more easily into my routine.

Fall came; the leaves fell and blew about in the salt breeze off the sea. The air turned chilly, with only an occasional day of relative warmth and calm. The heating was switched on in our offices; nobody hung about unnecessarily outside.

And still no news from Franz. No news is good news, I kept telling myself. If you're lucky you'll never hear from him again. I remembered his laughing promise to send me a postcard of his harem in Turkey and our vow to drink a hundred glasses of Kölsch in Cologne's Heumarkt after the war.

5

'Nütt! Your're wanted in the Kapitän-Leutnant's office immediately.' My heart skipped, and I pushed myself upright from my desk. Numb, I walked from the room. This could spell trouble. Several other people had been called to the commanding officer's room in the last couple of days, but nobody had said anything about what transpired there. Maybe it only concerned the operation of the office. But I hadn't liked the sneering tone in the corporal's voice. My mind raced, and I broke into a cold sweat as I knocked and entered.

'Close the door behind you.'

'Sir!' I stood rigidly at attention afraid my legs were moving with the shaking of my knees. The Kapitän-Leutnant sat at his desk, straight as a ruler. He even seemed to sit at attention.

'Seemann Hans Nütt.' His tone was harsh and official. 'You will account for yourself. Franz Ziemat from this establishment was your friend.'

'Kind of. You see we met . . .'

'He was your friend!' Now I knew I was suspect.

'I have information that you assisted in the desertion of Ziemat, Madowa, and Boschmann, who were to be transferred to the Eastern Front.'

What had gone wrong? Had Franz been arrested on the way to Turkey? Or had he simply failed to show up at the Russian Front, causing inquiries to be made? I felt as if I had been kicked in the stomach, but I kept my face expressionless.

He eyed me coldly, watching for any sign of guilt. There would be no quarter given. 'Madowa?'

'I beg your pardon, sir.'

'Madowa! Willi Madowa? You knew him?' he barked.

'Never heard of him, sir.'

'Of course you've heard of him. You made out his transfer papers a short while ago.'

'I don't remember, sir. There are thousands of transfer papers,' I stammered.

His fist slammed on the desk.

'You remember very well! You gave him false papers along with the other two.'

'I'm sorry, sir. With respect, sir, I don't know anything about false papers.'

'You're lying, Nütt!'

'Sir. I'm not. I don't even know the others, only Franz Ziemat.'

'How well did you know Ziemat?'

I shrugged, feigning innocence. 'Not really well. We had a few beers, went out with the girls. That sort of thing.'

'And you talked.'

'Well, yes. About girls mostly, sir. I don't know what you're getting at, sir.'

'You know very well. You talked about more than girls. How you could sabotage the war effort of the Reich! And how you could help that Communist and his friends to escape their duty! You socialist traitor!' His lip curled in distaste. It was as though he was swearing at me the way he said it.

My back stiffened. 'Sir, I deny that completely.'

'Don't lie. We have all the evidence we need.'

'Sir, I haven't seen Ziemat for months. I thought he'd just gone on transfer, as far as I knew.'

'Think! When did you last see him?'

'I'm not sure, sir. If I remember, it was when the leaves were falling. We walked home to our barracks and I remember the leaves were . . .'

His hand slapped on his desk, making me jump. He half rose and leaned toward me over the desk as he spoke in a hushed, controlled whisper. 'I am not interested in goddam leaves falling! I want to know exactly when you saw him, where you were, what you said, and what you did. You were preparing his escape, weren't you? Speak!'

I watched, mesmerized by the gold braid on his sleeve as his fist slammed up and down on the desk with each phrase. Pinned to my place by his stare, I had a wild impulse to tell the truth and beg for mercy. But I doubted there would be any. With the greatest difficulty I regained control. The truth could be devastating for Franz, and the others as well.

I told a tale about going out with Franz to a bar where we met some unknown girls. I said we drank with them and then went home to the barracks, with the autumn leaves falling around us.

'He was gone in the morning when I woke,' I concluded.

Steel-blue eyes beneath the perfect military haircut declared I was lying before he spoke. He laid his hands flat on the desk in front of him.

'I'll give you one last chance, Nütt. Admit you helped Ziemat and the others to escape and I'll do what I can to help you. Admit you were foolish, man! I don't think you really realized what you were doing. If you plead your youth and ignorance it will go easy for you. Otherwise, if you do not tell me now, we both know others will get the truth from you shortly. You will be shot as a traitor to the Reich. Come on, do you want to die for a single mistake?'

'Sir, I'm innocent! What can I say but that?'

'Think about it, boy. We are not unreasonable men. We know what it is like to be young and foolish. You didn't mean to be a traitor. You just helped a friend who fooled you into doing it. Those Communists are trained in brainwashing and psychological control. He made you do it, didn't he? He manipulated you, didn't he? You have no malice toward the Führer and the Reich. Now, come, admit it. Then I can help you.'

It was a tempting offer. Put all the blame on Franz. But what would happen to Franz if they had him? Or would it make any difference? They'd shoot him anyway. Why not tell him and take the chance? But then what would really happen to me? I remembered how he had called me a 'socialist traitor'. In a way, if I gave in, I would be denying my father and betraying my Social Democrat background. I realized suddenly how I hated this Nazi and all he stood for. And I hated his slimy method of trying to set me against my friend. I couldn't betray Franz.

The Kapitän-Leutnant closed the file on his desk. 'Well, Nütt, you've had time to think it over. Have you decided to confess?'

'How can I confess, sir? I didn't do any of these things you accuse me of.'

'Reconsider!' It was an order. He leaned forward. I stared at a point above his head.

He paused significantly. When I did not speak, he went on in a chilling tone. 'I have orders to send you to the interrogation prison for further questioning. You will remain there until you are either cleared or found guilty. I can only report that you stubbornly deny everything.'

My heart quaked and I felt my face draw tight with fear. The interrogation prison! Remembered hints and wild rumours flooded my mind as I stumbled out past the corporal. I was a prisoner, an enemy of the Reich. I was going to jail. Gestapo? Escorted down the stairs to the already waiting car, I was tempted to make a run for it at every corner and at every door, especially when I stepped outside. How vivid was the morning! The tang of the sea. Even the grey of the sky. I wanted to be in it, of it, to walk away and be part of the day. Suddenly I knew what it was to lose my freedom.

Although the interrogation prison was on the other side of Kiel, I was too stunned to remember anything of the drive. Nearly comatose, I sat, mind totally blank, until two marines hustled me into a large, rectangular brick building. They herded me along bare corridors and finally pushed me into a tiny cell. Nobody spoke, and the whole journey might have been no more than a dream. But that cell was my home for days, then weeks, and months. Time dragged interminably.

My cell was tiny, and mind-destroying in its sterility. When the shock partially wore off after my first night of imprisonment, I began to worry how long I could remain sane if left in that room. It was only about two metres by three, sparsely furnished with a flat, hard, steel bunk, a tiny sink, a toilet, and a little table. I recalled what I had read and heard of other prisoners and began to imitate the things they did to keep sane. I exercised daily, did breathing exercises, went on imaginary journeys, and practised mental arithmetic. I named all the countries and cities starting with 'A' on one day, then 'B' on the next. For brief periods I blanked out the horror of being a prisoner.

I couldn't talk to anyone, and that tortured me most.

After a few days I began to study the face of the guard bringing my meals, hoping he would talk to me or give some sign he noticed me, but he would not speak.

There was a peep-hole in the door by which people could observe me at any time from the corridor, but when I tried to see out of it I could distinguish nothing. The continuous spying obsessed and embarrassed me, particularly when I needed to use the toilet. I would have waited until night except that my cell was never dark. The overhead bulb burned incessantly. Once it burned out, and I savoured the sudden darkness; but in a minute the cell door was flung open and a guard rushed in to replace the bulb.

I strained to hear footsteps or conversation in the corridor outside, to hear other prisoners as they were led to exercise or interrogation, but my cell was sound-proof. At meal-times I would never hear the guard approach. The door would simply open suddenly and quickly, start-ling me, and the guard would enter carrying a tray, which he would set down near the door without saying a word or even glancing in my direction. Each day, with my morning meal, he would bring a set quantity of wax on a can lid, a brush, and a cloth, and I had to get down on my hands and knees and polish the stone floor of my cell until it gleamed.

Meals were regular and the quality was average, but there was never enough food. I lost weight, but worry and anxiety probably contributed to that too. At first I so hated being herded around that I did not make full use of my ten or fifteen minutes of time in the exercise yard. A guard prodded me to make me run. Then I began to realize that my muscles were becoming slack, and that exercise and fresh air would keep me fit and stop me from going insane. I began to run my fastest and exercise violently to make the most of my time. For the most part I tried to ignore the guards, hoping to give them the impression I didn't care what they thought or did. Every time, I hoped they would let me exercise with other young men for companionship and challenge; but I seldom saw another prisoner, and was never allowed to speak to one.

Then once, coming from the shower with my guard behind me I met a British airman coming in. He raised his eybrows and gave a small wink. In my whole time there that was my only human contact – and he was an enemy of my country. Somehow that exchange cheered me. I remembered it ever after, and watched in vain for that airman again.

From my tiny window I could peer out beween the bars at a brick wall and a part of the exercise yard below. I spent hours at the window, giving each prisoner an imaginary name and background as he moved about below. I waved at a man I named 'Frank' one day, but if he saw me he didn't respond.

One day my guard spoke, startling me so much that in my excitement I let my food grow cold. 'You may have books. I will bring them. Make a list of the kinds you would like.'

He left me a piece of paper and a pencil and went out. Excitedly I listed general headings, taking care to avoid any controversial material, such as foreign titles and authors. To read anything again would be wonderful. A door to the world would be opened and my mind could escape temporarily from my cell. I was amazed at their generosity. With books available, I felt sure I would never break down. Then I sat up straight, rigid with shock, suddenly realizing that I had been on the point of caving in, without knowing it. Silence. Silence and loneliness. Strong, healthy, good-looking, and independent, I thought I could get along well with people when I had to. And when I wanted them for something I managed well enough at getting my way. But now I was learning how much I needed others to keep me human. Just silence and loneliness could break me down. I remembered Pastor Harden's sermon on Peter sinking in the water when his self-confidence left him, and I began to pray again daily. The next day the guard brought three books. I didn't even notice that he never spoke to me, and I began to read voraciously, *Under Count Luckner as Seaman First Class.* Suddenly I was at sea again, having an adventure on a sailing ship.

Whatever the guard brought I read, and reread if nothing else appeared. For the first time in my nineteen years I was drawn into the world of ideas when the guard brought an anthology of poetry by mistake. I kept it as long as possible. I had always been physically active and had never bothered my head with books outside of my prescribed studies. But I learned more of value from those few books than I had in my years at school. In retrospect, I suppose the prison library was small and pathetically limited, but for me it was a vital escape and a means of remaining sane.

Two officers interrogated me at irregular intervals, and these interrogations began to assume a pattern. I would be startled by the sudden opening of the cell door. Each time, it upset me to know that they had probably spied upon me first. I would have to stand against the opposite wall, and salute the guard. 'Nütt, Hans, number 894365, Seemann. Suspicion of conduct prejudicial to good naval discipline and order, possible enemy of the Great German Reich.'

This was the prescribed routine every time the cell door

opened. The guard looked at me unfeelingly, stepped to one side, and jerked his head to indicate that I was to go out in front of him. In other circumstances it would have been comic.

I tried to steel myself for these occasions, to make my face a mask, but inwardly my heart thumped uncontrollably and my brain seemed to swell and reel. I rose, straightened my tunic, smoothed my hair, and gathered enough self-control to walk out with military briskness. The guard never touched me and he was unarmed; there was no escape from that place anyway.

We marched to a plain, nearly empty, stark grey room in a corner of the same floor as my cell. As I entered, I saw a table with two chairs behind it and a single chair in front of it. The guard left me standing at attention in the middle of the room and abandoned me.

After five or ten minutes the door opened again behind me and two men entered without speaking. They closed the door quietly and remained still for a minute or two while I felt their eyes drilling into the back of my head. Even during the first interrogation, I knew instinctively that I was supposed to remain as I was. The waiting was nerve-shattering.

Their footsteps approached from behind and my scalp prickled. They paused behind me, then walked past me, one on either side, to the table and sat down. I was left standing in the middle of the room.

Both wore marine uniforms and displayed the polished, tightly contained look of the Nazi. Seated, they studied me coldly and dispassionately. They were in their thirties, probably competing for promotions. The older of the two had light blond hair and very pale blue eyes that appeared depthless and impenetrable. I found him extremely frightening. Eventually he spoke, in a harsh whisper that I had to strain to hear.

'Seemann Hans Nütt?'

'Yes, sir.'

'Your commanding officer reports that you refuse to admit your guilt in aiding the desertion and escape of three marines from your barracks. It will not help you to lie any longer. We have in this prison two of those three, Boschmann and Madowa. Both have admitted that they received passes, vouchers, and other papers from you as did Franz Ziemat. We have those papers from all three, bearing the stamp of the office where you worked. You will now tell us the truth!'

My mind raced. If they had only captured Boschmann and Madowa, where was Franz? He was the only one I had talked to, and he had promised never to tell the other two of my part. If he was still free, my interrogators must be bluffing that they had evidence linking me to the false papers. But how would they have got hold of his papers too if he had escaped?

'Sir, I do not know any Boschmann or Madowa. I did not give them any papers. How could I when I don't know them? And I have not seen Franz Ziemat for months.'

Had Franz made it to Turkey or Greece, escaped to neutral territory? I prayed for both of us that he had got away.

'You did not deny that you had given papers to Ziemat. You gave them to him for the others too. Now admit it!'

'No, never! I did deny it. I never gave anyone forged papers.'

He pretended to yawn. 'Don't give us that line again. Each time you lie it is worse for you.'

'Sit down,' the other officer said. I noticed a duelling scar on his cheek, but his eyes looked softer.

He took over, rising to stand above me. Then I knew

that whether I was standing or sitting, they would keep me psychologically beneath them.

'Let us open the window and get some justice into the air.' There was silence until the window was open and I could feel the cool sea breeze on my face.

'How long have you known Franz Ziemat?'

'It must be about sixteen months,' I answered after a pause.

'Why were you friends?'

'I don't know. We just happened to meet in the barracks and chanced to talk.'

'Wasn't it because he was a Communist and you are too?'

'No, I am not a Communist.'

'You lie! Your father was a Social Democrat provincial leader and committed suicide to avoid facing justice for his crimes. They were the same as Communists before we eradicated them. Enemies of the Fatherland and the Führer.'

I was angry, despite my precarious position. The Communist Party had been born out of the left wing of the SPD, but it was far from being the same party. And the accusation that my father was a criminal particularly rankled. He'd been *driven* to suicide by the Brownshirt gangsters. I swallowed hard and struggled to maintain control. Then I replied hoarsely, ignoring the bait.

'We went drinking together and dated girls together. It was simply for fun. He was older than me, but we did not discuss politics. We both wanted to be ships' captains and he had been on a sailing ship too, so we sometimes talked about that. Mostly we just had fun together.'

The questions went on and on, going in circles, trying to trip me up.

Suddenly, 'You were homosexuals together.'

'No!'

Why would they say that? To embarrass me? To smear me? To rattle me? But it was not brought up again, although the accusation upset me.

'Did you have sex with girls together?'

'No. Never.'

They were fishing for anything to besmirch Franz and me. I began to believe they had nothing definite. But I could not be sure. They looked like men who enjoyed playing with other men's sanity.

If only I knew where Franz was!

In the middle of a stream of questions about the places Franz and I had visited, they both stood up disconcertingly, and the older one said to a guard who had materialized behind me, 'Take him away for now.' With that the interrogation stopped very suddenly. I realized later that they must have come to the end of the allotted time, but the abrupt halt left me shaken and sweating.

Obviously there would be other sessions. They had not believed me. I could imagine the widespread and ruthless search for Franz. If he made good his escape, the military police and the Gestapo would appear incompetent, and others might try to desert as well. Few men had spoken with affection of the Nazis around the barracks, but neither had there been any open criticism. Now, for the first time, I wondered how others felt.

I was marched back to my cell in silence. Nobody had threatened physical abuse, but I kept wondering if it might start. Mentally exhausted, I lay on my bunk the rest of the afternoon and evening. Only Franz could prove my story wrong. If they captured and tortured him he might be forced to tell. If only I could find out where he was!

Days and weeks passed, and I was interrogated four more times by the two officers. Always the same unexpected summons at different times; always the same questions, put in different ways; always a lecture against the evil Social Democrats and Communists, to which they swore I belonged. Until now I had never given politics any serious thought. Helping Franz had been an act of friendship. But now I began to take some pride in my socialist background, and began to view my assisting Franz as a political action against the Nazis. Throughout my formative years the Nazis had controlled Germany, and I had had to accept the fact, although I had never joined the Hitler Youth. Now, with time to think and under the pressures of my imprisonment, I questioned everything in Germany. Remembering again the fine people from many countries I had met while sailing, I wondered in what sense those people could be called my enemies. The illicit BBC broadcasts we had listened to at home had certainly tried to convince us that the German people should really be the friends of the British and their allies against the Nazis.

After many weeks in prison, I was again suddenly summoned. This was to be the shortest session.

When I entered the interrogation room I was left standing, but my pale-eyed interrogator, whose name I never learned, was already behind the table, alone.

'Seemann Nütt, you have persisted in your lies, and I can no longer help you.'

I was amazed at the word 'help'.

'You have this one last opportunity to admit what we already know and I may be able to help you in your sentence. Now speak, man!'

'I have nothing more to say. I am innocent.'

He trembled with fury.

'Fool!'

For a moment his self-control slipped. I had obviously disappointed him with my persistence: and the thought that I had cheated him – possibly out of a promotion – cheered me a little, despite his next words.

'You are a stupid young fool. Well, my fine young cockerel, tomorrow you will be court-martialled.'

He was incensed; the more he spoke, the more livid he became. I knew he wanted to hit me, to beat me, and I flinched mentally as he rose behind the table and leaned toward me. Probably only regulations saved me from a severe beating.

'You are vermin, a louse on the body of the Fatherland, and tomorrow at your court-martial I will say so. With your stupid stubbornness! Take him away.'

Back in my cell I lay on my bunk. I felt sick in the stomach. I couldn't eat or sleep.

The following afternoon, my door swung open suddenly. After the ritual, my guard made the usual gesture for me to go out ahead of him. As I did so, feeling unsteady, I sensed in his bearing a new remoteness, a withdrawing from any possible association with me.

The judge in his robes sat behind a desk on a dais. I was led into the dock on his left. My two interrogators sat across from me to the judge's right beside the prosecutor. A young Leutnant sat at a desk behind me. Other than these participants, the small, bare courtroom was empty, except for the guard at the only door.

There was a chair in the dock, but I was left standing. It became apparent that the young officer behind me was my defence counsel, although no one had told me so, nor had we ever met.

The prosecutor rose to speak.

'Your honour, this prisoner is Seemann Hans Nütt. We

have conclusive circumstantial evidence that he stole official documents to assist in the desertion of Franz Ziemat, Karl Boschmann, and Willi Madowa, three seamen, as described in the notice of trial before you.'

The judge didn't bother to look at the document; his eyes remained fixed on mine, penetrating me, trying to break me down with his icy stare.

'Seemann Nütt, the charges against you are aiding in the desertion of the three marines, and seeking to divide the forces of the Reich from within.' He quoted the number and clause of a section of the military criminal code that pertained to this strange charge.

Then the prosecutor called upon my interrogators to give evidence, and each went over different aspects of my association with Franz and my refusal to admit my guilt. I scarcely listened to the well-worn rhetoric, concentrating on maintaining my self-control. But suddenly, my heart leaped as I heard the one with the duelling scar, the one who had opened the window to 'get some justice into the air', say, 'The evidence is circumstantial only. Boschmann and Madowa are imprisoned here but say only that the documents were procured by Ziemat, and they do not know where he procured them. The prisoner refuses to admit the truth.'

The prosecutor protested immediately. 'Here are the stolen documents found on Boschmann and Madowa. They bear the Kiel office stamp on them. They definitely came from the office where Nütt worked.'

But my heart sank again as the judge seemed uninterested in this 'dispute' over the lack of proof involving me directly. The circumstantial evidence continued to pile up. Abruptly the judge swung on me again when the prosecutor finished.

'Accused, stand up! Do you have anything to say? The

evidence is clear. Do you still refuse to admit to the charges?'

'Your honour, I have nothing more to say. I have given my story many times, and it has not changed. I am completely innocent.'

Their anger swelled and swirled around me.

Then, without warning, obviously hoping to break me down by surprising me with a piece of evidence they had saved to the last, the prosecutor stooped behind the table and brought up a brown paper parcel. He flung it on the table, tore it open, and revealed a folded, bullet-ridden, blood-stained marine uniform. He snatched it up and thrust it toward me at arm's length.

'This,' he cried, 'is the uniform of Franz Ziemat, and you, his friend, killed him!'

I shook. My friend's uniform had always been a slight shade more faded than the other blue uniforms around it, and I was terrified as I saw it again. They had caught and killed Franz then. My best friend riddled by machine-gun bullets. I very nearly cried and broke down. Only the strongest resolve kept me on my feet facing them. In my mind I saw the stream of bullets tearing apart Franz's long, lean body. I knew I was as pale as death, but I could not let them break me now after getting this far. I managed to stay on my feet and say nothing, although I leaned on the rail and gripped it with all my strength.

'You have killed him as surely as you stand there,' he repeated, pointing his finger at me, and shaking the tattered tunic in the air, 'and yet you are so bold that you dare to face us, representatives of the Reich, and say nothing? His death is your fault!'

The judge took it up.

'Tell us the truth, Nütt. You gave him the papers, didn't you?'

I could not speak. If I opened my mouth, I risked breaking down entirely as I gazed at that uniform. They were all clearly exasperated that I had not finally succumbed. The judge was so angered that he half rose, thought better of it, sat down again, and leaned toward me. This was it. I felt dizzy and weak, surrounded by a ring of hostile eyes.

'You are found guilty as charged, Hans Nütt. The evidence is overwhelming. I see clearly that you are an obstacle in the path of the victory wagon of the Führer. We will get rid of such elements. The Führer must succeed. Elements like you have to be exterminated,' he ranted.'You are guilty as charged. You will be stripped of this glorious uniform you don't deserve to wear. When we have won the war you will be turned over to the civilian justice department.'

Behind me my defence counsel stirred. I had even forgotten his presence.

'Your honour,' he said, 'I plead for mercy for this man because he is so young. Perhaps his was an act of youthful foolishness and he is now trapped by his mistake. In my . . .'

'It will be considered,' the judge interrupted through thin lips. 'Court adjourned.'

In a daze I walked back to my cell, expecting to die very soon, the judge's word 'exterminated' echoing and re-echoing. How would they do it? I kept asking myself with horrified fascination. The executioner's axe? They had used it on some traitors already. Hanging? Surely as a member of the armed forces I could expect to be shot?

I was locked in again, with no idea of what would happen next. I passed a horrible night of fitful sleep, repeatedly waking from nightmares. Once I screamed when in a dream I entered a dank, dark chamber and saw a hooded executioner waiting for me, swinging a shining broadaxe.

At breakfast time the guard was accompanied by another man carrying a pair of shears. At first I was so distraught that I expected him to attack me with them. But instead, the man cut off the insignia of my uniform and the gold buttons from the front; symbolically I was no longer in the military.

Weeks dragged by. I wanted to have the whole business over with, and every time my cell door opened, I tried to prepare myself to die. But unexpectedly I was taken out one day and led to a visiting room. Incredibly, my mother and my brother Alfred were there to visit me. For the first several minutes we all stood silently, just holding each other and crying, until the guard made a threatening gesture and said, 'Sit!'

The chairs were arranged two on one side for my family and mine off by itself, probably so that they couldn't pass me anything. I sat down unsteadily as tears streamed down my face. My mother too wept silently, looking at me, and Alfred had his hands over his face, his shoulders heaving occasionally as he fought for control. He presented a pitiful picture, a shadow of the man he had been before being severely wounded on the Eastern Front.

'Mutti.' It was all I could say.

'Hansi, Hansi, my beautiful son! What have you done? Why are they keeping you here?'

'It is a mistake, Mutti, but I am all right. I will be sent out soon to a civilian court. I don't know where or when, but I am doing okay, and you must not worry too much. Perhaps I will be able to write to you.'

Our visit lasted no more than ten minutes, but I learned that my mother and brother were living comfortably enough. They had not been harassed because of me, except that my brother had been questioned about Franz. But, as he had never met my friend, there had been little he could say. There hadn't been any threats of reduced rations, or loss of home or citizenship, to either of them, which had been my biggest worry. They would become destitute if reprisals were made against them.

My heart was bursting with love, the ghost of my father strongly felt in the room, but we were not allowed to embrace before I was marched out. In my last sight of them for years, they sat there, their eyes full of tears, my mother's arms reaching toward me, as the guard marched me through the door.

Still no one told me anything of what would happen to me.

6

After a couple of days, two marine guards came again and took me from my cell. Exercise? Shower? Execution? They led me downstairs to a van waiting in the prison courtyard.

This is it. They are taking me to be shot, hanged, or beheaded. Where will it be done?

The van wound through the streets, but the windows were blacked out. Eventually the vehicle stopped, reversed, and stopped again. I closed my eyes. God give me strength, I prayed.

The door jerked open. A great rasping sigh of relief burst from me. I felt my knees begin to buckle and I almost fainted; then I recovered. We were at the train station.

Other prisoners, of different ranks and nationalities, stood in a closely guarded group near by. My guards marched me to the officer in charge. The sergeant-major signed a receipt for me, tearing it briskly from his pad. My guards saluted and left.

'What's happening?' I whispered to the first Navy man I saw in the crowd of prisoners.

'Silence!' The sergeant's voice echoed through the vaulted halls of the station. Heads turned, and I stared at the ground and shuffled my feet.

In a few minutes another guard and a porter arrived with a luggage trolley loaded with manacle chains. They shackled us two by two and marched us to our platform. In the eyes of official Germany I was a common criminal, paraded in chains in public with thieves and robbers. The manacles chafing at my wrists, the degrading spectacle we presented to passers-by burned into my spirit, searing, destroying. A man who has worn manacles is scarred forever.

Before we moved off, the officer in charge spoke with cold deliberation to his guards, in a tone we were meant to overhear.

'If any of them make any move to escape, shoot to kill.'

Each guard loaded his rifle in front of us, clicking a round into the breech.

The train took us south to Neumünster. At a filthy common jail, we were fingerprinted and photographed. The guards announced that there would be a judgement after the war on those of us in uniform, but there was no civilian trial, and I was never told what was to happen to me. For the first time, though, I did begin to believe that I was to live. I felt the challenge to survive and a fierce resentment at being treated like an animal. Not only was our prison filthy and filled with petty criminals from the entire Nazi-dominated area of Europe, but it was also crawling with bedbugs. I had scarcely fallen asleep the first night when I awoke with a terrible itch all over my body. I complained of it to a man near by as I scratched wildly.

'My God! This itch is driving me crazy.'

He laughed. 'It's just the bedbugs, fella. You'd better get used to them.'

I leaped from the bed, pawing wildly at my shirt collar, where I began to find the dirty bloodsuckers.

'They're filthy, and spread diseases of all kinds, don't they?' The thought sickened me.

The man gave a wry chuckle. 'Don't think it matters

here, mister. Nobody cares about us. If some of us get sick and die, there are fewer to feed.'

In a country that prided itself on cleanliness, how could our government leave us covered in bugs? I couldn't believe it.

'They're worse than you think, too,' he added. 'You've just had the first taste, so to speak.' He laughed hollowly at his own black joke. Then he pointed to a man I hadn't noticed in the gloom. The poor creature sat on a stool, his feet up slapping and brushing at his legs, the chair, his arms, his clothes. He murmured and whimpered, quite beside himself, close to total collapse as he vainly fought off bedbugs, and the sleep that would give them total control. I found out later that he was Jewish. A very rich man, he had owned a brewery in Berlin. The bedbugs were only the beginning of the persecution that would soon destroy him. Exhaustion finally overcame my loathing, but I only slept fitfully. Not only were the bedbugs devouring me, but my tonsils were swollen and inflamed.

Next morning, we awoke itching, swollen, and irritable. My neighbour called to me.

'Do this and we'll get some of the buggers.'

He took off his thin straw mattress, removed the loose bed boards, and tapped them on the floor. Literally hundreds of bloodfilled bedbugs fell out of cracks, and he crushed them under foot. We all followed suit in an orgy of revenge, stamping on them until the floor was red and slippery with the blood on which they'd glutted themselves the night before. It didn't help much. Each night, a new horde descended upon us, thirsting for our blood.

After several days, my tonsillitis was much worse. The pain and my lack of sleep made me almost delirious at times. Finally, I spoke about it to the guard, who seemed most humane.

'I am very sick, sir. My tonsils are very bad, and I can't swallow any more.'

'Let me see.'

I opened my mouth while he peered in.

'Mein Gott! That's terrible. I will report it and maybe they'll put you in the infirmary here.'

I was surprised that a place as bad as this had an infirmary. But I began to pray that they would take me. The guard's strong response made me feel certain that I would die of infection if I was refused treatment.

'Maybe because you are German they'll take you,' my German bunkmate whispered. 'You can thank God you're not a Pole.'

The following day I was taken into the infirmary and the abscessed tonsils were cut out. Much later, I learned that the infection should have been controlled first. But at the time I felt only relief, despite the pain, and luckily I healed quickly. They kept me in the infirmary the shortest possible time and then sent me back to the foul and verminous barracks.

During my stay in the infirmary, the Christmas of 1941 passed almost unnoticed. We prisoners preferred not to think of Christmas, particularly the food we'd once enjoyed at festive dinners. Here we had to accept thin soup, a slab of black bread, and a smear of jam made mostly of turnips.

Even after so short a time away, it was dreadful to return to the prison wing. Men were sick everywhere, the stench was bad, the bedbugs waited, and the crowding was awful. About five hundred prisoners were crammed together in a large, gloomy room that was designed for about one hundred and fifty.

I lost track of time, and don't remember how many weeks I was kept there. Then one day I was called out and the manacles were put on me. I was shackled with an army corporal. They were moving me out at last and I was thankful at least for that. As we were marched out, I could not bear to look back at the poor wretches left there, although, had I known what lay ahead, I would have wanted to stay.

A sergeant and two privates marched the group through the streets for about a mile to the train station. As it was early morning we were saved the embarrassment of having our countrymen see us. They loaded us into a special prison train, which took us to a prison in Lübeck. That night there was an air-raid and the thought of dying locked in a prison cell horrified me. I prayed to God to let me die a free man.

After a dreary, two-day journey we reached Berlin, our numbers swelled with more servicemen. Guards hustled us out of the station, striking prisoners with their rifle butts to pack us tighter into the waiting vans. Beside me a middle-aged Pole screamed in agony as a guard hit him in the kidneys, knocking him against another guard who slashed at him too, hitting him savagely in the groin. I was powerless to help him, much less defend him. They would have knocked me senseless if I'd tried.

Wedged in, I gasped for breath, hoping I wouldn't suffocate.

On arrival at the prison on the Alexanderplatz, each prisoner was handed a card with his name on it. A guard spoke matter-of-factly.

'Keep it on your person. If we have a bombing, we will be able to identify your body'

Our gigantic, two-roomed cell was crammed with about fifteen hundred men of every race, nationality, colour, and class. I spoke to Bavarian criminals, Norwegian professors, Catholic priests, and military officers. It was the filthiest place I had ever seen, and full of bedbugs too. Bunks were five tiers high. We were without blankets, pillows, or mattresses. The food was the worst I had ever tried to eat, just thin soup and dry bread, but we had to line up humbly while it was doled out under the critical eye of Gestapo guards.

I was kept in Alexanderplatz for three days, along with some of the servicemen with whom I had been transported. On the second night another man and I attempted to escape through a bathroom window. We had successfully bent two window bars a little way when there was an air-raid. Pandemonium broke loose. We abandoned our attempt as other men rushed in looking for a safe place to hide. Hope for an early escape waned, but I never let go the idea. Somewhere, some time, I would try again.

A group of us, mainly servicemen, were taken by train again to Hanover and then to Bremen, spending nights in two prisons, eating only thin soup. On the third day we reached Papenburg, near the Dutch border. Within half an hour trucks had trundled us to the gates of Börgermoor-Emsland concentration camp.

For the first time I guessed what my sentence was to be, although I was not told anything; the concentration camp for the duration of the war and civilian sentencing afterward. If the Nazis won, and if I survived the treatment in the camp.

7

The trucks stopped before the main gate with the Börgermoor sign in front of it. As we clambered down between rows of armed guards, we got a full view of the prison camp. A sickening stench hung in the air. High electric-wire fences surrounded squat, unpainted grey shacks arranged around a barren courtyard. Outside stood better-cared-for buildings which I took to be the guards' quarters.

Beyond, as far as I could see, lay flat, desolate, marshy land dressed in winter's drab. My soul shrank from the bleakness of it all. Lines of men worked the fields in the distance, and I could make out guards dotted around them. Inside the prison compound I saw a few ghastly-looking, emaciated prisoners at work around a long table of some sort. Later I learned that they were the rag-pickers who were too sick or weak for manual labour in the fields.

We were marched through the gate and lined up in the courtyard. Guards immediately ordered us to strip naked and pile all our belongings neatly in front of us. They were taking no chances with concealed weapons. The SS guards took our clothes, our wallets, rings, and money, everything. These items were put into a big envelope with our names and prison numbers on them.

'You will get these things back after the war, when you have been cleared of your crimes,' the commandant told us.

But the man next to me whispered, 'Don't ever expect

to see that stuff again, mister. It'll be sold for the SS coffers, if what I've heard is true.'

It was to be the only critical remark about the SS I heard in my whole time at Börgermoor. A fearful silence clamped down upon us. We began to distrust everyone around from that moment. Anyone could be an informer.

We stood about for a while naked and shivering, and I noticed that everyone there was thin. My own ribs stood out like those of a skinny boy. Little did I know that I was fat compared to what I would be a few months later. But I felt some pride in being stronger and more robust-looking than those around me. I should have the guts to survive this if these other men can, I thought.

We were issued cheap underwear, no socks (but a kind of wrap-around flannel to be tied around each foot, to slip into a wooden shoe), clogs, a shapeless black-and-yellow-striped prison uniform, a belt, and a round, black cap. It was clean but none of it was new. I wondered what had happened to the man who had worn mine last.

The barbers hurriedly cut one strip from front to back down the centre of our heads, leaving the rest of our hair hanging down lankly on either side. Perhaps this was for reasons of haste, but the result humiliated us even further; and if we escaped we would be readily identified as prisoners. We had few illusions about escape anyway when we looked at the high, barbed-wire electrified fences and the guard dogs ranging outside.

During this time I stood mute but already wondering if there was anyone I dared speak to.

Stripped of our once-imposing uniforms, we stood now in an ugly mockery of a military parade. The commandant stepped on to a platform and addressed us.

'Prisoners!' Automatically we sprang to attention.

'If you behave yourselves well in this concentration

camp, any one of you may apply, in a year or so, to prove yourself a worthy German soldier at the front. If you are fortunate enough to be accepted you will be sent to Bavaria to a special regiment, the Frontbewährung (Trial Regiment), for the Eastern Front.

'If you prove yourself to be a good soldier at the Front, then all of your past record will be wiped out and you will be accepted again as a full member of the military.'

There were no responses, only a few guarded questions and comments among ourselves later that night.

'Isn't it the Eastern Front where everyone is being killed?'

'Where have you been? Of course it is.'

'May be better than staying in here, do you think?'

'Maybe. It's possible.'

'Wonder what the chances of surviving there would be?'

'Who knows?'

'Do you suppose they would really clear your records?'

'Dunno.'

Then silence. No one wanted to risk any opinion. Our hopes and fears went underground.

We were assigned to individual barrack blocks, each housing about fifty men. Every bunkhouse had a 'Top Prisoner' or Kapo, and an assistant. The guards chose these men for their brutality and readiness to obey orders without question. They accepted for the sake of minor privileges, and the power over other prisoners which their position gave them. The Kapo and his assistant had bunks just inside the only door. Beyond them was a space for eating, with barren tables of unfinished wood. Rows of cupboards for our outside clothes ringed the wall. Beyond the dining room was a sleeping room, its walls completely filled with four tiers of bunks. Even on sunny days this dreary hole was cheerless and dank. In winter, the damp cold was so piercing that we could only get close to feeling warm in bed with every rag on.

The Kapo dominated every aspect of life in the barracks. I walked through the door and was hit by a bucket of cold water over my head.

'Son of a bitch!' I exclaimed in surprise and began to wheel, groping angrily for my assailant. Before I could turn, a heavy hand from behind wrenched me around and I came face to face with the Kapo. He thrust his jaw close to mine.

'Don't "son-of-a-bitch" anybody around here without my say-so. Don't breathe without my say-so. Don't crap without my say-so! I'm The Top and you don't do anything without my permission. Understand?'

I was being tested. Being one of the younger and stronger men I was singled out for the treatment. As I looked into the sneering face of the man in front of me, I was conscious of the assistant lurking behind me, and the SS guards patrolling outside.

I recognized instantly that if I was to survive I would have to accept whatever came my way.

'You hear me?' he repeated, snarling. He smashed me hard in the face with one fist, then straightened me up with the other. I found it almost impossible not to strike back, despite the odds. He'll kill me if I hit him back, I realized. I trembled with suppressed rage, only holding myself in check with the greatest self-control. But neither did I respond to his question, and he took careful note of that before pummelling the next prisoner. Knowing that I was a marked man, I resolved to tread carefully. Gingerly feeling for broken teeth, I stalked off to find a bunk, making it a point not to bow my head. A burning hatred blazed up inside me. I had a score to settle.

'Some place to sleep!' a man said under his breath to nobody in particular. 'But what can you expect?' He continued to mutter to himself, until he began to sob quietly.

I regarded him seriously. If he is talking to himself already, how long can he last, I wondered. How depressing to have him wandering around here like that! I determined to choose a bunk as far from him as possible. He went to a bunk near the door, so I quickly took one against the far wall in the corner. Later I was to cherish the illusion of privacy there, my back to the wall, with people on only one side of me. When quarrels or other problems arose I retreated to my corner. At times envious glances were cast my way; had I been smaller or weaker I might have lost my place.

A black uniform appeared in the doorway behind us as we chose our bunks. 'New prisoners. Listen! Your beds will be made perfectly at 6 A.M.,' commanded the Scharführer, or officer in charge of our section. 'If they are not, you will be punished for your sloppiness.' We stood at attention as he continued.

'Step out of line too often and you'll be put on commandant's report. You may think it's tough here, but God help you if you end up in the Strafgruppe (punishment squad).

'Your Kapo will issue your food and relay any information, instructions, or messages. All requests must be made to him.'

Smug and gloating, the Kapo stood to one side of the SS Scharführer. This Kapo and his assistant were to be our real jailors then, a fact that I felt boded ominously for me. I'll be getting the rough side of it, I thought. Alone and afraid, I would have to endure weeks and months under the man's control. Later I learned that the

Kapo's name was Stein and I began mentally to substitute Schwein (pig) whenever I heard it.

We had arrived at mid-morning, with nothing to eat for breakfast. By late afternoon I heard stomachs rumbling around me, and my own gnawed at me terribly.

'When do we get our other meals, do you know?' I asked a balding prisoner, who seemed to know his way around.

'If you don't work, you don't eat. Maybe around six we'll get something. But listen, boy, don't start thinking of food. It'll eat you up!'

Nobody even smiled at his grim joke. We already felt the consuming hunger which would soon dominate our thinking.

At about half past six three prisoners carried in large kettles and set them on a table inside the door next to Stein's bunk. He took them behind his curtain of blankets, savouring his power over us. The men milled about waiting while the soup was being ladled into smaller pots behind the curtain. Then the assistant announced,

'You will all go to the tables and stand there. On my order one man from each table will come up here with a tray.'

He spoke slowly, with a deliberate lack of concern about whether we ate or not, or whether the food was warm when we got it.

A number of younger men had followed me to the corner where I'd chosen my bunk. They now stood about me, so it was quite natural that all fifteen of us took a table together. We looked around silently at one another, then I nodded, picked up the tray, and joined the line in front of 'Schwein Stein'. May as well find out right away, I thought and began learning the ropes.

The man in front of me shuffled away and I stepped

forward, studiously keeping my eyes on the tray. I tried to give the impression of taking something from common waiters, being as calm, remote, and cool as I could. It was the wrong act to play, I was sure, but I couldn't pretend to grovel to such creatures.

The food was terrible. A small pot of thin soup with only a few vegetables and occasional scraps of fat and meat, and fifteen pieces of dark bread that were already crumbling at the edges. I didn't doubt what was happening to the thickest soup behind that curtain, as I reflected on how much fatter those two were than the rest of us.

'Schwein! Schwein! Schwein! Goddam bloodsuckers!' I swore softly under my breath as I returned to the table and distributed the meagre portions into the men's bowls as evenly as possible.

'There's little enough to go around, lads, so we'd better be completely fair to start with. It's the only way we'll survive without quarrelling.'

No one disagreed, and there was a hint of mutual respect that could grow. There was no trust or comradeship though; only fear and apprehension united us for the moment.

After the soup and bread we were given a jug of a brown liquid that passed for coffee. No matter what it was, we never wasted any. We were always hungry.

Much to my surprise, we were allowed to write one letter that evening. I wrote briefly to my mother that I was well and not to worry about me. We knew our letters would be read, if they were sent at all, so I didn't say more than that.

It was March 15, 1943. At about 9 P.M. I went to bed, ending my first day in a concentration camp. At least there aren't any bedbugs, I thought wryly, before turning to the wall to block out my tiny, ugly world so that I could sleep.

But sleep wouldn't come for hours. I stared at the rough boards in the darkness and thought of home. What was this war doing to my mother? Willy lay in an unmarked grave in Russia, Alfred was a war invalid, and I was a prisoner of the SS. How much did our fatherless family have to suffer? How long would I have to endure this place? And then what?

On that day, had I but known it, fighting was fierce on the Eastern Front and not everything was going Hitler's way. Hamburg, Stuttgart, Essen, Hamm, Munich and Nuremberg had all been heavily bombed, some of them even in daring day raids. Stalingrad had fallen over a month before and the Germans were not faring well in North Africa.

As I closed my eyes, my only thoughts were of personal survival. I wondered for the first time if an Allied victory might be the only way I'd be set free and a lot of other people released from their misery.

I was unaware of the lice that invaded my bed while I slept, to be 'the enemy within' for months to come.

Well before sunrise a loud, hoarse shout roused me. The single window yielded only a weak grey light by which we dressed and made our way across the compound to the latrines.

A stinking, ugly hole. Just a couple of damp, icy rails over an open ditch, one rail positioned to sit down over and other set to rest our backs against. We had to sit in a row, urinating and defecating en masse. There was no toilet paper, nor was any effort made to maintain hygiene.

It was to get much worse. After a few weeks, warmer weather came, bringing with it hordes of flies to breed in that devil's ditch. The stench grew much greater and I made my latrine visits as brief and infrequent as possible. Finally some lye was dumped in and the flies decreased, if not the smell.

Soon, however, the flies did their work anyway and dysentery ran rampant. The smell of sickness hung around the latrines and the bunk rooms. We were allowed a shave and a cold shower once a week, but this did little to keep us clean during the week, when we had no toilet paper and worked in the fields all day. At night guards would shoot anyone who left the barracks and we were reduced to using a stinking bucket for a toilet.

Dysentery hit nearly everybody, and soon there was a steady flow of men to the latrines or the pail. In the fields, during the day, we had to squat where we were. If we were lucky we might find some grass or leaves to wipe ourselves. Privacy was impossible anywhere. We were like animals.

On Sundays we did not have to work and we would bathe and be shaved. If they thought it was needed we would get a haircut too. What the camp called a bath was a quick ice-cold shower crowded with naked men and the rank odours from their bodies. For the shave we would sit on a chair, having soaked our beards, in water. Then, with precisely eight strokes, we would be roughly shaved.

We worked every day in broad, flat fields, around which our SS guards established real or imaginary lines, depending on the physical arrangement.

'Prisoners must stay inside this line,' the commandant ordered, 'or they will be shot dead. There will be no warning.'

Later that spring a man in another gang did try to

escape. The rumour was that he never got more than fifty feet across the line.

To begin work the guards spaced us out along the side of a field, an endless row of uniform gnomes, each with a shovel. Behind us, across the 'death line', was a row of SS guards, automatic pistols pointed toward our backs. Each guard had a truncheon ready to hand, thrust into his jackboot.

'You will dig from here across the field. Each man will keep up or he will be punished. You will work steadily until noon, when you will be ordered to stop. You will have thirty minutes to eat.'

Orders! Orders! Continuous threats of punishment. We stood there in the morning gloom and drizzle. I wondered how many of us would live to reach the other side of that field. We could barely distinguish a water ditch and hedge beyond it in the distance. I gritted my teeth and began to dig. They weren't going to break me or kill me off in this dismal place if I could help it. It looked like a continuous, flat graveyard as far as the horizon, and already I hated it.

Börgermoor was in the Ems district. It was nearly treeless, with frequent ditches and hedges that were the only vertical features in a never-ending landcape. How could I ever escape from here, where I could be seen for miles, without being shot or drowned in a ditch? I pictured myself a hideous, bloated corpse floating face up in a ditch. Vague ideas of escape had entered my mind and would stay to haunt me for months.

I began to observe every element of our daily routine, and to become familiar with the habits and idiosyncrasies of every guard. If there were chinks in their wall of control, I had to find them.

The digging was drudgery, the heavy, damp soil packed

from disuse and the winter's rain. By noon my back
ached and I felt tired. Blisters had already risen on my
hands. Some prisoners began to flag and fall behind a
little.

The first beating came just before our break. An older,
weak-looking man got more than five feet behind the
line, which we quickly learned was the allowable limit.
He saw the guard approaching from behind, pulling his
truncheon free, and the poor man made a frantic effort
to catch up. But it was too late. The first blow, on his
shoulder, sent him staggering to one side. The second,
across his head, knocked him forward, off-balance. The
third brought him to his knees. He tried to raise his arms
for protection, but blows struck him until he fell forward,
his forehead in the mud. The final blow thudded on his
back and kidneys. When he finally staggered to his feet
later I saw that he had wet himself, and I felt certain he
wouldn't last long.

There were no sounds during the beating except the
scraping of our shovels, the swish and thud of the truncheon, and the gasps and grunts of the unfortunate
prisoner. We dared not stop working, and watched only
from the corners of our eyes, with horrified fascination.
The hair on my neck rose with hate, fear, and anger.

'Schweine! Schweine! Schweine!' I hissed with each
thrust and turn of my shovel.

Lunch that day, and every day, was a single dry piece
of black bread. Nothing else. We chewed it slowly, sitting
on the edge of the unturned soil. After eating, I looked
for something to drink. Despite the misty morning I had
worked up a thirst from the work and the dry bread.
There was no water then, nor would there ever be. No
matter how hard the work or how hot the weather, we
never had a drink from morning until night. In the

summer, my thirst was often excruciating. We came back at night scarcely able to speak, our tongues swollen, our throats seized shut, and dashed for water at the camp.

We soon learned to drink our fill each morning, but we could never hold enough. At times men fell on the ground and drank from the ditches, but then the dysentery grew much worse from the stagnant water. A growing number of men unfit to work were sent off to the rag-picking gang. Night-time visits to the latrine bucket increased. The situation grew steadily worse and the stench became nearly unbearable in the bunkroom especially for those who slept near the pail.

Wagner, Number 506, the man who talked to himself, was the first to go. For nights he could be heard moaning, muttering as he blasted into the latrine pail. He could barely make it to the fields. One day he was beaten, and the next transferred to the rag-pickers to tear apart old clothes for making blankets. But he was too far gone even for the lighter work to save him. One night we woke suddenly. With a loud clang and splash the latrine pail had tipped. Something thudded on the floor. I heard nothing more and went back to sleep, too weak and tired to care.

Later, in the early dawn, an echoing shout brought us to our feet. There, lying in a pool of excrement, was the body of 506. He had died on the pail during the night.

Wagner was the first of our gang to die, but as we looked bleakly around the circle of faces surrounding the mess on the floor we knew he wouldn't be the last, and we were helpless to do anything about it.

'You two, 607 and 810, take him out of here and over to the main gate,' the Kapo ordered from the doorway. He turned away with a look of bored disgust.

I was number 810. Neither guard nor Kapo ever used

my name the whole time I was there. He chose me to do this degrading job to show his dislike for me. He would break me if he could.

'Get out on parade, the rest of you. You, 810, you can clean up this shit when you get back from breakfast. And don't be late for the work train, or else!'

I hated him and cursed him again under my breath. I would scarcely have time to eat and get my bed made before inspection. If my bed wasn't perfect I was in for a beating, and if I was late for the train my punishment would be even more severe.

We dragged out Wagner's body. I had no time to wash. After gulping my soup, I tucked my bread inside my shirt and hurried to clean up the mess and make my bed. Half an hour later I was in line for the train, sweat streaming off my face. The Kapo stared at me with a brutish look. It was a small triumph, but my spirits lifted at the knowledge that the Schwein hadn't broken me yet.

Gradually I realized that our SS guards hated their job. Not that they cared about us. Their work was boring, and assignment to prison-guard duty was at the bottom of the SS hierarchy. We took advantage of their lack of concern to steal vegetables while we worked in the fields. These we ate raw, and although they were dirty and probably contributed to dysentery, they helped to keep us alive. After months without fresh food, we revelled in the sweet, succulent taste of tiny carrots. We could barely control ourselves, and without the guards present we would have devoured the entire crop. As it was, we plucked a carrot whenever the guards looked away, scarcely breaking our digging rhythm as we did so.

By midsummer, most of us suffered from an accumulation of fluid in our feet and legs. Of course no treatment was given and we became very frightened of the swelling.

I began to worry that attacks of dysentery and other bodily weaknesses might break me, even though my will remained strong.

Number 805, Johann, in the next bunk, suffered terribly from the fluid. I watched him sit on his bed one day poking his finger into his puffy calf, watching in horror as the hollow remained for at least thirty seconds.

'What causes it?' I whispered. He didn't hear me.

'Johann! What causes it?'

He looked at me blankly, his eyes wide pools of fear.

'It's coming up,' he gasped. 'What happens when it reaches my balls?' His look pleaded with me to say something. Anything to staunch the flood of his fear.

I couldn't answer. In the last few days I had noticed the start of swelling around my own ankles. In near panic, afraid I might vomit, I hurried away.

All that day I kept asking what it was and what caused it. Finally, an older man, a former colonel, explained. 'In some it kills, but from what I know most people survive it. Just depends on how bad it gets. No idea what causes it though. If it's just starting on you now, I'd think your chances are pretty good, but I don't know about him.' He nodded towards Johann.

From that evening on, it was hard to avoid treating poor Johann like a doomed man. To compensate I began calling him by his name instead of his number. When we talked I tried to distract his attention to other things. As food was the principal topic of conversation, I would tell him of meals I had prepared for the Captain on the *Wega*, especially lavish ones for customs officers in foreign ports.

Johann always laughed. 'He was a clever old fox, wasn't he? I wonder where he is with his ship now?'

Such chatter worked for a while to distract both of us.

But at night I would hear him crying quietly before he fell asleep from growing weakness and exhaustion. In the mornings he would check his legs, then pull down his shorts and anxiously examine his genitals. I couldn't help watching, sharing his fear. A pall hung over our corner of the bunkroom. I checked too; fortunately my own swelling was hardly spreading.

One Sunday morning in Börgermoor we underwent our usual bunkroom inspection. As always, five or ten men were beaten with truncheons by the Kapo and his assistant because the bunks weren't squared enough for the SS sergeant. I thanked God again that I'd had thorough military training and could make my bed perfectly. 'Schwein' always fingered his truncheon when the inspector sergeant looked at my bunk, and I knew I'd get an extra beating if anything was wrong.

But this morning something was different. We were marched out for the daily count and commanded to remain in lines.

'You are wanted for a medical procedure,' the Scharführer said. 'Starting with you,' he pointed at the end man, 'one by one you will go to the medical officers over there.'

No explanation.

We craned our necks to see as the first man reached the table temporarily set up on the beaten earth of the compound. Two men in white smocks stook there, syringes in their hands. We saw the prisoner roll up his sleeve and pull down his pants and undershorts. I sensed some men around me cringe at the thought of the needle.

Then, incredulously, we watched one of the medics take a syringe full of blood from the man's arm, turn him around, and pump it into his buttocks. Quiet, involuntary exclamations burst from the lines.

'Jesus Christ!'

'What the fuck?'

'Goddam guinea pigs!'

We were silenced by a threatening gesture from the Kapo, who strode up and down the lines thumping his truncheon against his palm.

The following Sunday we were lined up again, and this time received an injection of a clear liguid into our biceps. It had no smell and seemed to have no effect. We even wondered if it was just water. We were never told the purpose of either of these 'medical procedures', and we did not dare ask questions. Prisoners had no rights at all. It became common belief that we were being experimented upon in some outlandish way. At nights when we stripped for bed, I looked for infection in the needle marks, before beginning the daily ritual of popping lice between my thumb nails. The big lice we found in our groin hair we called 'grandmothers'. They were always full of blood.

Several weeks after our arrival we came home one evening, tired and thirsty as usual. As we stood about the water barrel waiting our turn to drink, the main gate suddenly opened behind us and a new lone prisoner was unceremoniously thrust through it. He was even younger than me, I guessed, and hobbled with obvious pain in one leg. After he walked toward us a few steps he paused uncertainly, looking our way and then at the surrounding camp. No one moved.

Then, feeling drawn to him because of our age, I went forward.

'I can't really say, "welcome" to a hole like this, but my name is Hans and I can show you around.'

'I'm Heinz,' he said, obviously relieved that I had

bothered to speak to him. 'They just brought me here. I don't even know where I am.'

'Börgermoor-Emsland concentration camp.' Somehow I was embarrassed to say it, as though I was in any way responsible. 'We're near the Dutch border.'

I noticed by the downy fuzz on his cheeks that he must be very young, and he looked lost and frightened. But he's healthy and strong enough, I thought, as I sized him up, wondering why he limped.

After pointing things out that he'd need to know, I was going to take him to the latrine as he asked. But at that moment 'Schwein Stein' appeared in front of us.

'Get away, 810. You! The new one, 890, you come with me.' And Heinz was hauled away for 'the treatment'.

It turned out that Heinz was assigned to our barrack, so that I got to know him and he told me his story. He was only seventeen and had been called up the year before. After his basic training he had been shipped off to the Eastern Front.

'It was horrible. On the line there were so few of us I could scarcely see the others to my right and left. Then the Russians came in thousands and drove us back. Always back. All around me guys were dying. Each night when we regrouped there were fewer and fewer familiar faces and more new young guys like me. Christ, we didn't have a chance!

'Well, I could soon see how it was going to end for me around there: another rotten corpse in a few days. I'm too young to die.' He looked at me, his eyes pleading for understanding. 'Besides, I'm a farm boy. It's all I know and care to know. I don't wanna fight nobody.

'Well, one night I saved some bread from supper and after dark I went out like I was goin' to crap, and I put the bread over my leg and I shot myself. I didn't need to pretend to holler! I screamed to beat hell. Then when they picked me up I said I was hit by a sniper. I'd managed to throw the bread away in the dark, and I had my pants half down and the toilet paper out before I did it.

'Well, they believed me all right and I was sent back to the hospital. I was nearly home, I figured. In the hospital the doctor who treated me was very nice to me. He'd call me "son". Then one evening he came and sat by me and started talking. I was too stupid to see that anything was up.

'After a while he asked me about the Front and said he knew how terrible it was especially for a young guy like me. He said he'd be scared as hell if he was there. Then, sort of joking, he said, "I'm like your father, aren't I? You can tell me the truth. You shot yourself, didn't you? You put some bread over your leg so they wouldn't see any tell-tale powder burns, and shot through it." He was really sympathetic.

'Well, in no time I was blurting it all out. It was such a relief to tell somebody who understood and cared.' His short, choking laugh was bitter.

'Of course, the next day I was arrested and dragged right out of bed. My treatment stopped and I've been passed though a half-dozen prisons, until they dumped me here. No one has looked at my leg since. And no one will.'

He pulled up his pant leg and showed an ugly, oozing wound. The smell sickened me, and my stomach heaved at the sight, but I tried not to show it.

Because he was crippled, Heinz was put on the rag-picking crew, but he was right about the lack of treatment. His wound grew steadily worse. He limped more and the smell got so bad that no one wanted to eat with him. Those not used to it nearly gagged when they went near him during our Sunday showerbaths. None of us had anything to give him to put on the wound.

The end was predictable, although no one mentioned it. Gangrene set in. Finally Heinz collapsed in delirium and was taken away unconscious, as unceremoniously as he had arrived. We never heard about him again, but we were sure he died.

My twentieth birthday came and went soon after, but it was some time before I realized that I must be a year older. It made little difference anyway.

Food increasingly dominated our talk and our dreams. We grew thinner from hard work and privation. In two months I took my belt in two notches and wondered how long I could last. I was very frightened.

But in my third month summer began and we were able to pilfer from the fields. All body fat was gone, and so, with this bit of extra food, my weight seemed to stabilize.

One day I bent to drink from a ditch. My reflection horrified me. My eyes were sunk into my skull and my Adam's apple protruded grossly. I knew my arms and legs were scrawny, but I was shaken at the sight of my face. Others were even worse off.

I had dysentery and water on my ankles, but other prisoners suffered more severely, and some began to die. They would defecate constantly, then eventually collapse and be taken away to the infirmary, either to recover or die. I don't know if they received any treatment. I doubt it.

Some time in July the 'water' reached Johann's genitals and he died, convinced his manhood was gone, although with most prisoners the swelling was not fatal until it reached their lungs.

Two days later his bunk was occupied by a young Wehrmacht corporal, formerly an artist. I'd have preferred the bunk to stay empty longer.

'Why are you here?' I asked.

He ignored the abruptness of my question, and to my amazement had me laughing in a few minutes. I'd forgotten what it was to laugh.

'You won't believe why I'm here. I'm an artist. Before the war I drew newspaper cartoons for our local paper, but I was kicked off the paper by the Nazis. Well, I was pretty sore about it, and it was all Hitler's doing, so I drew a cartoon of him.

'In the picture I showed the Führer with Lilli Marlene. They're both in the nude, except he's got the top half of a uniform on. He's got his belt in a loop around his elbow, and her leg is hoisted up through it so as he can go straight into her, and he's screwing her hard with a long, skinny cock like a pencil.'

I gave a stifled gasp at his audacity, and then I laughed until I cried.

While I wiped away my tears of laughter, he continued, 'For a caption I put the tune:

> *Von der Kaserne, vor dem grossen Tor,*
> *Steht 'ne Laterne, und steht sie noch davor.*
>
> *Mit dir Lilli Marlene.*
>
> (In front of the barracks, by the big gate,
> Stands a lamp post, and it stands there still.
>
> With you, Lilli Marlene)

'Well, I hung the damn thing on my wall, and wouldn't you know some grubby little bastard reported me. I was arrested, and . . . well, you know the rest . . . so here I am.

'If I can find him after this bloody war is over I'll have his balls for bookends.'

It was good to talk openly like that, and to laugh, even for a few minutes.

The artist's story was incredible, but I also met men in Börgermoor who were there only for having intercourse with Jewish, Polish, or Russian girls. Even though the girls were willing. After all, the master race had to be kept pure.

Summer dragged on into fall. The weather grew damper and we began the harvest, often soaked to our skins. The bunkhouse was even drearier, and we began to dread the approaching winter. Each day we rode to the fields on the open cars of a little train, no matter what the weather. Luckily it seldom snowed for long in that part of the country, but the constant damp and chill brought on an onslaught of colds. By early December many of the colds bordered on pneumonia. I was lucky not to get one.

Despite these miseries and the drudgery, I noticed that most prisoners had begun to accept the life in Börgermoor. I began to doubt they would even try to escape if the chance came. I talked to them less and less, not wanting their attitude to rub off on me. I wanted out of there. Anyway, I risked being betrayed for an extra ration of food if I even mentioned escape.

Most of our time in the fields was now spent in digging potatoes and mounding them up for winter. We laid a pad of straw first. Then we picked over the potatoes carefully to avoid later spoilage and piled them neatly on the straw, covered by a smooth layer of soil, piled up to carry off the water. It was while we were spreading the last of these layers that life took a sudden turn for the worse for me.

8

'Stupid blockhead! That's not good enough.'

I leaped to attention from my crouching position by the potato pile. I hadn't heard the Scharführer come up behind me. My mind had been far away in Aunt Gerda's kitchen, eating her Obsttorte.

'Pardon, sir?' I was confused. What had I done wrong?

He was instantly enraged. I should have kept silent.

'Fool! I said it's not good enough.'

I realized he meant my potato piling. I surveyed the pile, looking for flaws. I had helped with several piles before and thought I was quite good at the job. There were no bad ones showing, and the pile was pointed and even for good drainage. I could see nothing wrong.

'Don't stand there, you ass, get busy and fix it.'

I didn't know what to do. I bent to work but couldn't find anything to improve.

'It's fine, sir,' I blurted, again standing erect.

He was livid. 'Goddam pig! Don't contradict me.' He hit me with his truncheon; with his boot he kicked at the pile. Potatoes rolled in all directions. I wanted to tear him apart with my hands.

'You need a lesson, I can see. What is your number?'

'810, sir.'

'Fix that pile, and do it properly. And have it done before quitting time if you know what's good for you.' He spun on his heel and marched away.

I was devastated. I knew I'd made an error but didn't understand what. If only I'd kept my mouth shut. What had I done? I knew that pile had been good. As I worked feverishly to rearrange the potatoes, I pondered the problem. What will happen to me now? A beating. I'll get a beating tonight for sure. And for nothing, too. What had brought it on? It almost seemed planned.

Suddenly I remembered the Kapo in conversation with the commandant that morning. During roll-call parade they had stepped to one side. They looked up and down the lines, and now I remembered how 'Schwein Stein' had looked at me. The bastard, I thought, he's got me into this. Something's up.

That evening the dreaded call came. The Kapo swaggered into the centre of the eating area, his signal that he had something to pass on to us. Silence spread. His smirk showed he was gloating.

'810! Report to the guardhouse. Immediately.'

My stomach dropped, but I was determined to show no emotion. I rose from the table and walked straight past Stein, pretending he wasn't there. I caught one or two surreptitious winks as I went out the door. Stein wanted to see me grovel, or at least show how shaken I was, and the prisoners were encouraging me not to give in.

The commandant sat behind a table. As I arrived, another prisoner had just been beaten. He crouched on the floor, gasping for breath, trying to struggle to his feet.

'209, if you plot any more escapes you will be shot.' The commandant's voice was low, cold, and emotionless. As the man struggled to his feet and was pushed from the room, I saw spatters of blood on the floor. They won't break me down like that, I swore to myself. I steeled myself for the worst.

'810?'

'Yes, sir.'

'Today you did poor work. You argued with an officer and you disobeyed his order.'

'But . . .'

'Shut up! Give him ten.'

'Sir, I . . .'

'Shut up!' He was suddenly furious. Spittle flew from his mouth as he leaped to his feet, red-faced, and shouted at me. The transformation shocked me. 'Pig! I see you need a bigger lesson. Give him ten and transfer him to the Strafgruppe. We'll see how you do there, you traitorous bastard!'

I think my beating was more severe because I had angered the commandant by trying to speak. The first blow hit me across the neck and shoulders from behind and made me stagger. Then they seemed to fall on me from all directions. Somehow I managed to stand still except to shield my face. I clenched my teeth to stifle the screams inside me and prayed my skin would not be broken. Even in that moment I feared most the lingering infections that I had seen on others. I know I received more than ten blows; it seemed to go on forever. Tears broke from me involuntarily, but through it all I felt triumphant that I hadn't gone down and crawled before these demented creatures.

When it stopped I was laced with fire. Nausea rose in me and I nearly broke from the pain. The room went out of focus and sweat poured from my body. When I could see straight, I looked down to see if I'd wet myself – many men did from these beatings. Another small triumph; I had not.

'Out! Out!' I was poked from behind.

I staggered through the door and across the compound toward the Strafgruppe barrack. The cool night air and

the drizzle cleared my head a little and I was able to walk
erect again by the time we reached the door.

'This is your place now,' the guard crowed behind me.
'We'll see how long you last here, traitor. Go get your
outside clothes and bring them here.' He leaned against
the wall and lit a cigarette while I went to my former
barrack. My bunk-mates looked up, no shock on their
faces. Beatings were nothing new. The Kapo was there,
but I ignored him and went to my locker. Paul, the artist,
stood near by.

'Am I bleeding?'

He knew what I meant. 'No blood coming through,' he
whispered. 'You're lucky.'

'Hurry up!' the Kapo shouted. I wanted to kill him
more than ever.

The Strafgruppe barrack was exactly like the other
one, but there was a deeply depressed feeling about it.
My new Kapo took me to an empty bunk.

'211 died last week. You can have his.' It was all he
said by way of introduction. Almost all of the other
prisoners were already deep in exhausted sleep; there
was scarcely a curious glance in my direction. No one
spoke, but I was too deep in misery to notice. The pain
had subsided slightly and I crept on to the wooden boards
of my new bunk and lay on my stomach. Gingerly taking
care to avoid pressing the sorest places, I tried to take
stock of my bruises. At least I'm not bleeding, I kept
thinking. Open wounds might kill me. Finally I fell into a
drugged sleep, thanking God I was relatively unharmed.

By luck, the following day was Sunday and I was able
to recuperate partially before going out on the work
gang. I knew already that the 'punishment squad' was
carrying railway ties. The rumour had got round the camp
that each man had to carry two at a time, and run with

them. When I heard of it I had wondered how they could manage to survive a single day. Now I would find out.

I was too embarrassed by the welts across my body to want to go for a Sunday shower. But a former Luftwaffe sergeant in a bunk near mine said, 'You'd better shower. It's not much, but it'll help your bruises go down before you go to work. We've all seen bruises before.'

As I stripped for the shower I watched the faces of the others for a reaction. There was none. I examined the parts of my body I could see. The long, angry red welts stood up and criss-crossed my back, buttocks, legs, arms, and shoulders. One curved around my thigh; the end of it leaving a bruise on my penis. I trembled, knowing I could have died or been emasculated if it had hit me squarely on the testicles. I knew nothing would be said if I died: my body would simply vanish from Earth. I thanked God for sparing my life. At that point only my faith kept me going.

Even in my deep misery I couldn't help noticing that the naked men in line with me were walking skeletons. My own weight I guessed to be about 125 pounds, down sixty from normal. As if he was reading my mind, the sergeant behind me said, 'You're young and very well built, boy, but you won't last two months in here. Either we get sent back or we die.'

It was a terrible jolt. Remembering how wild and furious the commandant had been the previous night. I felt sure I'd never be sent back. Besides, I was certain that he and the Kapo had picked me to fill the place left vacant by the dead number 211. I've got to escape! I've got to escape or I'll be dead before I'm twenty-one, I thought desperately.

Next morning, when I picked up my first railway ties

my arms strained under the weight. This was going to be tougher than I thought.

'Run! 810, run!' my new Scharführer barked.

By the time I reached the railway car I was gasping for breath.

And there was no purpose in the work.

We each had to carry two ties at a time for a distance of about a hundred and fifty yards to the end of the rail line. We ran nonstop. A huge pile of ties had been dumped from a barge beside the canal and we had to carry them to railway cars for loading. It was plain that the sole purpose of placing the ties there was to give us punishing work. The canal bordered the railway too, and the pile could have been dumped right beside the track only a few feet away. The senselessness of this drudgery numbed my body and mind.

By mid-morning I had become an unthinking automaton, no longer conscious of my body's exhaustion. Yet I kept my place equidistant from the man in front of me and the one behind. There were four guards along our route and a fifth stationed atop the tie pile, all well armed with Mauser rifles and Lüger pistols. Each guard was provided with an aluminum rain shelter that faced our work line. The guards slouched on their benches, watching us in utter boredom. Occasionally they would make jeering calls or loud, snide remarks about us. I came to ignore them. Much more important was the Scharführer, who was responsible for our work. At intervals he would stride up and down beside the line of prisoners, threatening us. By mid-afternoon we were really worn down and the whole Strafgruppe of thirty had noticeably slackened pace. He was getting very agitated, anxious to maintain face in front of the guards.

'Work, you bastards! Run!'

We picked up the pace again, driven by fear of the truncheon he took out and smacked against his jackboot. But inevitably a man stumbled and slowed, and his two ties tipped off balance. As I passed him I heard his rasping breath and saw the panic in his eyes as he strained to reposition the ties on his shoulders. In his desperation he moved too quickly and dropped one. Instantly the Scharführer was on him. The first blow lashed across his neck and down over his face near his eye. I didn't dare stop to help him.

At the railway-car door I dropped my ties and began to trot back to the pile. As I passed him again, the prisoner had just regained his feet with his ties on balance. He began to stagger forward. Blood flowed from his face, and at first I thought his eye had been knocked out. A large, bulging bruise stood out purple beside the socket.

He'll be dead soon, I thought. My God, My God! That's me in a few weeks. 'You won't last two months,' the sergeant had said. I couldn't afford to give in to exhaustion. The incident shocked me back into conscious thought.

The next day it grew colder, and it rained on us as we rode the train to work. All around me men were coughing and shivering, eyes red-rimmed and sunken. We began our trot in the drizzle. The guard on the pile wore a raincoat and hat and turned his back to us and the rain. I looked beyond him. If I broke and ran, it was a good hundred yards to the first cover, a barren hedge. Beyond it lay a ditch, then a field and far away another ditch.

It was hopeless. I'd be cut down in seconds. There was no possible escape. As I trotted back and forth all that day I felt completely desolate. I'm going to die! I'm going to die! It kept running though my mind in time to my jogging.

That night, in my sleep, a body floated face up in the canal and the guards jeered at it, 'Get up and work. Let's see you get up and work now!' As I drew nearer I saw that the face was my own, and I woke sweating with shock.

My third day on the punishment squad started out even colder. As we rode toward the canal, snowflakes drifted down on us and I shivered with the damp chill beneath my winter coat. It was December 9; I had been in Börgermoor nine months. Will I see 1944 or will I die by then? I wondered. I won't live to be twenty-one. My mother will never hear of me again. Her face and my brothers' faces drifted before my eyes and I wept silently, uncaring.

When we jumped down to go to work our wooden shoes clicked harder than usual on the partly frozen ground. The sky was low, dark and pregnant with stormy cold. The wind picked up as we marched to the pile of ties to begin. 'If it was hard before, winter's going to make it much worse.' It was the sergeant at my elbow. He looked haggard and old.

That day was excruciating. When we stopped at noon to chew our rye bread, we soon began to shiver as our sweat cooled quickly in our meagre clothing. We huddled together, steam rising from our backs. Working exhausted us, stopping froze us. When I can't take it any more and there's no hope, I'm going to make a break for it, I decided. I'd rather be shot than be driven into the ground, dying a slow agony.

I'd never believed I could feel so desperate.

PART TWO
On the Run

9

I woke with a start and looked around. The sights and smells of the farm reminded me that I was a free man. I felt refreshed and comfortable. My clothes were almost dry, and there were no signs of a cold or the pneumonia that I could have expected after the events of the last twenty hours. I stretched lazily. 'You're a free man, Hans Nütt,' I gloated, then suddenly had to grab my belly; dysentery affects free men too.

Bodily functions taken care of, I looked at the sky. It was another dull day, grey, with snow falling gently; it covered the ground to a depth of half an inch. I looked down at my feet, bruised, scratched, filthy; I had to obtain shoes somewhere soon. I looked around me. In an empty bay at the end of the shed stood a heavy four-wheeled farm cart, and on it lay a pile of potato sacks. I went over, took down a sack, tore it into strips, and wound them around my feet until they were covered.

I tried a few cautious steps. I could walk, although not very comfortably. But my feet felt wonderfully warm. Luxury is relative to one's previous condition; in my position, those bindings of sacking represented an enormous improvement.

I sat down at the back of the shed behind the cart and debated what to do. I was hungry again, but that was nothing new. I could put up with hunger, if it meant staying free. My clothes were the great problem; the longer I kept my camp uniform, the greater were my chances of being recognized and picked up. Should I hide in the straw until nightfall, then set off again, moving only when it was dark? Or should I take a chance, walk boldly up to the farmhouse, and throw myself on the owner's mercy?

The farmer who opened the farmhouse door was about fifty years old, a stout man, clad in farm overalls and heavy boots. 'Who the hell are you?' he demanded, staring at my filthy clothes and the sacking around my feet.

'I escaped yesterday from a concentration camp.'

He grabbed my arm and dragged me into the kitchen. 'Come in, come in, don't stand out there.' He peered all around before closing the door, as wary as if his house was on a busy city thoroughfare. 'Here, sit down.' He ushered me to the table, a plain wooden table in a simple but spotless kitchen. He appeared to be the only person at home.

'I need new clothes,' I blurted out, desperate.

'No, don't ask me for that. I can't give you any. But I'll feed you.'

'Thanks. I'm very hungry.'

He put bread and cold meat before me. 'Eat up. You look starved.' He watched me tear at the bread and meat like a wild beast. My instinct was to cram it into my mouth and swallow it at once, before it could be taken from me, and I had to force myself to slow down and chew the food. Each time I looked up, he smiled at me and gestured at the food, as if to say, 'Eat it all, there's plenty.'

When I had finished, he smiled at me again, a naturally jolly man. 'You escaped, eh?'

'Yes, yesterday.'

'Good, good. Wait here.' He disappeared into the scullery or pantry off the kitchen and reappeared with an open bottle of beer and a glass. He put them in front of me and sat down, still smiling broadly. 'Beer. You celebrate, eh?'

It was the first beer I had seen since my arrest over a year ago. I picked up the bottle and poured, watching the liquid bubble and sparkle and leave a frothy head. I held up the glass and looked at the Dutchman. He nodded vigorously and grinned. I drank, savouring the clean, biting taste in my mouth so much that I was reluctant to swallow. I knew that beer was the last thing a man with dysentery should drink, but I didn't care. It seemed right to celebrate, and I relished every drop.

I stood up somewhat unsteadily from the table. 'You can't give me any old clothes?'

'No, I'm sorry. I don't have any.'

'Well then,' I waved at the table, the plate, the empty bottle and the glass with some froth still sticking to its sides, 'thanks.'

'It's nothing. Good luck.'

'Thanks again.' I left and kept going west. Within half an hour I was paying dearly for that bottle of beer, but I had no regrets.

Soon I came upon a dirt path about five feet wide between the fields, and began to follow it. Conscious of my suspicious appearance, I was frightened of meeting anyone. In that almost featureless countryside there were few places to hide, but I could see anyone coming from a great distance.

Once committed, I had to go on. The snow had eased, and the thin cover on the ground was melting. My feet were sore where the sacking rubbed on them, but I forced myself to ignore the discomfort. There were no signs of Germans, or of anybody else. It was a sparsely settled area with few roads, and at that time of the year there was little work to do in the fields.

After a couple of hours, I saw another farm ahead of me in the distance. I slowed down and approached cautiously. As I came closer, I noticed a man ploughing near the farm with a team of horses. He failed to notice me until I was quite close, when he heaved on the reins to stop the horses, turned and looked towards me. He made the sign of the cross. I couldn't blame him, for his routine was now disturbed by the appearance of a skeletal, wild-looking man in filthy, tattered clothes with his feet wrapped in torn sacking. What my face looked like now, I could only guess.

As I turned off the path and approached him, he stood dead still and crossed himself again, his eyes wide with astonishment and fear.

'Can you help me? I need clothes, particularly shoes.' I pointed at my feet.

He looked down at my feet, then back at my face. He pondered for a few seconds, shook his head, then said, 'Go to the shed by the house. That's where I put my old work-clothes. Maybe you'll find something there.'

'Thank you. You're very kind.'

'I never saw you, remember that!' he replied, immediately turning back to the plough and the horses.

I hurried into the farmyard and soon found the shed he meant. Inside, piled in a corner, was a heap of old clothes. I rummaged through them and found an old brown jacket made for a man double my size. It almost went round me twice but I tucked it into my pants. Then I went through the heap again, but I couldn't find any trousers or shoes. The distinctively striped camp trousers would still betray me.

In desperation, I rooted around the shed. On a shelf

by the door I found half a can of creosote and an old
paint brush. I got them down and struggled with the lid
until it came off. Without taking off my trousers, I
covered them with the strong-smelling creosote, applying
it thickly until the yellow stripes were obliterated. They
were a mess, but they would no longer give me away at
first glance.

Jacket, trousers of a sort. Now I needed shoes. I
rummaged around again, but found only an old cloth cap
which I stuck on my head. At least it would hide the
prison haircut until I could do something about it. Things
were better, but not by much. Without shoes I would still
be conspicuous.

As I left the shed I was seized again by diarrhoea. I
dashed over to the outside toilet and relieved myself.
When I came out, I could scarcely believe my eyes.
Beside the backhouse was a jumbled pile of boots and
shoes. I crouched down and examined them. Feverishly I
tried on every one of the half-dozen pairs until I found a
pair that fit – more or less. They were old, cracked, and
dry, but I put them on with more joy than a millionaire
trying on new, hand-made shoes.

Now I was ready to continue my journey with more
confidence. I looked like a scarecrow, a hobo, a tramp, a
madman even. But no longer like a concentration camp
prisoner.

'Find what you wanted?'

I jumped around, startled. It was the farmer. I had not
heard him enter the farmyard.

'Yes, yes, thank you,' I stammered. 'I'll leave now.
Thank you.'

'Perhaps you should eat first,' he replied. He had
recovered from his earlier fright, had thought it over and
decided to help me. He was a brave man.

He fed me bread and cheese, and smiled nervously as I ate. 'Thank you again,' I said, as I picked up my cap to leave.

'God bless you,' he murmured, and crossed himself again.

A couple of hours later, I saw a small village ahead. It was dusk, and the few creatures in the landscape were growing indistinct. It must have been about five in the afternoon. Again I had to make a decision – whether to avoid the village altogether, or to risk asking for food there.

I was to find before long that the physical exertion of walking several hundred miles, sometimes without food, was nothing compared with the stress of constantly weighing up my situation and choosing one alternative over another. There was no room for error or miscalculation. If I made only one mistake, a single misjudgement, I would be recaptured and killed.

Common sense told me to avoid the village, especially when I saw evidence that a German army unit was billeted there. I could see some of the officers exercising their horses in a meadow not far from the close-packed houses of the village. Yet I felt sure that the Dutch people of the village would help me. I had stopped at three farms since my escape, and, at each, people had assisted me with varying degrees of willingness, with no sign that they would consider betraying me. I made up my mind and sat down, waiting for the darkness to deepen.

Shivering with cold, I studied the village. I estimated the population would be about one hundred, not counting the German troops. It was a small settlement, typical of a remote agricultural area, and I could imagine that the populace would not welcome the occupying German troops forced upon them. Dr Goebbels's propaganda boasted of the friendly reception accorded our troops in Western Europe, but nobody believed him.

Getting to my feet, I peered at the nearest house through the gloom. It was a small cottage rather than a house, the sort of place a farm labourer would live in. More to the point, it looked too small to have room to billet any soldiers.

I flexed my cold-stiffened joints, slunk through the dusk, and knocked on the door of the cottage.

10

'My name is Hans Nütt. I have escaped from a German concentration camp. I need food, clothes, shelter.' My half-forgotten Dutch was coming back to me.

'Oh, I'm sorry, I cannot help you, because I'm alone.' She saw the look of disappointment on my face. 'Yes, my husband got deported to Germany to work in a factory there.'

'I'm sorry.' I thought this slim young woman was going to turn me away. I couldn't blame her.

'But the mayor will help you – he's a very good man and he hates the Germans, the Nazis, the SS, the Gestapo.' The words came out in a rush. It was clear she felt the same hatred and would do nothing to aid the conquerors of her country. 'The mayor of our village will certainly help you.'

'Thank God. How do I get there?'

'I'll take you. Just a minute.' She grabbed a coat and closed the door. 'Come with me,' she said, taking my arm, ignoring the pervasive odour of creosote around me.

She led me along the garden path, through a gate in the hedge, and up to the front door of the large farmhouse next door. She knocked and waited. A lady in her fifties opened the door, and as soon as the young woman explained who I was, I was ushered quickly into the mayor's office.

The man in ordinary working clothes who rose from the desk was in his middle fifties and overweight. He grasped my hand and told me to sit down. In a few words I explained who I was.

'You can stop worrying,' he said with a smile. 'Yes, I will help you.' He paused and muttered to himself. 'Food, clothes, papers.' He turned to me, 'You wouldn't happen to have a photograph of yourself?'

'A photograph?'

'Yes.'

'No, I don't. I don't have anything.'

'Pity. If you had a photograph I could issue you with identification papers. That's one bit of authority the Germans left me. Oh well, let's get started anyway. We'll give you new clothing – well, not new, but certainly a great deal better than what you have now.'

We both laughed. My gamble in coming into the village was paying off.

'Take your cap off,' he commanded. I obeyed. He stood up and came to where I was sitting. 'That haircut will give you away at once. Wait here a minute.' He went out and I heard him giving orders in the kitchen.

'You need a haircut badly. I've sent for the barber,' he explained as he returned. 'Let's go into the kitchen; my wife likes to keep this office tidy.' I picked up my cap and followed him.

In a few minutes the village barber arrived. He studied my hair for a few seconds. 'Ah, what a mess! Fancy just cutting it like that!' He took out a pair of hand clippers and set to work, making no comment about the mud, lice, and other debris in my hair.

'That's the best I can do, I'm afraid,' he said a few minutes later. 'Don't tell anybody it's my handiwork.' He laughed as he put his clippers away. 'Advertisements like that I don't need.'

He left, and the mayor's wife showed me to the

bathroom. 'Throw all your old clothes out,' she told me. 'We'll burn them and give you new ones. Do you have lice?' She didn't wait for an answer. 'You most certainly do. Never mind, we'll get rid of them.'

And without another word this obviously middle-class woman calmly hauled away my filthy, lice-ridden clothes to burn them. I was filled with admiration for this couple who, at the risk of their own lives, tried to help me and acted so matter-of-factly about it, as if it was perfectly natural to assist an escaped prisoner while there were enemy troops only a few hundred yards away.

The bathroom off the kitchen contained a large enamelled tub and drew its hot water from a huge old-fashioned gas heater, which lit with a hiss and a pop when I turned the tap on. With reluctant fascination I took a look at myself in the mirror while the tub filled. The haircut improved my appearance, but otherwise I looked like a demon from some medieval vision of hell. My eyes were sunk deep in their sockets, the skin was drawn tight over my cheekbones, and my lips were without colour. The rest of my body was emaciated; imprisonment in the concentration camp had removed most of my flesh and left the bones protruding. The swelling around my ankles still remained, and my legs were covered with angry blotches where the creosote had soaked through my trousers.

I soaked in the bath for a little while, then scrubbed myself from head to toe, taking particular care to rid myself of every louse. I let the bathtub drain, rinsed the tub, then filled it again and relaxed in the luxury of my first hot bath for many months. I felt a great sense of well-being, of confidence, of hope.

When the water was nearly cold, I got out and dried myself on warm towels. I shaved thoroughly and carefully, dried my face, and opened the door. My joy knew no bounds when I saw what was piled neatly on a chair outside.

Clean underwear, clean shirt, clean socks, a clean blue one-piece mechanic's coverall, a brand-new cap, and a pair of very old-fashioned high-laced boots made of soft leather. They fitted me perfectly. Except for the cap, nothing was new, but it was all clean and had plenty of wear left in it. I pulled on the jacket, picked up my cap, and went through into the kitchen.

'Bravo! You look quite the gentleman,' the mayor's wife called out.

'I just don't know how to thank you,' I stammered.

She left the pot she was stirring on the stove and came and placed a hand on my shoulder. 'Don't worry. We understand.'

There were four of us at supper, the mayor, his wife, his son, aged about seventeen, and I. We sat and ate as if there was nothing out of the ordinary; conversation was polite and restrained.

It was a simple, nourishing meal such as I was used to at home, but these simple family surroundings did more for my peace of mind that anything a doctor could prescribe. I felt my confidence growing; everywhere I turned, I found people ready to risk their lives to help me. I hoped the same would be true of my whole journey to Switzerland or Spain, from where I hoped to reach England and safety. It was hard to believe that yesterday's fugitive, barefoot, wet and stinking, dressed almost in rags, was now sitting down, bathed and shaved, in clean, lice-free clothes, to a meal at a table set with fine white linen.

After we had finished our meat, potatoes, and veg-etables, followed by a delicious milk pudding, the mayor gestured for me to follow him into his office. We both sat down, he behind his desk and I in a comfortable armchair where my only wish was to fall asleep. But the mayor's words shocked me into full consciousness.

'You've a long way to go yet. The SS and the Gestapo won't give up, you know. I can help you in some ways, but mostly you are on your own.' He reached into his desk drawer and offered me a cigar from a box. 'No? Your're welcome to one.' He lit his cigar and leaned back before continuing. 'The first thing to remember is that you don't have any papers. Pity you didn't have a photograph; then I could have given you genuine papers. You must get a set of papers as soon as you can. The Germans are constantly checking people's identification papers. You don't have any, so you must avoid travelling by train or bus, and it would be better if you don't take a ride with anyone.'

'I understand. I must keep walking.'

'Unfortunately, that is true. Now, you might be able to get hold of some papers if you are in an air-raid. It's not the nicest way, but you can try to get them from a dead person. I can't stress too much what danger you are in until you get a set of papers. So you must always be careful. Avoid cities and large towns. Keep away from railroads and main highways. As far as possible, keep away from any road that can carry motor traffic. Now, how good is your geography?'

'Good enough to tell me to keep going west.'

He sat back and roared with laughter. 'If you do that you'll end up in the North Sea.' He hunted in the bookcase by his desk, found a battered school atlas, and turned to a map of Holland and Belgium. 'Come over here and look. See, this is where we are.' His finger moved to the west until it rested on the sea coast. He looked up and smiled. 'See, this is the way to go.' He traced a route across Holland and Belgium into northern France. The route was more to the south than to the west.

'I see,' I murmured.

'Good. Now, one other thing. You may be able to hitch a ride on a freight train now and again, but be careful. Don't ever fall asleep on a train, however safe you think you might be. You never know where you might end up. Always pick a slow freight, never an express: expresses always end up in big cities.'

He puffed on his cigar thoughtfully and considered a couple of minutes before adding, 'When you get into Belgium there's a small town called Achel. A priest there, Father Vlaminck, will help you.' He wrote the priest's name and the name of the town on a piece of paper. I reached forward to take it.

'No, memorize it.' He waited while I did so, then lit a match, and burned the paper in the ashtray. We watched silently until it was consumed. Then he stubbed out his cigar in the ashes. 'One can't be too careful, you know. I don't want you giving away the good father if you get caught. One last piece of advice: you can probably trust most village priests if you get into trouble. Almost without exception they are anti-German.'

'I'm German, you know. Why are you helping me?'

'The sin is not in being German but in being Nazi. If I were to hate all Germans, I would be no better than the Nazis, who hate the Jews. You tell me you were in a concentration camp, so that's good enough for me. They don't put their friends there.'

His wife brought in a tray with cups and a pot of coffee. 'Not the real thing, I'm afraid, but if you use your imagination . . .' She smiled and left. As we drank our 'coffee' I told the mayor about myself and he listened intently. By the time I had finished it was late.

'Time for bed. Let me show you to your room.'

'I'd rather sleep outside. I don't want you to be caught with me in the house; it's too dangerous.'

'Oh nonsense!' he replied. 'The Germans are all fast asleep by now. But, if you insist . . .' He shrugged his shoulders.

'I'd rather sleep in the barn, if I may.'

'Of course. It's up to you. It's not every day we have visitors.'

He showed me through a door which led to the barn, and I made myself comfortable on a pile of hay beside the horse stalls. I hadn't told him the real reason for wanting to sleep out in the barn – I was terrified of a diarrhoea attack during the night. The toilet was outside in the yard, and I hated the thought of making a mess in the house which had afforded me such hospitality.

It was as well I did so, for almost immediately after falling asleep I was attacked by agonizing abdominal cramps and had to rush for the outhouse. It was the first of several visits during the night, but between attacks I slept like a child.

Early next morning, before it was properly light, the son came into the barn and fed the horses. 'Breakfast's ready,' he called out cheerfully. I followed him into the house, where I ate a simple breakfast with the family.

'Time to go,' I said finally, reluctant to leave these kind people.

The mayor's wife handed me a canvas bag. 'One or two things for your journey,' she said with a warm smile. I shook hands with everyone, put on my brand-new cap, and turned to go.

'After the war . . .' the mayor called.

It was not yet light and nobody seemed to be about. I had only gone about a hundred yards when I heard the mayor calling me back.

'Here, take this,' he ordered, handing me a three-pronged farm fork.

I looked at it, puzzled.

'Carry that and it will always look as if you are going to or from your work.'

We smiled and shook hands for the last time. As I walked along, thinking of their wonderful kindness and bravery, all I could do was to say a silent prayer for the mayor and his family.

A couple of miles down the track I was following, I examined the contents of the canvas bag the mayor's wife had given me. Inside I found food (a piece of smoked ham, about a pound of sausage, a loaf of dark bread, and a dozen boiled eggs), a knife, a fork, and a spoon, a packet of cigarette tobacco and papers, a small amount of Dutch money, and pages torn from an atlas showing all the countries of Western Europe, including England. It was difficult not to sing and whistle as I continued on my way.

Follwing the mayor's advice, I used only minor roads and paths, and avoided all places with large populations. It took me two weeks to walk across Holland and Belgium. Dressed as I was and carrying my farm fork, I no longer looked like a fugitive. I let people assume I was a travelling labourer. At that time there were many such transient workers – Czechs, Poles, and Belgians – working on farms or assigned to construction of the Atlantic Wall defences against invasion along the coast of France. At night I slept in barns.

One day about noon, I stopped at a lonely farm to ask for food. Through the doorway I saw an elderly couple feasting on a huge ham, and my mouth watered as I anticipated being offered some of the juicy meat. Instead, the old man led me over to a brick pig barn at the rear. In the front corner stood a huge copper kettle, in which potatoes and turnips were being boiled up for the pigs.

The old farmer lifted the lid. 'Help yourself,' he said and went back to the farmhouse.

Still thinking of the succulent ham, I took my knife and peeled the skins from a handful of potatoes. Suddenly I noticed a milk separator against the other wall, with a pot of cream under it. I took my spoon and spread fresh cream over my potatoes and feasted on them until I could eat no more. It was not as tasty as the ham would have been, but it was much better than going hungry.

After I had licked my knife and spoon clean, I went back to the house. 'Thank you so much for your hospitality.'

'That's quite all right.' No questions about who I was; my disguise was effective.

About a mile from the farm I paid dearly for my greed and self-indulgence as the worst diarrhoea of my life gripped me. But to my surprise I didn't feel weak afterward, as I had after attacks in the camp. I realized that I was beginning to regain my strength and that the effects of the dysentery were leaving me at last.

One night I was foolish enough to stay with a group. I reached a small town in the evening and, instead of going round it and sleeping in the country, I approached a barn-like building. I crept in quietly, and then froze as I was confronted by the sight of about twenty or thirty men in shabby work-clothes sitting on bales of straw, eating their supper. They looked up as I entered.

It would have looked suspicious for me to turn around and leave, so with assumed casualness I sat down and pulled some bread and cheese from my canvas bag. From their conversation I knew they were Poles. I spoke to one of them in Dutch, and he replied in German, a language spoken by several of the men. I discovered they were a forced-labour gang that the Germans employed on street repairs.

'What about you?' one man asked.

I held up my farmer's fork and yawned. It would be wise to end this conversation.

He pointed upwards. 'There's lots of hay up there.'

'Thanks. Good night.' I picked up my bag and my fork and crawled up the ladder to the loft.

Early in the morning, before it was yet light, I felt somebody shaking my shoulder. I started to protest, but a hand clamped down over my mouth.

'Listen,' he hissed, 'don't make a sound. I've come to warn you. Our group leader is very pro-German and he might report you. Don't stay here once we leave. Get out fast.' He removed his hand and crawled away in the darkness before I could thank him.

As soon as the group left for work, I picked up my possessions and headed out of the town quickly, taking care not to be seen for the rest of that day and resolved to be more careful in the future.

I tried to beg a good meal each midday or early in the afternoon. For evening meals I ate small snacks from the food in my canvas bag, or sandwiches given me by a farmer or his wife. My course was not direct – I had to make detours around populated areas, and wait and reconnoitre before crossing any railway lines, main highways, or river bridges that lay across my route. Yet I was making good progress, sometimes thirty miles a day. If the weather stayed good for that time of year, I could keep moving on my route to a neutral country. I looked frequently at the creased pages from the atlas and tried to decide whether to make for Switzerland or Spain, but I was unable to make up my mind and decided to postpone my decision until I reached France.

I crossed from Holland into Belgium in fine style. I was looking for a barn to sleep in when a freight train rumbled slowly along the nearby line and stopped at a siding to let an express freight through. Clutching my canvas bag and my farmer's fork, I hurried across the field, my heart beating at the opportunity. I stopped at the foot of the embankment and listened, but all I could hear was the wheezing of the locomotive. I peered into the darkness; from what I could see, it was an ordinary freight train. I decided to take a chance. Crouching down, I moved along the embankment to a point halfway along the line of boxcars. A pause. Still no sound. I scrambled up to the line and onto the platform at the end of one of the cars.

Laying my fork down carefully so as to make no noise, I clasped my canvas bag securely and crouched down. Another train, a passenger, went by before the locomotive on my train groaned and puffed as we set off. I did not realize we had crossed the border until, at one of our many stops, I heard the railwaymen speaking French. I was in Belgium.

Cautiously I peered around the end of the boxcar. By the feeble light from the signal box I could make out some details of a railway official's uniform. It was different from those I had seen at our stops in Holland. I felt a sense of jubilation, and I had to warn myself to be cautious. Two borders crossed, two more to cross, and I would be free! I was halfway through my journey.

The next time the train slowed down, I threw my fork off and jumped down after it. It was about three o'clock in the morning. After hunting around a while, I found a barn to sleep in. I was tired and hungry, but that was no longer important.

11

A couple of days later I was close to the small town of Achel which the mayor had mentioned. After long thought, I decided to risk visiting Father Vlaminck. It was an insignificant town, and I soon found the church with the priest's house next door.

Without a clear idea of what I should say, I walked up the brick path and knocked on the door. A black-robed priest in his late thirties opened the door and looked at me inquiringly.

I greeted him in French, 'Bonjour.'

To my amazement he answered immediately in German, 'Bitte, kommen Sie 'rein (Please come in)!' He opened the door wider and ushered me in. Then he led me to his study and quickly produced coffee and biscuits. I was unable to speak at first, flabbergasted that he recognized me as a German.

But he continued speaking in German and did not seem the least discomfited at finding me on his doorstep. I found my voice and told him about myself, mentioning the Dutch mayor. He followed my story intently, occasionally interrupting to clarify a point.

'I'll try to help you,' he said when I had finished my account. 'I would like to have you stay in this house, but unfortunately that is not possible. You see, they've billeted a German officer here. You can understand what a risk that would be.' He must have seen the look on my face. 'Don't get upset. He's not in the house now. He won't be back before evening, so we've lots of time.'

Father Vlaminck gave me some Belgian money, but I found even more valuable the advice he offered. For a priest he displayed an astounding knowledge of the location of German checkpoints and how to avoid them. In addition, he told me where I could jump on a freight train, and where it was best to get off. He discussed all this quite openly and without any outward signs of tension. I was positive I was not the first fugitive he had helped.

Before I left, he gave me food to take with me and dismissed me with a cheerful wave. I was beginning to realize the extent of organized resistance to the German invaders and the determination of the resisters not to let their spirit be crushed, no matter how great the military might ranged against them.

It is natural to think of occupied countries as teeming with enemy troops, but I learned that this is not so. Once the conquest is completed, the victors will keep only enough troops in the occupied country to ensure civil order and to guard against invasion. This was particularly true in Germany's situation, where troops were constantly needed for the Eastern Front. It was impossible to maintain unceasing surveillance over every train or bus, and the Germans had to be satisfied with guarding strategic targets.

Father Vlaminck's advise was invaluable. I was soon close to the border between Belgium and France, a border that was now largely non-existent because Germany occupied both countries. But my excitement at the prospect of entering France was tempered by anxiety. I was sure that every Frenchman felt hatred for all Germans. I felt I could not hope to find Frenchmen distinguishing between pro-Hitler and anti-Hitler Germans, and feared that I would not receive any help if it became known that I was one of the hated Boches. In the end, I decided to pass myself off to the French as a downed American pilot. This was a desperate gamble, but the risk of a local Frenchman knowing how Americans spoke and acted was remote, far less than it would be if I pretended to be English. At that time there was no television and few American films in France. My ploy might just work.

Very early in the morning of Christmas Eve, 1943, I crossed from Belgium into France, brought close to the border by freight train the night before. I had remained hidden all day and until midnight, knowing that the countryside ahead was the last country between me and freedom in Switzerland or Spain, and that I had to be very careful. But I saw no guards or checkpoints, and I crossed into France without incident.

Going down a minor country road later that day, I stopped to roll a cigarette. I had just got it lit when a farm cart drawn by two heavy horses trundled around the corner. Seated on the box was a short, wiry farmer of about forty-five, wearing a long blue peasant's smock.

Pulling on the reins, he greeted me with a smile and asked, 'Where are you going?'

I had to play for time. 'Guess!' was the only thing I could think of to say. He did not seem put out by my evasive answer.

'Oh, from your accent I can tell you're Belgian.'

I was relieved that he did not recognize me right away as a German, and immediately I decided to try out the role I had planned for myself. 'No, not Belgian.'

'Dutch?'

'No.'

'Polish?'

'No.'

We both laughed, caught up in the spirit of the game.
'Russian?'
'No.'
'Well, what are you then?'
'I'm an American. A pilot.'
He leaped down from the cart and embraced me. 'An American? My God! How did you get here?'
I lifted my cap so that he could see my hair. 'As you can see from my haircut, I was in a prisoner-of-war camp in Germany. I escaped, and here I am.'
'My God! I must help you. Where are you going?'
'I'm trying to get to Switzerland or Spain and then back to England.'
'Would you like to come to my home? My family would be very honoured to meet you.'
'Sure, certainly. Thank you.'
He thought for a few seconds. 'Just wait here for ten or fifteen minutes. I'll be back. I have to go to one of my fields, then I'll take you home.'
'Okay.' I was delighted. My ruse seemed to be working. I rolled and smoked a cigarette while he was gone.
He must have hurried, because he was back in less than ten minutes. Smiling, he reached out a hand and helped me up on the cart beside him. Then he turned and lifted the straw. 'Look!'
Under the straw was a sleek, plump hare. 'That's for tonight, for supper.' My mouth watered at the prospect.
Approaching the village, I was seized by fear. 'Perhaps I should get under the straw?'
'Why?' he laughed. 'The Boches will never notice you.'
'There are Germans in the village?'
'But of course. But it's Christmas and they won't see you. They never bother us much anyway.'
I remained tense as the horses pulled the cart slowly

into the village. From a distance, I heard the strains of a traditional German Christmas carol and I had to turn aside to hide my tears from my companion.

The horses turned unbidden into the courtyard of a farmhouse. Two boys in their teens came rushing out to hold the horses' bridles and looked at me inquiringly. Their father jumped down, beaming.

'Guess who I brought!'

They continued to stare at me, but said nothing.

'An American pilot!'

The two boys came round to me and shook my hand enthusiastically. 'Bonsoir, monsieur,' 'Enchanté, monsieur.' They rushed into the house to tell their mother.

Just then we heard the roar of approaching aircraft engines, and the farmer and I looked up in time to see a group of British airplanes fly over. Pointing at them, he smiled. 'Vos camarades! (Your friends!)' I grinned and nodded, and we went into the house.

Dropping the hare on the kitchen table, the farmer proudly introduced me to his wife, who quickly set bread, cheese, sausage, and milk before me and begged me to eat. There was a lump in my throat as I realized how delighted these simple people were to help an ally, even under the noses of the Germans.

'We must celebrate this happy occasion,' the farmer beamed. He sent his wife out on her bicycle to the next village to buy apéritifs and wine, as well as other Christmas luxuries, and got me to help him skin the hare and prepare it for cooking. Then he insisted we go into the living room and sit down there. From the appearance of the room I could tell it contained the family's few treasures. Clearly, I was an honoured guest.

We chatted for a few minutes, then there came a knock on the door. The farmer answered and ushered a stoutish sixty-year-old man into the room. 'Monsieur le maire,' he announced respectfully.

As the mayor spoke very little English, we spoke French. My French was not fluent, but I knew enough to conduct simple, if often ungrammatical, conversations. So I was able to reply when the mayor asked me who I was and where I was going that I wanted to reach a neutral country such as Spain or Switzerland and then return to my unit in England.

'But that's no good. Completely impossible.' The mayor frowned. 'We must be realistic. You'll never make it.'

I stared at him incredulously. After my escape and my journey through Holland and Belgium without being stopped and asked for my papers even once, I believed the rest of the journey would be as easy. But the mayor's next words were harshly realistic.

'You must realize certain facts.' He counted them out on his fingers, for emphasis. 'One, your French is far from perfect. That could cause you difficulties and draw attention to you. Two, you have no identification papers, and there are checkpoints across the country. We might be able to get you some, but it will take time. Three, France is full of German soldiers and the Gestapo. You know that if they catch you it is all over.' He drew his finger across his throat to emphasize his point. I needed no reminder.

'What do you suggest I do?' I asked soberly.

'You must wait here for a little while, where you are safe.'

The mayor was the first of a succession of visitors; the schoolmaster, the priest, and several others, none of whom spoke English. They all asked the same questions and then told me my own plan would not work. Each visitor also talked with my host, Monsieur Régis, before leaving, but I couldn't hear what was said.

When the last visitor had left, Monsieur Régis spoke to me again. 'We have a much better idea than the one you suggested. We have a friend who is a doctor, and he will get you back to England safely.'

'Are you sure?'

'Absolutely. If he says he will get you back to England, you are as good as there already.'

'But how. . .'

He raised a hand to silence me. 'No questions. It doesn't pay to know too many details.'

'I'm sorry.'

'I know. Don't worry about it. Do you want to talk to this doctor?'

'Yes, I would be very pleased to.'

'That's good. He'll probably call in here later tonight, and you can meet him then. Now, it's Christmas; let's forget about the war. After you, monsieur,' and he ushered me back to the kitchen, where the supper table was laid ready.

As we sipped on our apéritifs, I tried to sort out in my mind what was happening. My visitors had probably all come separately to avoid arousing suspicion, but there was some organized resistance group here, of that I was sure. I could not tell if the farmer was a member of this resistance group, but whether he was or not, he certainly knew whom to contact. I wondered about the doctor who could apparently spirit people off to England so easily.

Supper interrupted my musings. It was a meal such as I have never eaten in my life, and I was thankful I was free of dysentery as I devoured the mouth-watering hare and pork. My wine-glass was constantly refilled in spite of my protest, and, had it not been for the huge meal, I would soon have been completely drunk.

While we ate the family asked me all kinds of questions about my life, bombing raids on Germany, life in the United States, and what it was like in the prisoner-of-war camp. I answered as best I could, making up answers when their questions touched on subjects outside my experience. The questioning ceased when the father sent his boys out to finish the chores that had been interrupted by my arrival and his wife brought a pot of real coffee to the table. I inhaled the rich aroma with delight.

'We keep the real coffee for special occasions,' she said.

'Like Christmas and special visitors,' her husband added. He went out and came back with a bottle of calvados, from which he poured three small glasses.

'À la victoire!' he cried, raising his glass.

We joined him in the toast to victory. A few minutes later his wife was clearing away the dishes when we heard a car pull up outside.

'The Gestapo!' I whispered, jumping up, ready to flee.

'Sit down. It's the doctor; I know the sound of his car.' He left to greet this latest visitor and I waited in trepidation until the farmer returned and beckoned me into the best room, where he left me alone with the doctor.

'Hello,' he said in English. 'I'm Dr Monet. Let's sit down, shall we?'

Of medium height and slim build, the doctor seemed to be in his late thirties. 'Before you return to England, I need certain details from you. You don't mind?' He pulled out a notebook and pencil.

'No, not at all. Go ahead.' I tried to talk in what I believed to be an American accent. His English seemed perfect.

'Name?'

'Jim Witt.'

'Date of birth?'

'November 3, 1922.'

'Rank?'

'Flight Sergeant.'

'Type of plane you were flying?'

The questions went on and on – the base I had been operating from, my service number, the prison camp, my home address in the United States, and many others – and he wrote down all the answers I had made up as I had neared France.

Halfway through the interrogation he looked up from his notebook. 'That's a funny kind of English you speak.'

'It's the way we talk in San Francisco.'

'Hmm. I see. Well, let's continue.'

I sensed, even from the way he sat, that he was a military man, and throughout the interview my suspicion grew that he was a British agent operating in occupied France.

Finally, he closed his notebook. The interview was over, but we chatted for a while. At last he stood up. 'Thank you. I'll be in touch with you again soon and let you know what's happening. Please don't get up. I want to have a word or two with Monsieur Régis.'

He left the room and switched at once to speaking perfect French. After a few seconds, I could no longer make out the words as they lowered their voices. I guessed they were talking about me. A few minutes later, I heard his car start up again and I went back into the kitchen.

The family stood huddled together, their faces pale, their movements nervous and agitated. It was easy to guess that the doctor had told them I was probably not an American, warning them they might have a Gestapo agent on their hands.

'You must be very tired by now.' Monsieur Régis broke the heavy silence.

'Yes.'

'May we show you to your bedroom upstairs?'

'Thank you.' I followed him to the plain but comfortable room he indicated.

'Good night. We'll see you tomorrow,' he said as he closed the door behind him.

Instead of undressing, I lay down fully clothed on the bed. It was invitingly soft, but I felt too scared to sleep. I could imagine the turmoil the doctor's words had caused the family. They had set out to help someone they believed to be an ally; now they could be in danger from the dreaded Gestapo. The house was quiet. Perhaps they were all sleeping.

But perhaps the farmer was sitting at the bottom of the stairs, with a loaded shotgun across his knee. If they thought I was a Gestapo agent trying to infiltrate the underground, I was as good as dead. I expected the door to burst open any second while a trained Resistance assassin rushed in and cut my throat. My terrified mind toyed with these violent images, merging incongruously with memories of Christmas at home, the decorated tree filling the whole house with its spicy tang, the presents, the carols.

I discovered silent tears running hot down my cheeks. It was time to control my fears. I sat up and tried to think.

My story and assumed identity as Jim Witt would not stand investigation for a moment, but who was there to investigate it in France? Maybe I had misinterpreted the situation, and what the doctor had discussed with the family did not concern me at all. Maybe he was passing on some bad news that had nothing to do with me.

Yet the doctor had been suspicious of my story, however much he had tried to conceal his doubts. If he was a British agent, as I suspected, I could assume he was in radio contact with London. And London could soon check my story and prove it false. Once the doctor heard from London that he had an impostor on his hands, he had very little choice. I could only be a Gestapo man, who had already found out too much. The farmer and his family, the mayor, the priest, the schoolteacher, and the doctor would all be identified as underground members and would be tortured and shot. The only alternative course of action would be to order my death.

It was taking too much of a chance to remain; I had to flee. For a few minutes I listened attentively. All was quiet. I could try opening my door and creeping down to the kitchen, where I had left my canvas bag, but that risked running into some other member of the household. I would have to open the window, creep through it, and jump down to the ground.

If the window could be opened. I tiptoed across the room and reached up, fingering one side of the frame. Hinges. That meant the catch that fastened the window was on the other side. Slowly I groped around until I found the brass catch. I grasped it and turned it slowly, a fraction of an inch at a time, listening for the squeak that could betray me. There was only a slight rubbing noise, and at last the handle was clear. I prayed that the hinges wouldn't squeak when I pulled on the handle.

They didn't. The window didn't move at all. Panic seized me. I felt all around the frame for a second catch or a bolt. There was none.

Sweating, I reached out and moved my fingers around

the frame again. Then suddenly I noticed the setting of the hinges and breathed a sigh of relief. Instead of pulling, I pushed gently on the handle, and the window swung open easily on well-oiled hinges.

I stepped back, checked that my cap was in my pocket, and listened. There was no sound. Could I assume nobody was watching? Maybe they had heard me at the window and thought I was just wanting fresh air; maybe they were waiting to make sure I really was escaping before they killed me.

The temptation to remain and take my chances gnawed at me again but I rejected it. As silently as I could, I swung my legs out of the open window and dropped to the courtyard below just outside the kitchen window.

12

Silence.

I strained to see through the darkness.

I could see nothing, nobody. I grabbed my farm fork from beside the kitchen door and ran for my life. I ran for hours, just as I had when I escaped from the concentration camp.

When the bells summoned the faithful to church on Christmas Day, 1943, I was lying concealed under a pile of wet leaves in a small copse several miles further west.

Too terrified to move all that day and the following night, I kept wondering what had happened in the morning when they found me gone. Did the doctor flee? And what about the farmer, the priest, the schoolmaster, and the others? Did they go into hiding or did they try to follow their normal pattern of life, hoping against hope that the Gestapo would not suddenly descend upon them? I tried to imagine the priest saying mass that morning. Was his mind on the service? Were there Germans in his congregation, Germans who might form a firing squad for him in an hour or two? I desperately regretted not having been able to leave a note of explanation behind, but written material was highly incriminating evidence, and I could not take the chance of a note falling into the hands of the Gestapo.

'You've been exposed,' I told myself bitterly as I tried to make some plans. My mind kept returning to the warning the mayor and the others had given me. It was true: my French was not good enough for me to pass as a

Frenchman, and I had no identification papers. The odds were impossibly stacked against ever making it into Spain or Switzerland. It seemed easy enough to get in touch with the French underground, but should I reveal myself as a German, as a hated Boche? I dared not.

There seemed only one choice open to me. I would head for the coast, where I hoped I could steal a boat and make for England. The odds were not in my favour, but I couldn't think of any other way to escape the trap that seemed to be closing around me. It was better to take my chances on the sea and die there than to be taken alive by the Gestapo. And my capture would harm others, too. I had no delusions – they would torture me until I told them who had helped me.

Throughout the day I slept in short snatches, but the need to stay alert kept me awake most of the time. Early the following morning, I set off cross-country. I had eaten nothing on Christmas Day, nothing since the sumptuous meal of pork and hare on Christmas Eve. My stomach groaned with hunger, and at midday I begged food at a farm. I let them assume I was a Polish worker on my way back to work on the Atlantic Wall.

That night, I crept into a barn to sleep, leaving before the farmer was astir. A couple of days later, I was in the Pas de Calais area, moving cautiously to avoid any human being, French or German. My confidence was growing, and that may have led me into indiscretion near the village of Bomy.

I saw the village from a distance and turned aside to avoid it. But I could see no signs of Germans in the vicinity and turned back for a closer look. Perhaps it would be safe to beg food there. On a small rise at the edge of the village was a farmhouse that looked promising. I did not see the girl by the espalier until she called and waved to me.

'Bonjour,' I replied. She was about eighteen and attractive, the sort of girl I had gone out with in Kiel.

'What nationality are you?' she asked.

Her question startled me. 'What do you think?' I was playing for time, trying to think.

Her reply left me speechless for a while. 'You must be English.'

'Why?'

'I've been watching you. You walk the way a soldier does when he's marching.'

Playfully, foolishly perhaps, I answered, 'No, I'm an American pilot.' The same answer that I had given a few days earlier, and that had nearly cost me my life. Why had I said it again? Because of my hunger, and to impress a pretty girl?

'You must come in,' she said immediately, apparently unshaken by my reply.

She took me by the arm and led me to the farmhouse, where she called for her father. He appeared from the shed where he had been repairing a bicycle and she told him who I was.

'Where are you going? What will you do?'

The same questions as before. Committed to the deception now, I gave the same false answers.

'Come into the house,' the father said. 'Yvette, go and get some wine from the cellar.'

Yvette reappeared with a bottle of red wine and her sister, who was about a year older and just as beautiful. Then the two girls went into another room, leaving their father and me to drink the wine and smoke fiendishly strong cigarettes we made from the tobacco leaves hanging from the ceiling.

At about half past five I glanced out of the window and saw that it was getting dark outside, with a mist rolling in from the west. I stood up, knowing I should get out before I fell into the same mess again.

'Thank you for your hospitality. I must go now.'

'Oh no, don't go.' He called Yvette and Élise and told them what I intended.

'It's an awful night outside.' said Yvette. She looked at her father.

'I know,' he replied. 'I told him not to go.' He turned back to me. 'You can sleep here. We have a spare bed for you.'

I should have refused politely, but I looked outside at the cold, misty weather and then at the warm fire that made the farmhouse snug and inviting. I said to myself I would be a fool to go out and find some barn to curl up in for the night. Perhaps I was far enough from the Régis family to be safe now.

'Thank you, then. I'll leave in the morning.'

After supper, we sat and talked by the fire. The hatred of the Germans, the despised Boches, experienced by the French came through repeatedly in the way they pronounced the words and the look in their eyes as they spoke. Loss of freedom spurred their resentment, but they were confident that one day they would be free again. An often repeated phrase was 'Après la guerre (After the war)'.

That night, for the first time in many months, I slept in a proper bed with clean sheets.

After breakfast the next morning I said I was ready to leave.

'There's no hurry,' yawned Monsieur Lamotte. Yvette poured me another cup of what was called coffee in those days. I had the feeling they were unwilling to let me go, and, lulled by the homely kitchen scene, I rolled another cigarette and sat for a while.

About a quarter of an hour later. I heard the creaking of a heavy cart outside. 'C'est Marcel,' Élise called out and went to open the door.

A huge man of at least 220 pounds came in and sat down at the table.

He looked at me. 'You English?'

'No, American.' I was trapped now and had to continue the deception.

'Where are you heading for?'

'Switzerland or Spain.'

'No, no, no! That's impossible.' He went on to give the reasons that were now becoming depressingly familiar.

'I thought of reaching the coast and stealing a boat,' I ventured.

'Oh no, not that! You don't have a chance that way. I've got a much better idea. I have a friend in the next town, and he has very good contacts with London.' He noticed my look of amazement at the casual way he referred to these clandestine activities. 'Oh yes, we can talk to London. My friend can get you over there safely. Would you be interested? If you are, I can arrange it.'

It seemed likely that Monsieur Lamotte or one of his daughters had contacted Marcel while I slept; his arrival was certainly no coincidence. And I could only answer, 'Yes.' I had trapped myself again.

'You really can do it?'

'Oh yes. Last September we came across an English pilot who had come down and evaded the Boches. With the help of my friend we got him back to England.'

'He may have been one of those who flew over yesterday afternoon,' joked Monsieur Lamotte.

'It could be,' Marcel replied.'We've got to get pilots and other air crew back so that they can fight again. An aircraft can quickly be replaced, but it takes months to

The flat, grey terrain around Börgermoor-Emsland concentration camp where Hans spent nine months before his miraculous escape

Hans's friend and partner in the French Resistance, Jacques Matton. This photograph of Jacques was taken some years after the war

Another Resistance colleague of Hans in Isbergues, André Leleu

A popular Resistance meeting place was the Café Boniface in this building in Lillers. This photo was taken in the late 1950s when Hans Nütt revisited France and the sites of his Resistance work

Jacques's house (bottom right corner) in the neighbouring village of Guarbecque

A _Lynde_ , le _6 mai 1943_

Signature :

Picavez

Empreinte
digitale

N° 213

CARTE
D'IDENTITÉ

15 FRANCS

Nom _Jeansson_
Prénoms _Laurent - Jean_

Né le _3 février 1919_
à _Roubaix_
demeurant à _Lynde_
Rue _du Bois_ N°
Nationalité _française_

SIGNALEMENT

Taille _1 m 74_   Nez _ordinaire_

Cheveux _blonds_   Forme générale du visage

Moustache _néant_   _ovale_

Yeux _marrons_   Teint _ordinaire_

Signes particuliers _néant_

Above: This document was supplied to Hans by the French Resistance, identifying him as a Frenchman named Laurent Jean Jeansson. The card was a basic piece of identification carried by all French citizens during the war

Canadian soldiers with young André Desquesnes, son of Resistance worker Marie-Louise Desquesnes, in 1944

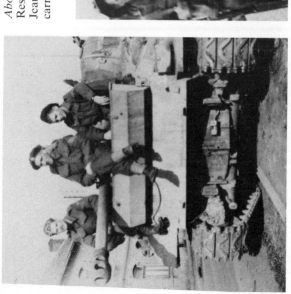

Canadian soldiers on the first tank to enter Isbergues in September 1944

Hans Nütt in front of Marie-Louise Desquesnes's house in Isbergues after the Liberation in 1944

Marie-Louise's house, where Hans spent almost a year working for the French Resistance

Marie-Louise and her daughter several years after the Liberation

The Liberation of Brussels. September 3, 1944, with the Allied Forces passing the Royal Palace. Hans was in Lillers at the time

train a new pilot. Now to business. I'll pick you up tomorrow morning. I take it you can ride a bike?'

'Yes, of course.'

'Good. Then we'll cycle to the next town and meet my friend. He'll see about getting you back to England.'

During the night, I began to have second thoughts about Marcel's plan. It seemed too much to hope that I could carry off my deception. By morning, I had almost made up my mind to flee. After breakfast, returning from the outside toilet, I looked around the yard for my farm fork. It was a talisman; it had brought me good luck from the moment the Dutch mayor gave it to me. But I couldn't see it anywhere.

'Ready to go, Jim?' Marcel was standing behind me, holding a bicycle.

'Er, yes.'

'Okay. Say goodbye to the girls and let's go.'

They gave me a packet of lunch, a bicycle, and a kiss on each cheek. We called 'Après la guerre' to each other, and I left with Marcel, riding straight through the village, as if the nearest Germans were a thousand miles away. All I left Monsieur Lamotte's family to remember me by was a Dutch farmer's ancient fork and the recollection of a skinny young man masquerading as an American pilot.

The day was cool, with mist hanging over the fields and hedges, and despite my apprehension, it was pleasant cycling along the country trails with Marcel.

After twenty miles or so we passed the Isbergues sign and cycled for several minutes on cobbled streets, arriving at last at the main street. A medium-sized town, I estimated. Houses leaned into the picturesque cobbled streets. We stopped abruptly before a little corner restaurant called Café Boniface and quickly went inside. An attractive young brunette sat alone on a stool, a cup of coffee at her elbow.

'Jacqueline, how can I find Jean?' Marcel asked hastily.

They whispered together and then Marcel said, 'May I leave my friend here to stay with you?'

'Yes, of course, why not?' Jacqueline's black eyes shone with interest and intrigue.

'Guess who he is.'

'I don't know.'

'He's an American pilot.'

'Oh, no! Really?' Jacqueline exclaimed delightedly. 'You are more than welcome, monsieur. It's an honour. Come this way, please.' She glanced quickly through the window and the open door, then took my arm and led me speedily around the bar and into the back rooms. 'I am Jacqueline Boniface. My parents own this place. We will help you to reach your destination. You Americans eat steak and chips, don't you? Can I make you dinner?' Before I could answer, she began to prepare a meal while I watched her, aware of her femininity, wondering what I had stumbled into, and how far it would go. We chatted while we waited, and I gave my story again. At least it's good practice on the details, I thought.

Two hours later, Marcel returned. A short, rotund individual puffed along behind him. A rather comical-looking man, he had slick, dark hair and a cherubic face, and wore riding breeches and high brown riding boots.

'Jim Witt. Monsieur Jean Yvon.'

'Bonjour, Monsieur Yvon.'

'No, no! Just "Jean". We use only first names, so that we cannot give much away if we are caught.'

A stream of searching questions followed. Jean's appearance belied his keen intelligence, and if I hadn't been well rehearsed he would have found me out. In case

I ever sounded German, I told him I spoke the language fluently. I said my grandparents came to California from Germany and that we sometimes spoke it at home. I was sweating when he finished.

'I am sorry to have to ask so many questions after many others have done so, but we cannot be too careful, you understand? Will you drink a Pernod with us?'

I nodded in relief, my mouth dry with tension.

I was introduced to Jacqueline's parents and then, a little later, Marcel led me out into the twilit street where our bikes were waiting. Jean came out and joined us. 'We will go to Guarbecque now,' Jean said. I was mystified, but we rode off into the deepening night.

Guarbecque, I discovered, was a continuation of Isbergues. Again we came to a main street, but this time we went to the rear of a railway hotel and slipped our bikes into a private park. We entered silently by an unlit back door and passed through into a bright salon, where about thirty men and women turned toward us expectantly.

'This is a party in your honour,' Marcel said smilingly. Embarrassed at my own duplicity, I wanted to hide. If only they could accept me for what I really was!

'Vivent les États-Unis!' they toasted me. It was the first of many toasts. I don't know how I managed to drink with everyone and yet stay sober and keep up an approximation of an American accent. Soon I noticed that Marcel and Jean were singing loudly. They were receiving special attention as my hosts, and basking in reflected glory. At times I was tempted to shout out that I was an impostor and throw myself on their mercy, but I doubted that they would show any.

We toasted De Gaulle, Roosevelt, Churchill, the American Air Force, the British and Canadian forces, the

French Resistance, the Republic, and each other – everyone who was helping to throw out the Boches.

Finally we left. My companions were uproariously drunk, and they wobbled on their bikes singing 'Bonsoir, Irène' while I prayed that no German patrols would stop us in that condition. Back at the Café Boniface, Jean and Marcel each took an arm in order to lead me to the room where I would sleep. But it was actually I who had to help them up the stairs.

'Bonsoir, Jim Witt,' they crooned as they tried to put me to bed.

I fell asleep giggling, grateful but wondering again where the charade would end. Jean had said they would be checking up on my story and arranging another 'interview'. In the meantime I was supposed to relax and recover from my escape and my journey.

The next morning, Jacqueline's father, Monsieur Boniface, led me to his closet. 'You are my size, Jim, and you need a suit. You take this one to get you started.'

It was obviously his best. I was deeply touched.

'An old one, Monsieur Boniface, will be just fine.'

'Oh no! For what you have done for us, and getting out of that terrible POW camp. No, you have this one. I can get another.'

He gave me a shirt and tie as well.

'But dress in a hurry, monsieur. Jacques, whom you met at the party last night, is waiting downstairs. He'll take you to meet the mayor and the chief of police. They will provide you with papers. And we have arranged for you to go to one of our photographers for the necessary photos. You will be French by noon.' He laughed so heartily I had to join in.

I remembered Jacques. He was a dark, solidly built, athletic-looking man with sharp features. I was struck by his composure. Despite the fact that he obviously enjoyed the party, he was always in command of himself and somewhat watchful of others' well-being.

The mayor had the papers waiting.

'It is a pleasure to meet an American pilot, Monsieur Witt, especially one who speaks French. And German too, I understand?'

'Yes, speaking German helped me to escape from Absfelder camp.'

I explained again that I had been shot down over Pomerania. The police saw my parachute and captured me as soon as I landed.

'It must be odd to fight your grandparents' people.' It was the police chief, looking a little sceptical.

'No,' I replied firmly. 'It is the Nazis we fight and their criminal system, not the German people.'

'Oui, it is so,' put in the mayor. 'One doubts that all the German people support the damned Nazis.'

I wanted to tell him that some German people opposed the Nazis and that I was one of them.

From there, Jacques took me on his motor bike to a photographer, and then to a clothing store.

'It belongs to Madame Lacoque. She is a great lady, very elegant and distinguished. Her son Pierre was taken by the Boches to a slave-labour camp somewhere in Germany.'

Madame Lacoque, a tall, greying, dark-eyed woman, waited in a room at the back of a large building. The sun shone warmly on the yellow bricks as we entered.

'Come in, Monsieur Witt, I am pleased to meet you. My son Pierre is about your age. I hope some day you can meet him. But now, Jim, it is my pleasure to help an ally of ours. Come with me, please.'

Madame Lacoque rose with graceful dignity and led

me into a men's salon at the front. 'I have four such stores, so you must choose what you wish from these.' She waved a hand at a rack of clothes.

'But madame . . .' I stammered.

'There is nothing to worry about. You have no money, of course; it does not matter. We will choose three suits, a coat, a hat, and underclothes for you. And you will take this.'

It was a new leather wallet with a bundle of banknotes inside. Later, when I counted them, I found she had given me a thousand francs.

I was dumbfounded. What generosity!

'I will repay you somehow, some day,' I said.

'You have done so already, by fighting our enemies who spread their evil tyranny over free people everywhere. You are a young man of character who will fight them again, once you are back in Britain. Our organization will get you there. A few clothes from me are nothing compared to your contribution to victory.'

A choking feeling rose in my throat as we left with my new wardrobe. How could I show my appreciation of this wonderful lady's faith and trust?

I felt very sorry that her son had been stolen away; it hurt me that my countrymen were responsible for her misery. But the worst was yet to come for Madame Lacoque. A few weeks later she lost her only daughter as well. A brave girl of eighteen who was a very good courier, she died while out carrying a message, the accidental victim of an Allied bombing raid.

Even when the war did not actually end a young life, it could still change perceptions and deaden normal emotions to a degree I found frightening. At a friend's house one evening I met a young girl named Janine. She must have been about seventeen or eighteen but could have passed for even younger.

'Are you a courier?' I asked

'No. I am an exterminator.' She spoke matter-of-factly.

'A what?' I was shocked.

'An exterminator. I meet Gestapo men and invite them for a walk. When we are alone, I shoot them. I have killed five so far. They were getting too close to our people.'

'What do you feel?'

'Nothing.'

'Doesn't your conscience bother you?'

'No. It never bothers me. If I didn't kill them, they would kill some of us. They are *cochons*.'

I was deeply affected by Janine. Killing had become a way of life to her; human response was gone. I tried to picture her leading a normal life after the war but could not. Would I become so accustomed to death that I would no longer feel any reaction?

I imagined Janine as my executioner if I were unmasked. She would dispatch me with equal coolness. I shuddered at the thought.

I stayed with the Boniface family for several weeks and my strength and vitality grew daily. I ate with an enormous appetite and Madame Boniface had to get an extra food-ration card in order to feed me enough. That wasn't too hard, though. There seemed to be plenty of black-market food available, as well as quantities of tinned meat the French had hoarded when the British pulled out in 1940. There was always butter, and sometimes coffee. Certainly we ate better than the people in Germany.

'Mon Dieu, but you can eat! Dear Jim, the Boches treated you so badly.' She treated me affectionately, like a mother.

At night Jacqueline, her father, Jacques, or Jean would take me for a walk. Whoever accompanied me always wore a coat and kept at least one hand inside a pocket, grasping, I was sure, a gun. We never talked of this precaution, but I assumed it was both to protect me, and to subdue me if I proved false. They were obviously instructed not to take any chances.

But I felt no desire to run away. I was well fed and clothed and was enjoying the respite from my flight from the Gestapo. Besides, it was still January and travelling was difficult and miserable. I hoped desperately that the Resistance would get me to England, where I believed I would be safe. If only I could reach there before either the Gestapo or the underground discovered my true identity.

After our walks, we would gather in the Boniface living room, where Monsieur Boniface put out the lights. Behind drawn curtains, grouped around the radio which was kept barely audible, we listened to coded messages on the BBC, carrying instructions to the Resistance. The dial was always carefully turned to a French station before the lights went on again. If the Gestapo caught anyone with a radio set on the BBC frequency, an arrest was inevitable.

I was amazed at the extensive organization of the underground. In a month I had been in the homes of a dozen Resistance members and had met a hundred more. On a walk one evening, I commented on this to Jacqueline.

'You know many more than I do, even,' she replied. 'We don't want to know them, as you can understand. Our job here is intelligence work: we gather all the military information we can in our area, and it is radioed to England to be pieced together in London. It's for our

own protection not to know too much. I don't even know
the Resistance people in the next town.' The longer I
knew Jacqueline the more I admired her. She had a calm
wisdom beyond her years.

One evening, Monsieur Boniface took me out into his
garden, where we walked and smoked under the stars,
chatting for some time, as we did occasionally. Then we
sat quietly for a while before he broke the silence again.

'We are so small in the universe. Nothing really,' he
said. 'Yet we have no choice but to play out this war and
grasp at the life that comes our way. A young man like
you, Jim, must seize his chances for experience and love
in such dangerous times as these. If, as you say, you'd
like to improve your French, the best place to do it is in
bed!' I had to laugh, but my heart skipped a beat.

With that, he led me inside and left me in the living
room before the fire.

'I'm off to bed,' he said, yawning elaborately.

I sat a while looking into the flames, wondering again
what would happen to me. Presently Jacqueline came in
from her night-time courier duty. She looked happy with
herself; obviously the night had been successful.

'Will you have a drink?' I asked, suddenly shy.

'Why yes! A Dubonnet, if you will.'

She came to join me at the fireside. As the firelight
glowed in her hair I realized the full significance of her
father's words, and I put my arms around her and kissed
her. She drew back in surprise, looked searchingly into
my face, then returned my kiss. Then she stepped back,
looked at me frankly, smiled, finished her drink, and
walked silently from the room.

Now what have I started, I wondered. But I was too
excited to worry. It had been over a year since I had felt

sexually aroused at all. I went to sleep that night dreaming of Jacqueline in her bed down the hall.

I woke in the morning with a sense of excitement and a greater feeling of well-being than I could remember. Jacqueline was out all day, but I looked forward to the late evening with her by the fire.

When darkness came, Jacques appeared to walk with me. I was in high spirits and we walked briskly out to the edge of town and back. As we neared the Café Boniface again, I began hoping that Jacques wouldn't stay long and that Jacqueline's parents would go to bed.

But a stranger was waiting with Monsieur Boniface. He was a captain in the Resistance. I was to be moved to another house, subjected to another interrogation!

'You will come with me now,' the captain said.

There was scarcely time even to say goodbye to the senior Bonifaces before the captain hustled me into the darkened street. Jacqueline was not there when we left. I did not see her for several months, and then too seldom for our relationship to grow. At any rate, all thoughts of romance were driven from my mind by a new close call.

I was taken to another Resistance member's house where I met Charles, the area chief of the underground. Charles was a pleasant, kindly-looking man of obvious intelligence. I guessed that he was somewhat past middle age, but he carried himself so well that he seemed younger. He was the kind of leader I felt I could trust immediately – he would never shirk a duty, and his courage was unmistakable.

'We will do the formal clearance check on you now, Monsieur Witt. I have here a questionnaire to fill out. It will be sent to London, and in a month we will receive an answer. If you are cleared, we will arrange for your speedy passage to England. Should you prove to be an impostor, then you need not be told what we must do with you. We cannot take any risks. The Gestapo and their collaborators are all around us.'

There was no use arguing. At least I was practised in my story. My tension built as the questioning started all over again. I had thought I was finished with all that, and safe for the moment. The old fear gripped my stomach and I thought I might vomit, but with a great struggle I managed to calm myself enough to read the form.

The questionnaire was long, with thirty-six questions. Besides the expected ones about my military career and my capture, I was asked my home street address, school name, family and friends' names, and even the names of pets. Eventually it was finished, and taken off to be sent to England. They've got me, I thought desperately, but what other chance have I got?

For the next month I lived in that house, astonished when I found out that two German officers were billeted there too, just down the hall from me. And furthermore, the wine cellar down below was a Resistance arms dump, with even the wine barrels filled with ammunition! Despite my own precarious position, I had to laugh silently when we would sit in the lounge in the evenings; the German officers tried hard to be friendly to their avowed enemies, while unknowingly sitting above a cache of their own stolen arms, and talking with one of their own escaped prisoners. The family must assume I'm genuine, I thought, if they leave me alone with these officers.

My French had improved greatly and was never questioned by any German. Perhaps they thought I was originally Alsatian. Sometimes the officers would speak in their home tongue, confident nobody understood. 'These French are so self-centred,' the German captain said one evening. 'Can you imagine them ever getting an organized resistance going?'

'Never,' the lieutenant replied contemptuously. 'It's no wonder we overcame them so fast. You can see that they no longer have what it takes.'

I hastily dropped the book I was pretending to read and went quickly from the room, coughing and spluttering to cover my exit. In the kitchen, I told my host what had been said and we both collapsed in hysterical laughter.

'Keep listening,' he said. 'You never know when you'll hear something useful.'

The German military maintained a strict, official correctness toward the French to win them over if possible, and to show their superiority. Our two officers had obviously been told to be congenial toward us at the house. I had heard that a few young girls in nearby towns had been raped by German soldiers after the fall of France. Their families lodged formal complaints to the German commandant, and the soldiers were found and shot. Such behaviour was beneath the dignity of the master race.

After about a month, I was out walking one evening with my host, who kept his hand always thrust into a coat pocket, when his teenage son came cycling down the cobbled street after us. He skidded to a stop beside his father. 'Come back quickly,' was all he said.

All the way back I was near panic, barely able to conceal my anxiety. When I arrived I found Charles waiting with a stranger in the kitchen. 'Meet Lieutenant Jones from Texas. He's just been shot down too.'

I was keenly aware of their searching looks as I shook hands with the Texan.

'My Gawd, it's good to see another 'merican. What's

the matter with these people? None of them speak English.'

I had to laugh, and Charles relaxed visibly. The Texan showed me his papers and seemed not to notice any strange accent to my English. He told me of growing up on a ranch, and I told him I spoke the San Francisco slang of my home suburb. But he didn't seem at all interested; he was so happy just to speak English again and to talk about himself. Throughout our encounter I was very frightened, but I managed to keep from betraying myself as several other underground people came in to meet the Texan and to ask questions.

The American left in the morning, after sleeping hidden among the arms in the cellar overnight. My hosts were more trusting and relaxed with me after my meeting with him, but I worried constantly about the reply to my questionnaire. At times I was sure I was about to be killed and I flipped a coin in an irrational attempt to decide whether I should try escaping, but it said to stay. I couldn't see how I was going to make it all the way to Spain without help anyway. My mother often came to me in my dreams. Her one son was dead in Russia, and I feared another was about to die in France. I hoped Alfred would survive the war to take care of her, and to give her grandchildren.

I was eating luncheon gloomily one day, my nerves stretched to breaking point, when Charles burst into the room. Before the panic could even rise in me, he shouted, 'Congratulations, my dear friend, Jim! Your papers are perfect.' He waved a stamped document in his hand.

It must be a trap! But there was no doubting Charles's genuine enthusiasm. Dumbfounded, I just sat there until Charles grabbed and pumped my hand. Was it possible that there was another Jim Witt from San Francisco who fitted my description, all thirty-six questions? Had somebody slipped up and stamped the approval without checking my story? Perhaps the British were waiting to trap me when I got to London? But why would they leave me free to report on Resistance activities to the Gestapo in the meantime? I never did learn the truth.

'Hurry, my friend. Get your things together. I've been ordered to send you on to Lille this afternoon by train.'

We arrived in Lille at three o'clock and went to a hotel, where we were to meet a Monsieur Maurice. My escort spoke to the waiter, who answered vaguely that his boss was out and unavailable. We sat down with a cognac to await Maurice's return. At six, the waiter was still vague, so we ordered dinner. At nine, the waiter told us we'd have to leave because he was closing.

'But we have come specifically to see Monsieur Maurice. Our friend here has an important meeting with him.' Feeling a little desperate now, my Resistance companion whispered, 'He is an American pilot.'

'Mon Dieu! Why in hell didn't you say so?'

With that, we were hustled through the velvet curtain behind the bar into a comfortable sitting room, and immediately introduced to Maurice.

'I apologize for this error, gentlemen. But, you know, we can't be too careful. This is one time when our concern tripped us up.' We all laughed. 'We knew you were coming, Monsieur Witt, but we weren't sure how. A message came that 160 pounds of beef was arriving from the hotel, but we weren't certain how you'd get here.'

I spent a few quiet days at the Hotel Versailles and then one afternoon Maurice said to me, 'We are having a reception tonight. I am preparing a special white bean salad myself, which you will enjoy, I'm sure.'

At seven I entered the private dining room. Maurice was waiting for me and came over. I could see about thirty people gathered around, and the table was set with white linen.

'I have a big surprise for you,' he said. 'Come with me, and be seated.'

I didn't know whether to be frightened or excited.

'For this dinner I have, myself, prepared my special white bean salad,' he repeated proudly, as he took me by the arm and led me to my seat. For a different reason than he would have expected, I will never forget that salad.

We came to my chair. 'My surprise!' said Maurice with a flourish as he pointed to three men seated across the table. 'These are three American pilots. You will be happy to meet some of your countrymen.' He introduced me to two captains and a lieutenant. Frozen, I stared at them for an instant. I had felt so safe, and now this!

With the greatest effort of will-power, I forced myself into my seat, pretending to be happy. 'God, have mercy on me,' I whispered under my breath.

We chatted for a few minutes about being shot down and about our experiences in escaping to the underground, while Maurice personally served the salad, beaming at all of us. We began to eat.

'That's a strange accent you've got.' It was the lieutenant, plainly suspicious. Before I could give my story again, he went on, 'Can I ask you some specific questions about flying?' He set down his fork. My bean salad went dry in my mouth and stuck in my throat.

I waffled, pretending to have lost my memory in the POW camp. But I couldn't answer anything; it was obvious I was lying. One of the captains was listening closely to our exchange, his face becoming stony and set.

'Let's get the hell out of here,' he said, rising hastily and pushing back his chair.

Silence spread instantly across the room. Suddenly there was a scraping of chairs. The room emptied, leaving me alone at the table, my bean salad choking me.

I heard the dreaded word 'Gestapo' as the door clicked shut.

PART THREE

Inside the French Resistance

13

This is it! This is the end!

The words drummed through my head. I expected to die. But there was nothing I could do. I was trapped in that room with bean salad stuck in my throat. Time passed. I don't know how long it was before the dining room door opened again. Paralysed by shock, I couldn't move.

A French Resistance colonel entered with Maurice behind him. I could see the tip of a pistol barrel the colonel held behind his back. Maurice's left hand bulged in his pocket. He had the look of horrified revulsion I had seen once long ago on a man's face at the Hamburg zoo, as he stood in front of the snake pit watching the pythons. I was close to the end, but that look of revulsion twisting Maurice's face was all that I could think of. Could anyone really see me that way?

Without speaking, they strode to the opposite side of the table from me. My head swam. I tried to stand up but I couldn't. I knew I had to speak first to buy time, afraid they'd shoot me there and then.

'All right, that's it,' I blurted. 'I may as well put my cards on the table.'

'We know who you are. You are a Gestapo agent!' The colonel brought his pistol into view.

Desperation made my mind clear and gave me the right arguments.

'You can shoot me if you like. But if I was a Gestapo agent this hotel would be surrounded right now. You'd never leave the place alive. Also, you know I had lots of chances to talk to the Boches at the last house.'

'That's true!' the colonel said, shaking his head as though to clear it. 'Who are you?' His pistol wavered but didn't go down.

'I will tell you the truth, then you can do what you like with me.' I took a deep breath. Hope began to rise in me again. God, if only they'll believe my story, incredible as it must sound to them.

'I started to cover up my identity when I got to France, pretending to be an American. Then there was no way to stop. There was the Gestapo on the outside, and the underground on the inside. I was caught. I was afraid to tell you the truth for fear you'd reject me. I'm German, I admit it.'

Maurice gasped, and the colonel's gun steadied again. 'But I've been an anti-Nazi ever since they drove my father to suicide when I was a small boy. I was nine months in a concentration camp for helping a friend to desert. Then I escaped through Holland and Belgium to France, and finally reached here. You know the rest.'

Silence. An unending moment. Emotions chased one another across their faces, and I could almost see their minds questioning, testing, estimating.

Then, 'Fantastique! Mon Dieu, I think that could be the truth.' Maurice shook his head, marvelling. He pulled out a chair and sat down, laying his pistol on the table. 'How have you survived, Jim?'

'You have fooled us for months,' said the colonel quietly. 'But I understand.' He regarded me calmly, uncocking his gun and returning it to his shoulder holster. 'I suppose your story must be true. It is too fantastic to be a lie. But we will check it out.'

I expelled a huge breath, feeling as though I hadn't

breathed for half an hour, and said a silent prayer of thanks. Perhaps now I could stop running.

'We will contact London,' the colonel said. 'If they will take you, we will send you over soon. They may not, you realize, and if they don't we will have to exterminate you.'

Maurice looked shocked. I stood up trembling.

'But why now?' I was suddenly near to tears.

'You know too much, Monsieur Witt. Because you have been passed from one group to another, you know even more about the underground than I do. We cannot let you go. We must guard you. If the Gestapo catch you they will torture it all out of you. And then we will all die. There is no other way, Jim. We cannot take such a huge risk. But we will plead for you.'

Spontaneously, he reached across the table and shook my hand. Maurice followed suit, the look of amazement still on his face. 'I will call the others,' he said and hurried to the door, highly excited.

'Come in! Come back in. We have such a story for you.'

The others filed in again, glancing curiously and very cautiously from me to the colonel and then to Maurice.

'Our friend Jim is German!' Maurice said with dramatic flair. Several people half rose from their chairs. Mouths dropped open. 'He has escaped from a Nazi concentration camp and has come to us for help to get away. He is not one of the Boches, even though he's German.'

Maurice told my story and several people laughed outright. Then many of them came to shake my hand, even including the three Americans.

'Christ, it must be hard for you, fella!' The lieutenant brought me a glass of wine. 'I hope to hell the Limeys take you over. You could be very helpful to them you know.'

I had never thought of that before. To help the Allies? The enemies of my country? No, not the enemies of my country – the enemies of my enemies! I hated the Nazi system as much as they did. Why not do it? Why not help the Allies? Germany couldn't win the war anyway, I was sure of that. Maybe I could help to end it faster and save some lives on both sides. Why not help to wipe out that terrible, dishonourable, destructive system?

But maybe the British wouldn't have me. Maybe they wouldn't trust me. I'll probably spend the rest of the war in a prisoner-of-war camp, I thought, if I'm not shot here. Oh, God, please make the British take me.

The strain was taking its toll. In the next few days several grey hairs appeared on my head. Confined to my room, I could scarcely eat or sleep. I had finally told the complete truth, but now my life might be snatched away anyway. If only the British could see my sincerity!

I paced my room endlessly, moving the bed to the middle of the room so that I might walk around it. To this day the pink floral pattern of that wallpaper is imprinted on my mind. I slept a little during the day, but at night I kept waking in a sweat, and the hours dragged until sunrise. The nightmare of facing a firing squad haunted me, although in reality I knew that they would probably finish me quietly.

I was given good food, but I could scarcely eat. I concentrated on walking and exercising to wear myself out and numb my brain. Maurice invited me often enough and escorted me to the bathroom. He was very sympathetic but said little of my predicament. I was offered books but couldn't concentrate enough to read them. Days blended together and I cannot remember exactly how long I was confined there.

One morning I was pacing around my bed, three paces, two, three, two, and around again, when I heard Maurice's key in my lock. I stopped on the far side of the bed when I heard the sound and leaned against the edge of it. Maurice poked his head around the corner of my door. 'The British want you!'

He bounced into the room, half crying as he clapped me on the back. 'I am so happy for you, my friend!'

Suddenly weak at the knees, I sank onto my bed, not trying to hide my own tears. In the long flight from the concentration camp I had been forced to conceal my identity. For months I had played a part, but now that I was Hans Nütt again I could restrain my feelings no longer. Even as I wept, I began to laugh almost hysterically while Maurice stood over me beaming. Then I jumped up and hugged him, swinging him off his feet. Laughing and crying, we ran down the stairs.

'A drink to celebrate!' Maurice shouted.

We burst into the private dining room to find the colonel and several others waiting there, their glasses already filled.

'A toast to Jim.' Maurice grabbed his glass. Everyone stood up. 'Vive Jim Witt!'

I stopped, stunned that they could be so generous. A lump in my thoat, my heart surged with love for them.

'You are very kind. I don't deserve it. I hope that I can repay you,' I stammered.

'Ah Jim,' the colonel said, 'you have lived through hell here. And nobly too.'

The next morning I had the worst hangover of my life, but by noon I felt exuberantly happy anyway. Somehow I'm going to do something worthwhile in this war, I decided. I'll have to convince the British when I get there.

That evening, a dozen of us gathered again in the dining room. There was still a festive air as we sat down to dinner, and I laughed more freely than I could remember doing in years. When we had finished eating, we sat back with coffee, liqueur, and even cigars. Significant looks passed from one to another around me. Something was afoot.

'Jim,' the colonel began, 'there is something we want to ask you. It is not necessary for you to answer now. We have talked it over here in our group. We would like to ask you to stay with us and not go over to England. There is a lot of German troop movement through Lille, and the Germans are building fortifications, perhaps even rocket sites, near the coast. Because you speak the German language, know their military, and could pass for one of them, you would be very useful here. Will you stay and join the Resistance? We would like you to be one of us. We need your kind of courage, and just as much, your skills.'

I was too surprised to speak for a moment. Why not stay here and help these wonderful people? I remembered Madame Lacoque. Perhaps I could repay her and the others for all their kindnesses. I wouldn't be in active combat against my countrymen, just doing intelligence and interference work.

Then I thought of my brother Alfred. What if he was sent here? I couldn't fight against him. What if I said no? Would they let me go to England or would they shoot me? I felt sure they'd let me go.

But Germany couldn't win. Why not end it all quicker? I remembered my thoughts when the American lieutenant had said how useful I could be. My excitement grew. I was on my feet.'I will, mes camarades, I will! Hitler and his gangsters are an affront to all mankind. They are destroying my country and yours. There is no freedom or honour left. I will help you in your Resistance to bring it back.'

Suddenly shy, I laughed at myself, but the others ignored my embarrassment. Tears glistened in everyone's eyes.

'The group we belong to is called the British War Office Forces Françaises Intérieures. There are also de Gaulle's Free French and the Communists. We are all fighting the Boches. Our group reports directly to London, and we get our orders from there, so that they can co-ordinate our efforts. We get whatever supplies we need by sea and air from England. German military papers also come from there when we need them. You can help with that, Jim.'

I was being recruited into the Resistance immediately. They trusted me completely, and I now belonged in a way that I never had before.

The next day I reported to Charles, who was now my area chief, in Isbergues. 'We work in pairs,' he said. 'Jacques has a motorcycle, so I will put you with him for long-range work. We are glad to have you, Jim. There are so many things for you to do.'

Jacques, who had acted as my guide when I met the mayor and chief of police on my first day at the Café Boniface, was a calm, intelligent partner. Together we watched German military activity in an area of rough country, spying with field-glasses on a suspected rocket site. Because the site was cordoned off, we moved in as close as possible on foot after hiding the motorcycle a mile or so away. We had excellent German field-glasses, and from our vantage point in a clump of trees I was able to identify the numbers of personnel, their unit, the make of trucks, and cargo markings. It was almost certainly a rocket site!

By casually criss-crossing the trail of the incoming convoy, we found they approached their destination by a circuitous route from the south-west. We reported our findings to Charles and asked for an underground report on German unit numbers in the area of the Belgian border. In two days we learned that the trucks were loading at the railroad yards in Roubaix. We discussed plans with Charles.

'I think we should go to Roubaix,' I said. 'We can learn more if we go to the railroad up there.'

'Okay, go. They list the freight on the side of the railroad cars, a kind of manifest. If you can get close enough to read them with your glasses it might confirm what we suspect.'

We took the train to Roubaix, where we met a middle-aged woman in the Resistance. She led us to a nearby railway hotel. 'You have a room on the top floor, which overlooks the yards. It was the closest we could get and still give you good cover.'

My heart beat in anticipation. Our vantage point turned out to be so perfect that we both laughed. As each train pulled in, I read and translated every label I could, while Jacques scribbled down the details.

Toward evening we struck lucky. 'Hey, Jacques, get this down quickly. This is what we've been looking for.' A dozen cars were headed for the rocket site. I read the labels and passed the information on to Jacques.

Eventually I laid down my glasses. 'It must be what we want, but I don't understand all of it. There are many terms not commonly used. And I suspect it's camouflage labelling too.'

'British intelligence will piece it together. Thank heavens you could read that stuff. If that's not for a rocket, I'll eat my shirt,' said Jacques. 'They're obviously building some big new military device.'

Back in Isbergues, Charles enthused over our discovery. 'We'll find every rocket site in the whole of Pas de Calais, and the Allies will bomb them to hell before the Boches get them built.' He was right. Daytime bombing of the sites began shortly after and continued constantly.

The next week, when Charles approached me, his eyes glinted with merriment. 'They want us to re-route some of the trains for the rocket sites, as well as some of the material for the Atlantic Wall that Rommel is building up against any invasion. We're going to send them down south. That will slow construction and cut down their anti-aircraft effectiveness. Some big raids must be coming across the Channel, and we want them to get through.' He stroked his moustache to hide a grin. 'And you, my friend, are going to re-route them!' I looked at him, astonished.

'How in the world?'

'The papers are here. They are perfect, and it's all very simple. You will dress as a German corporal, and when the train comes into Roubaix you will go to see the engineer. You will address him like a haughty Prussian corporal and send him to Reims.' He began to chuckle.

'Yeah, laugh, it's me who's got to go up there! That's a risky business.' I was both exhilarated and frightened, but eager to try it. Charles pointed at the expression on my face and doubled up. He tried to speak, but couldn't get the words out. Suddenly, I imagined what I must look like and began to laugh too. When Jacques came in, he found us still leaning against the wall giggling. And when we tried to explain the reason we were laughing, we just burst out laughing again.

Poor Jacques looked from one to the other, then pulled off his beret and sat on the table to wait for us to finish. 'It's a picnic, it is, not a war. A bloody goddam picnic,' he said, drumming his fingers on the table. And we started hooting all over again, until Charles grabbed his fly in mock horror and made a dash for the bathroom.

I learned my lines and studied the station sketch, and less than a week later, I waited nervously in the rail yards at Roubaix. It was as easy as Charles said. The French engineer shrugged nonchalantly when I gave him the change of orders – he didn't care where he took the train.

After that success, we became quite bold, and I sent trains hither and yon. I became a specialist in this kind of activity. Charles would receive the necessary papers printed in German and French, which were always perfect forgeries, and I was never seriously cross-examined. Later, we took advantage of this excellent cover and I would occasionally go right into the stations at night and check the sides of the cars. By this method we were able to transmit much more accurate details of important shipments. London seldom gave any feedback on the information we radioed, but after we had confirmed the existence of two more rocket sites, Charles came in one night and announced to us, 'London says "Good work". I guess you two can feel happy about that.'

Jacques worked in a vehicle parts factory and, of course, reported any useful information he was able to discover there. But, because of his job, he could not work on intelligence during the week. So I became part of a flexible team, joining up with any one of a half-dozen others, depending on where I was staying at the time and what the job was to be.

I had three sets of papers in different places, for use in various situations. My Resistance identification card especially was a source of pride to me – I was as proud of my number 407 in France as I had hated my number 810 in Börgermoor. If only the Scharführer could see me now, I gloated, he'd die of apoplexy. I also had a document which said that I had been discharged from a prisoner-of-war camp when the French troops were demobilized. If I was stopped by the Germans, this document was necessary to prove that I hadn't escaped from a German concentration camp.

We kept careful track of troop movements. I identified every military unit, including their vehicles, arms and everything else we thought could be helpful. Prostitutes who consorted with the Germans were enlisted to gather what information they could, particularly on matters such as morale and expected troop movements. Other women were also encouraged to lead the Germans on to gain information. Cleaning ladies in the German military office were told to go through the garbage cans, and the brave women faithfully relayed crumpled but legible messages from Berlin or Regional Headquarters, despite the risks involved. Many of these valuable messages were brought to me for translation, and then the information was speedily radioed to England.

'There is a drop tonight, and our help is needed,' Jacques told me one morning before he left for work. 'Two of our people who regularly meet the British planes which drop our supplies are being watched by collaborators. Will you come?'

'Of course. You needn't ask.'

About ten o'clock, Jacques picked me up on a dark street corner and we drove quietly out into the countryside on his motorcycle, through a tangle of country lanes.

We stopped beside a copse of trees on a lane lined with stone walls. The night was clear and silent.

'Are we doing this alone?' I was shocked.

'The others are here,' he whispered back. 'Come.'

We pushed the motorcycle into the scrub beside a gate, went through a pasture, and entered the trees, moving slowly. Suddenly Jacques stopped in front of me. '336 and 407,' he said in a normal tone that sounded loud in the night, making me jump.

'Then we are all here, and the coast is clear,' a voice answered from low down in front of us.

In the pale light it was eerie to see a patch of the earth rise as the ground opened. Six people climbed up out of a hidden trap-door and we shook hands.

'The plane comes in five minutes. Here is your light, 407. Remember, you do not recognize us and we do not recognize you. We use only numbers for these operations.' The broad-shouldered man speaking to me as he handed me a heavy flashlight was obviously in charge. 'We go out to the field there away from the road and spread out in a hundred-metre circle. When we hear the plane, we turn on our lights and hold them straight up only. That way they can see them easily from above but the light is not very visible from the ground. There is a shade around your light, as you can feel.

'Come, I'll take you to your place.' He took my elbow and guided me toward the field. 'The pilots are quite accurate usually, and there is no wind tonight, which helps. When the stuff lands, we simply carry it back here to our storage area below the trapdoor as quickly as possible. That's all we do tonight. Then we clear out immediately. Three of us take the supplies from here later in small amounts. You will get some English cigarettes soon,' he said, laughing, as he left me standing alone in the night.

I was amazed how simple it was. We heard the plane's motor, we flashed our lights at him briefly, a 'chute came down, the lights went out, and in another ten minutes we were back on the motorcycle riding away, with several canisters stashed away below ground. For security reasons we were not told what they contained. Jacques kept the headlights off until we were well away from the drop site and turning down another lane. Then I began to breathe easier, suddenly aware how tense I had been. Every shadow had assumed the shape of an SS man, and I imagined what they would have done to me if I had been caught. I felt more vulnerable that night than I had since joining the Resistance.

While eating dinner one blustery evening at the house with a Resistance arms cache in the cellar, where I had once stayed, I was introduced to Paul. 'He is our expert in stealing arms from the Boches, but he doesn't have a bloody clue how the arms work, and he needs your help to figure them out,' Charles said, laughing.

'Please come downstairs and see what you can do,' Paul asked rather sheepishly.

In the wine cellar, Paul showed me wine casks filled with German hand grenades, the heady wine smell overpowering the reek of cordite. I was astonished to see how many cases they had stolen.

'But they are no good,' Paul complained, frustrated. 'We cannot use them. We tried to blow up a munitions dump with them, but the bastards didn't go off.'

I picked up a grenade and glanced at it. 'They look fine to me,' I said puzzled. 'Where are the detonators?'

'The detonators?' he repeated.

Slowly it dawned on me. 'Didn't they put in the detonators when they used them?'

There was a pause, then Paul said sheepishly, 'I guess

we are good at stealing from the Boches, but we need someone like you to show us how to use them.'

I tried hard to suppress my laughter, and to cover my smile, I pretended to look around at the cache of arms. Almost immediately I noticed a box of detonators at the back.

'There they are,' I said. 'These grenades are not like yours. They have to have one of these detonators put in before you can use them.' I took a detonator and showed him how to screw off the cap and slide it into place. 'They are manufactured separately for safe transport. You put this in, pull the string, count twenty-one . . . twenty-two . . . twenty-three . . . and then throw it.'

From that night on, I added the duty of weapons instructor to my growing list of duties. I taught men and women what I had learned in my basic training about the use of grenades, sub-machine-guns, and weapons of all kinds. It was convenient for us that the British Sten gun and the German Schmeisser used the same ammunition!

The local Gestapo office was enlarged to try to counter the growing threat from the Resistance, but we continued our work. My load of translations increased and although much of the information made little sense to us, we sent everything to London. Each bit of information was part of the jigsaw puzzle being pieced together in England. We never knew whether something that seemed insignificant to us might dovetail with information from somewhere else. At any rate, we were sure that there was little the German military did in our region that we didn't manage to report before long.

The arms cache in the wine cellar grew. 'How do you manage it? I'm astounded at the volume you've got!' I exclaimed to Paul one day after a session with some newly captured ammunition.

'Huh! This is nothing,' he said. 'We've got much more camouflaged in fields, under barns and chicken houses, and in just about every other unexpected place you can think of. And the Boches are constantly amazed at the amount of dynamite we've got. They think we're stealing it from them. Every time we blow up something they send frantic messages to Paris about it.' He grinned like a schoolboy. 'Little do they know that we can make explosives on every farm using only diesel oil and nitrogen fertilizer.'

I had to laugh at their ingenuity.

Occasionally I met pilots being passed along to the Maquis in southern France. These Resistance groups spirited them across the Pyrenees to Spain and Gibraltar, and from there they were passed on to England. Pilots were at a premium; there were more planes being produced than there were men to fly them. Other Allied fugitives were simply kept at camps hidden in remote places, but pilots were rushed along the 'railroad'.

My friend Marie-Louise Desquesnes was very active in helping these pilots and other servicemen on their way south. She was a hairdresser in her early thirties, a brave and kind woman who used her profession as a front for meeting with and passing on Allied soldiers and agents. Her husband and small son, both called André, were strong supporters of the Resistance. Marie-Louise was in contact with her younger brother, who lived in the Pyrenees, and the two of them were responsible for many successful escapes.

'I worry about you,' I said to her one day. 'You've been doing this dangerous work too long. One of them could be a Gestapo agent, and this time you could be the one who . . .' She knew what I meant.

During the winter, a pilot had parachuted down near

Aire-Sur-Lys, where he was swiftly taken under cover by
the local Resistance. He spoke perfect English and his
story of being shot down was quite typical. Everything he
had and wore was English; even his laundry labels had
been checked when his clothes were cleaned for him. He
was very grateful to the Resistance for his rescue. As I
had been, he was moved from house to house to prevent
detection and he met a number of people. Finally, when
they were ready to send him south to Spain, the pilot
disappeared.

The next day, everyone he had been in contact with
was rounded up and immediately shot. The pilot had
been a perfectly disguised Gestapo agent. He dealt the
Resistance a heavy blow.

Marie-Louise and I were chatting in her kitchen the
day of the executions. Suddenly her husband, André,
rushed into the house, wild-eyed and waving his gun.
'You are one of them too, you son of a bitch!' he shouted
at me. His voice dropped to a hoarse whisper. 'I'm going
to finish you now, before you get us all too.'

I backed to the wall, shocked and incredulous, as he
levelled his gun at me. He had left us that morning a
normal man, and now returned a raving maniac.

'What is the matter with you?' Marie-Louise regained
enough composure to ask. He ignored her and came on
menacingly toward me.

'André!' she screamed, darting forward to grab his
arm.

He looked at her. His wild eyes were red-rimmed from
crying.

'That English pilot at Aire-Sur-Lys,' he said, his voice
cracking. 'He was a Gestapo agent. They've shot over
fifty of our people.'

Marie-Louise trembled. Her face went ashen grey, and tears ran down her cheeks. Then she remembered me.

'But Jim is not one of them! André, you cannot believe that. The water in his legs, André! He was a prisoner.'

'I'm not taking any chances. He knows a hundred people. You don't know why he has water in his legs.'

I looked around. I could not escape; I was backed tight against the wall. Mesmerized, I stared down the barrel of the gun, too shocked to feel fear.

André jerked away from Marie-Louise and came towards me.

'I am not an agent. I hate the Nazis!' I shouted hoarsely.

'You are! You admitted you are German when you were trapped. Now admit the rest!'

I saw his thumb cock the gun.

Suddenly, Marie-Louise was between us.

'André! I know how you feel. But I'm certain in my heart that Jim is not one of them. I cannot let you kill him. You have a right to be suspicious, and upset over what has happened. But this is wrong! Before you kill Jim, you will have to kill me, André.'

She stepped backwards toward me until I was almost hidden behind her.

André looked at her in amazement. There was total silence in the room for what seemed a lifetime.

'You know the risks, Marie, you're crazy!' He paused a moment. 'But then, you are never wrong in your heart. Oh God, am I wrong?' He swayed back and forth. Tears streamed from his eyes. My life hung in the balance while my heart pounded painfully.

Finally, he lowered the gun. 'I want to believe you. I have always liked Jim. I considered him a friend. But I can't let such things stand in the way of my duty.' The gun barrel came up again.

'Remember, the British said to send him over,' Marie-Louise said quickly, pressing her advantage. 'They must believe his story. And look at the things he's done to help us. He is truly one of us now, André.'

'I want to believe you,' he repeated, then his voice broke. 'My God, what a horrible day! I have just come from Aire. I saw all those families we know.' He threw himself into a chair, put his face down on his arms, and sobbed at the horror of what had happened. The gun clattered across the tiled floor.

I staggered to the table, completely shaken, and collapsed onto a chair. For a moment I thought I would faint. I stared into space, my mind numb. It was the second time in France that I had almost been shot. Marie-Louise leaned against the mantel shelf, her face in her hands.

I don't know how long we remained that way, nor do I remember very clearly how we finished the evening. A suspension of thought carried us through somehow. We went individually and early to bed, and slept as though drugged well into the next day.

After that, I worshipped the earth Marie-Louise walked on, and hated to see her take risks. But she only replied, 'Jim, I take no more risks than you or many others. And that I must do until this mess is over.'

When the rift was healed and life returned to normal, I said to André, 'Your wife is a tremendous woman. I would give my life for her.'

'Ah! So would I, my friend. Between us we must take care of her. She saved us both. If I had shot you, I would have shot myself.'

Within the year, André died of tuberculosis, and I

tried to watch out for Marie-Louise more closely. I always went to her for haircuts, which gave me a chance to talk to her and see if I could help her in any way. She was stoic in her grief, never letting it keep her from her avowed duty. As the air battle increased in ferocity, more and more Allied pilots passed through her home, many of them even younger than I.

Throughout the spring of 1944, the pace of our activities increased. The French were sure now that the Allies would eventually win, and they were extremely anxious to finish the war and see their country free. Resistance members talked of coming out in more open combat. They wanted to blow up bridges and rail lines, but I argued against it.

'No! No!' I exclaimed every time I heard such talk. 'You don't know how well trained they are; they would kill far more of us than we could of them. Please, you must wait for the invasion. It's bound to come before too long. If you blow things up, it will hurt you more than the Germans. Wait for Allied instructions, or you might hamper the total effort. Let Paul's unit take care of that with their explosives. It's their job. We make ourselves more useful, vital even, gathering intelligence no one else can provide.'

But they grew more impatient as spring wore on. Sporadic fighting broke out here and there as the Resistance became bolder and more impatient. They often suffered heavy casualties, and Charles sombrely acknowledged that our group had been right to restrain our activities.

I was grateful Charles was such a fine leader. He had also become a good friend and we occasionally talked about doing something together after the war, perhaps buying a sailing boat, and leaving all this chaos behind. But it was not to be.

One of our greatest fears was infiltration by the collaborators. With victory in sight, more people were joining the Resistance, seeing a chance to help or wanting to be on the winning side, and it was difficult to keep up with screening them, as well as carrying out our intelligence work and the training of new recruits. Any one of the new members could be a collaborator. And one of them was.

One day Charles was approached in the street by a young woman who said she had been sent to see him by the mayor of Aire-Sur-Lys. She wanted to join the Resistance, and the mayor had told her that Charles was the chief for the area.

We never found out exactly what happened between the two. The mayor had sent Charles recruits before, and perhaps Charles assumed that because she knew the mayor was in the underground, she must be telling the truth. We don't know how much checking he did before confirming that he was the chief. That evening, however, the girl disappeared. The Gestapo took Charles and whisked him away to Paris, where the Resistance people we contacted saw him taken into Gestapo headquarters on the Avenue Foch.

If the Gestapo broke Charles they would have us all. We feared for our lives, and prayed for Charles. We knew what they would be doing to him and our lives hung suspended for several days. We debated whether to flee, but where to? Then the report came from Paris; Charles had been shot.

The group met in requiem. We knew Charles hadn't exposed us under torture, or there would have been a lightning raid. There was no doubt what we'd do if the

Gestapo came, but there was little actual discussion of suicide. As we parted, Jacques spoke for all of us, 'A damned good man!' His voice broke. 'We'll drive every bloody Boche back into the Rhine.'

In the weeks that followed I worked long hours and many nights I hardly slept. Days blended into one another as the hectic pace of training and intelligence work continued. There were demands for my help in many places at once, and I was so busy that it was almost June before I realized it. We had all hoped to celebrate Christmas in a liberated France, but now that seemed very unlikely. Why didn't the Allies invade and drive out the Nazis?

Expectations rose to fever pitch. We knew that the Allies could not give warning of place or time. When there was to be an invasion, it would just happen. There couldn't be any risk of alerting the enemy.

We heard rumours that German counter-intelligence had changed their earlier prediction that the invasion would be in the Pas de Calais area, and now plumped for Normandy. But this Abwehr assessment was scorned by Berlin, and Hitler reprimanded all his counter-intelligence branches in our area, as we discovered from a careful study of the garbage retrieved by our indomitable cleaning ladies. As we had no foreknowledge of Allied plans, we were in the dark too, but we enjoyed these signs that the enemy was rattled.

Nor did it help the Germans to see the faces of the Frenchmen around them. In addition to the old scarcely veiled contempt, there was now an expression of triumph and expectation that could no longer be hidden.

'Bientôt (soon),' everybody seemed to whisper. 'Soon France will be free again.'

While we waited, we continued to gather intelligence for the British. And made sure our weapons were ready.

14

The Allied invasion of France took place on June 6, 1944.

At about noon, Jacques rushed up to me, his face beaming, to tell the news. 'It's true! It's happened! The invasion! In Normandy!' We flung our arms around each other, knowing that the liberation of our area could not be long delayed.

Instructions poured in from London, and we toiled at a hectic pace gathering and transmitting intelligence. The Allied bridgehead expanded with sickening slowness until Caen fell. Then Allied armour poured out across France. The British Second Army hit Amiens on August 31 and rolled on towards Brussels.

Then suddenly, First Canadian Army tanks reached our area. Proudly, we pinned on our Resistance armbands and hoisted the flag of Free France outside our homes. Now, at last, we could fight in the open. After relatively little fighting, the tanks pushed through rapidly on September 6, chasing the retreating German army. Their movement was so fast that significant pockets of German troops were left behind, holed up in various strongholds. They were obviously a dangerous threat to the civilian population.

We hadn't known what our role would be when the Allies reached us, but now it was clear what we must do. The pockets of German troops had to be routed out and POW camps set up. I was told to report to a Captain Danel who was put in charge of clearing the German troops from their local headquarters, a baronial manor house set among thick trees in a large estate just outside the town of Lillers. It wasn't going to be easy, I thought, when I arrived at the scene shortly after noon.

Captain Danel gave me a captured German pistol. 'We won't expect you to use that, Jim, except in self-defence. But we certainly need your military expertise and understanding of German weapons. This clump of trees will have to do for our headquarters.'

He looked up and frowned. 'What are they doing?' he exclaimed, pointing toward his Resistance men. 'Get the hell down!' he yelled at them. A large group had left their hiding places in a ditch and stormed up the drive toward the manor house. They were more enthusiastic than experienced.

'My God! Stop them. They'll all be killed!' I shouted, seeing all too clearly what could happen.

Just then, heavy fire burst out from the trees around the estate. More sharp-shooters in the upper storeys mowed down the Resistance men, vulnerable and exposed in the open. A few tried to take shelter behind scattered trees and bushes. Others turned back, only to drop grotesquely on the grass. It was over in a few minutes. We were stunned. Half our men slaughtered in a few seconds.

Before we could regroup properly, to vent our horror and fury, German artillery positioned by the front corners of the house opened up on our position, and we all dived for the bottom of the ditch beside the road.

'Jim! What do you think?' It was Danel beside me.

'Their sharp-shooters are well placed. They've obviously been prepared for this for some time. It seems as if they expected attack from this side, since they have their artillery drawn up here.' I tried desperately to collect my thoughts, to guess what the Germans were planning.

'You're right. If we come in from the north, the ground is more open, but if we wait a few hours until dark we could reach the trees and have some cover.'

'Yes,' I reasoned, 'then they'll have to move their artillery to the back of the manor with horses. But if you send in a group from here to kill the horses, we can put their artillery out of commission.'

'We've got to do that to get on an even footing. We'll never get near otherwise,' he agreed.

The plan worked. After dark, our commandos moved in, with the main body swinging to the north and digging in at the edge of the trees. At dawn, the men on the north flank opened up. Another group shot the horses, which were hitched up to move the enemy artillery. By late afternoon, the battle appeared to be going our way.

With Danel I circled the manor, following ditches where we could. Our men were still taking crazy risks at times, but for the most part we were now well organized and Danel was pleased. We left the last ditch and emerged onto the road beside the car he had been given, on our way to fetch more ammunition. Suddenly, Danel dropped to the verge, bleeding profusely from a chest wound. Even at that distance a sharp-shooter had reached him.

Hastily, I dragged his unconscious body back down into the ditch, ripped the sleeve off my shirt, and pressed it against his wound. The only hope of saving him was to drag him over a hundred metres along the ditch to where trees screened the road, and then carry him up the road. We were alone – no one was nearby to help.

The ditch was shallow, and I had to bend double to drag him along. The captain had obviously been identified as the man in charge and whoever had shot Danel was watching for us. Every time my back raised at all, shots whined close and I had to get down on my knees. But I was afraid the captain would die if I didn't hurry. Frantically, I puffed and pulled, and we finally cleared the ditch. Danel was unconscious and bleeding, but still alive.

Luckily I didn't have to stagger far with my burden before a car stopped, and we rushed to the hospital. After an anxious hour they told me that Danel would live. It was a great relief; he was a good man.

I left the hospital immediately and began walking back through the town toward the battle zone, shaken up by the narrow escape. People were celebrating and cheering in the streets, and I was offered many drinks as I went along. Occasionally I received suspicious glances too, as it was known that German soldiers were deserting their units and taking up various disguises. I had lost my beret in the ditch as I dragged Captain Danel to safety, and my tall, fair head must have been noticeable in the crowd. However, I wore the French Resistance armband and the Cross of Lorraine, and some people cheered me for that; at one house I was literally dragged inside for a drink.

'You are heroes, you in the Forces Françaises Intérieures! One drink with us!'

After I finished a cognac, I begged off and said I had to report back to my unit, but I didn't tell that we were engaged in a battle. I would have had to explain about taking the captain to the hospital, and I didn't want to appear to boast. As I left, a little man from the back of the room followed me quietly, but I scarcely noticed him and turned away up the street. The cognac quieted my nerves, and I felt calmer as I walked along. At the next corner I turned into a lane that would take me by a short cut into the country toward the manor house.

Suddenly four men leapt out from behind a wall and

surrounded me, their guns pointed steadily at my chest. Stunned, I stood absolutely still. They were obviously very excited and jittery. My God, I thought, here I've come all through the war and now I'm going to be killed by the very people I've helped!

'Against the wall! Hands up!' It was the man who had followed me from the house, 'We know that you are a Boche. I know your accent.'

'I am a member of the FFI-WO. You can see my armband.'

'You killed one of our men and stole his jacket. Where is your ID?'

'At the place where I am staying.' I was sweating.

'A likely story! If you are FFI, where is your gun?'

'I left it at the battleground. We are taking the old manor house from the Boches.'

'If you are FFI you would be there. You are trying to sneak away in disguise.'

'No! I just took Captain Danel to the hospital. I saved his life!'

'Ha!'

I watched their fingers trembling on their triggers. Suddenly I was angry.

'You bloody fools! Who do you think you are? Judge and jury? If you kill me you will be shot for murder!'

They blinked and hesitated. I pressed them.

'Take me to the hospital and find out. You'll see.'

'They've got some other Boches at the city hall. Let's take him there. He'll get his due sooner or later if he's lying.'

'He is lying! I recognize a German accent, I tell you. Shoot the bastard Boche now.' The little man spat out the last words, hatred flashing from his eyes.

'Pierre! I am in charge,' said a taller, younger man.

'We will take him to the city hall. You can guard him while I go to check; shoot him if he tries to get away.' The little man was forced to yield to his leader, and I began to breathe again.

They fanned out behind me and marched me to the city hall. I hoped we'd see someone who knew me on the way, but I had not spent much time in Lillers, and everyone I knew was fighting at the manor house.

At the city hall I was shoved roughly into an empty room. They ordered me to sit on the floor while Pierre and two of the others sat by the door. Their guns pointed at me menacingly. I closed my eyes and prayed. An hour went by, and the little man smirked triumphantly. I began to hope desperately that the man in charge hadn't met with an accident. Time dragged.

After nearly two hours he returned, and entered laughing. 'You were right, Pierre! He is German. But he's also on our side! And he did save the captain.'

'Come!' he turned to me. 'The mayor would like to see you. And for our part, please forgive us. We appreciate what you have done, but you know we can't be too careful.'

I couldn't answer. Weak-kneed, I climbed to my feet and tottered after him to the mayor's office. I resisted the temptation to kick Pierre as I passed him.

'Monsieur Witt! I apologize for this dreadful error. On behalf of the citizens of Lillers, please accept my apologies.' The mayor pushed out a chair and offered me a cigar and a drink. 'We are preparing a citation in your honour for saving Captain Danel, and also for your excellent work. You are truly a remarkable young man. They tell me in Isbergues that you are only twenty-two years of age. Oh yes, I know the whole story. Quite remarkable! I can imagine how you felt about this incident today.'

He spoke at some length, beaming over me, while I sat getting drunk from emotional exhaustion and cognac on an empty stomach. I wanted desperately to go home and sleep.

Finally he let me go, providing his car to drive me back to the battle. I arrived in time to begin the questioning of the first captured prisoners before they were taken to a POW camp.

To my amazement all the German officers were provided with Red Cross doctors' papers. It was obvious that they had hoped to escape, and to abandon their soldiers. But I made it clear that we knew they were not medical doctors.

That evening, I had the satisfaction of taking part in the liberation of Isbergues, where I had spent so many months underground with the Resistance. The next day I was on my way to the town of Béthune when I came upon a large contingent of dispirited soldiers in German uniforms camped on the edge of a slough. They had no artillery but quite a large number of horse. I walked up to them wondering how long they had been there.

'I would like to speak to your captain. The war is finished here, and you must lay down your arms,' I told a corporal in German.

He looked at me blankly and shrugged his shoulders without understanding. I repeated my orders, and he shrugged again. I was amazed. Then it struck me that none of them looked German! They led me to their captain, and I tried again.

'The war is over. You must lay down your arms. It is no use fighting – you will kill and be killed needlessly.'

'I do not understand very well. Have the Germans given up?'

'They have been driven far back toward Germany. Those still here have given up, and you will be safer if you do too.'

'I understand. We give up to you. We are weary of this war. It is not ours. We haven't had orders for days.'

At his command the whole unit stacked their weapons on the road. I stopped the first car that came by and sent the driver for help. His eyes popped at the pile of weapons.

'You mean you disarmed all of them? Alone?' He drove off shaking his head.

The captain told me his men were all Ukrainians who had volunteered when the Germans overran their territory. I felt sorry for them, uneducated, bewildered pawns of war, particularly later on when I learned that a million such men were shipped back to the USSR, and all of them were shot. At the same time, I despised the captain as a traitor. As I questioned him, it became obvious that he had taken the easy way out; he had had the chance to go underground and resist the Nazis, or even just hide, but he had chosen the coward's way out.

Continuing on to Béthune after this incident, I found the British already in control, and so I helped with interrogation of prisoners. Dozens of them sat in the street, waiting abjectly, scarcely aware of their surroundings.

After a long session of questioning, drained emotionally and physically, I went out for fresh air and dinner. Just outside the town, to my horror, I saw the British artillery set up, pointed at Isbergues, and ready to fire. Breaking into a run, I rushed up to the commanding officer.

'What is going on?' I nearly screamed at him.

'We are preparing to shell Isbergues. It is full of German military.'

'No! Stop! The only Germans there are under arrest. You mustn't fire. My friends are there too.'

'Who are you?'

'I'm in the Resistance. I came from Isbergues this morning. I can prove it. Just come with me and we'll drive over there.' I was nearly wild with anxiety.

'Stand by. Don't fire!' he shouted. 'All right. We'll check.'

'Thank God!' It was all I could say. We drove to Isbergues, where all was quiet, with the Resistance clearly in control.

The captain turned to me. 'They're damned lucky you came along, old chap! If you hadn't we'd have levelled the bloody place. I wonder who the stupid bastard was who told us that story?'

It was the last straw. I just turned my back on him and walked away. Mentally exhausted I went home to bed and slept for fifteen hours.

POW enclosures were set up immediately an area was liberated, and the long process of sorting prisoners began in earnest. A form had to be filled out on each one: 'Name? Rank? Number? Unit?' I spent endless hours interrogating prisoners, identifying, classifying, and cross-examining. It was draining, depressing work.

One morning a German soldier was brought in under heavy guard. He was accused of beating and shooting an elderly couple without provocation. They had both survived their wounds, and now made a positive identification.

'You've got to help me,' he begged me.

'I am not your judge, only the interpreter,' I replied.

'You must be responsible for your own deeds. I can only tell you that you will have a fair hearing before a Resistance tribunal.'

The trial took place the same day. The evidence was conclusive and damning. The soldier broke down, swore he was sorry, and begged forgiveness.

'What mercy did you show these poor old people?' the judge replied stonily.

The sentence was death by firing squad. The soldier deserved it, but it was all I could do to say the words to him in German. I felt I was sending a countryman to his death, even though I had nothing to do with the verdict. The man had to be dragged from the courtroom to face the firing squad.

Another day I was taken to question some German officers who were captured in Rommel's Atlantic Wall fortifications. I was amazed at the Wall's vastness and complexity. No wonder the Germans had been able to hold on so well and wreak such terrible destruction on the Allies. The bunkers were enormous, equipped with heavy artillery. Cannons rode smoothly on rails. Barrack shelters were located deep underground, with elevators and direct access to the bunkers.

While I marvelled at these examples of German ingenuity, I wished fervently that it could have been put to some noble purpose. It sickened me to have the world despise my homeland, when its potential was so great. I wanted to tell the world that it was only the Nazis and their demigod who led some of the German nation astray; that we could be a great people.

But in the ensuing months the German reputation would sink even lower as the horrible atrocities of Belsen, Dachau, and Buchenwald were revealed to the world. I

was devastated, and wondered what horrifying details
were yet to be exposed.

The German army hung on in Brest, Dunkirk, Le
Havre, and St Nazaire until the end of the war, casting a
shadow over all of western France. No one could relax
entirely with the enemy still there. We prayed that Hitler
would soon capitulate. I longed to go home to see my
mother.

One day a message came that the British wanted me in
England. Jacques brought it to me. He was my new
commander, now that Charles was dead.

'Do you want to go?'

'Not particularly. I'm happy enough with what I'm
doing here. I like you all, and I'm very busy.'

'Then you won't go! It's as simple as that. I will just
send them a message that you are staying here.'

That evening Jacques returned. 'They were quite irate.
I just said that you were not going, and that was it.'

I laughed at his boldness.

'We have a right to make some decisions too,' he
asserted. I wondered what the outcome would be for me.

Eventually, worn out from doing interrogations and
feeling the need of a change and some physical activity, I
requested reassignment for a while, and Jacques sent me
out on patrols with a partner. It was a welcome change.

One afternoon, we came back into the town after
patrolling our regular route to Aire-Sur-Lys. A large,
noisy crowd packed the main street.

'What is it?' we asked a man.

'The goddam collaborators! They've got them.'

'They're not killing them?' I was aghast.

'No, they'll try the buggers in court. Right now they're
getting a haircut and their own special parade.'

We pressed in closer. The collaborators, men and women alike, had been shaved bald by the Resistance. Now they were being loaded on horse-drawn wagons to be paraded in the streets. Already eggs, tomatoes, and garbage were flying, and catcalls filled the air. A band broke into a mocking tune, 'See, the Conquering Hero Comes', and led the wagons up the street. My scalp tingled from the vicious whispers and calls around me. There was an ugly mood in the air. With only a little provocation, I believed, the crowd would have torn the collaborators apart; I turned away, sickened. There was no doubt the collaborators deserved their fate, but I just wanted the conflict to end and all the hatreds to fade away.

PART FOUR
Spy School

15

The cell door closed behind me. Almost silently, quite undramatically, but I was a prisoner again.

I still had my armband and my papers, but they had taken my sub-machine-gun away. The major didn't say I was a prisoner; he simply gave no explanation at all.

The cell was clean and, as cells go, comfortable. The bunk bed was similar to the one I had slept in in the military prison in Germany; the light was subdued but not gloomy. I sat down on the bunk and tried to make sense of the events of the day.

The jeep had driven up while I was on a road patrol with my Resistance partner, and it stopped near by as we checked the papers of a middle-aged couple. The Allied forces were stationed only in the major centres of population, leaving the French Resistance to carry out routine police work and supervision, including the checking of baggage and identification papers.

I waved the couple on. 'Au revoir, m'sieur, madame.' Then I looked up at the three men in the British jeep, a major and a captain of the military police and a senior member of the local Resistance. They got out and approached.

'You are Jim Witt?' the major asked me in French.

'Oui, c'est moi. Can I help you?'

'We'd like you to come with us for questioning.'

'I see.' I shrugged. It was inevitable, I supposed, now that the front had moved on so rapidly, that loose ends would be tidied up. I turned to my partner and shook hands with him. 'See you soon,' I called out as I climbed into the jeep.

As the captain swung the jeep back in the direction of St Omer, the major reached over and picked up the sub-machine-gun from my lap. I looked at him, then at the French Resistance officer. He shrugged his shoulders in resignation, but his eyes flashed angrily.

By the time we reached the outskirts of St Omer, it dawned on me that I was a prisoner. The major talked of inconsequential matters and treated me courteously, yet there could be no doubt that it was pointless to resist. He had received orders to take me to headquarters. One glance at the man told me he would never hesitate to carry out his orders.

The town had suffered a great deal of damage during the liberation. Some of the familiar streets we passed along were now little more than heaps of rubble, but the centre of town was relatively unharmed. A few windows were broken at the city hall, where the jeep stopped, but otherwise the building appeared intact.

The major left us when we arrived and the captain showed me into his office. He immediately switched from French to German.

'You are really Hans Nütt?'

'Yes.'

'What nationality are you?'

'I'm German, of course, but, as you see, I have French papers because I'm a member of the French underground.'

'But, legally, you're German?'

I agreed. This officer was surely too intelligent to believe that a man's nationality determined which side he fought on with no regard to ideas of right and wrong?

'What's going to happen to me, Captain?'

'In a day or two you'll be transferred to England and . . .'

'What? You can't mean that!'

'Why not?'

'The French leaders I've worked with for over a year told me repeatedly that my background and my loyalty to France would make me very valuable to them in the post-war period.'

'In what way?'

'I'm not sure, but I would guess they meant in the occupation of Germany.'

'Hmm. I see. But at that moment you are a German citizen, and I'm afraid we'll have to follow orders and ship you over to England.'

'Orders?'

'General Eisenhower has ordered that all aliens we come across are to be sent over to England.'

'But what about this?' I jabbed a finger at my Free French armband. 'I've a job to do here.'

'I'm sorry, but we have our orders.'

'Do my superior officers know I'm here?'

'Of course. They had to help us find you.' He took a packet of cigarettes from his desk drawer and offered me one.

'Thanks. Didn't they object to all this? Captain Danel and the colonel, my area commander?'

'I don't know. The major would deal with that. All I have to do is to establish that you are Hans Nütt and that you're German.' He stood up. 'And we've established that, haven't we?' He shook my hand courteously, but that was little consolation when a corporal took me down to the cells.

Now, sitting on the bunk in my cell, I began to feel angry and frustrated. I had not made any definite plans for the future, having simply assumed that I would continue working with the French until a free Germany existed once more. But now a frightening possibility had occurred to me. However kindly and politely the British treated me, I was still a prisoner. And prisoners of war were kept in camps. I realized that in England I might be put with a group of other German prisoners of war. Among them would be some Nazis, perhaps even SS men. It was not difficult to imagine them viewing me as a traitor to the Führer and the Fatherland, and staging a form of 'court of honour' which would sentence me to death. They would not hesitate to exterminate me. I would not be safe in a British camp.

I reached into my pocket and took out the papers the French underground had given me. To them I was a useful ally because I believed in their cause and had proved it by bearing arms against my own countrymen. The French did not bother about my real identity. To them I was Jim Witt, an identity I had come to believe in myself. It had surprised me to hear the captain refer to me by my real name, which I had not used for well over a year.

A soldier brought me supper but politely refused to answer any questions. I lay down on the bunk and finally slept. When I awoke next morning, I was confused for a moment until, with a sinking heart, I remembered where I was. A different soldier brought my breakfast on a tray.

'How long do I have to stay here?' I asked in English.

'Don't ask me, mate. You'll have to ask one of the officers.'

'Can I see an officer, then? What about the captain?'

'He'll send for you when he's ready.'

'When will that be?'

'Don't ask me, mate.' He was friendly and considerate,

showing no signs of hostility. My colleagues in the underground always made a joke of English politeness, but in my present situation the politeness was no joke. It masked my real predicament.

All day I sat in my cell waiting for the captain to call me. I passed the time reading old newspapers and magazines the soldiers gave me, trying to concentrate but repeatedly finding myself thinking of a POW camp, where my fellow Germans would certainly discover my wartime sympathies. The captain sent for me late in the evening just as I was getting ready to sleep.

'Please sit down. Cigarette?'

'Thank you. What's going on, Captain? You said I was going to be sent to England.'

'Yes, you are. Sorry about the delay. It can't be any too pleasant in the cells.' That damned politeness again. He opened a file on his desk. 'You stick by your story that you are Hans Nütt.'

'It's no story. It's the truth.'

'Quite, quite. We just have to be sure. Well, I can tell you that we're sending you over to England. You'll leave early in the morning.'

'Am I being sent to a POW camp?'

'I really can't say. You'd have gone today, but Colonel Leclerc of the Resistance insisted on seeing Major Hawkins about you.'

'Oh, why?' I felt a stirring of hope.

The captain smiled. 'You seem to have proved very useful to the underground. Colonel Leclerc spoke very highly of you. It was quite a scene in fact, especially when he banged on the table and insisted that you be released immediately.' He must have seen the expression of hope on my face. 'Sorry, old chap. It didn't work. The major refused to give way, although he couldn't present the colonel with a fait accompli by sending you this morning before the colonel got here. The meeting went on all afternoon, and Colonel Leclerc left in a very foul temper.'

'I'd like to talk to Colonel Leclerc.'

'I'm sorry, that's not possible.'

'He's my commanding officer. You must let me speak to him.'

'I'm sorry. The matter's settled.'

'Doesn't it matter to you that I fought with the French Resistance? Look, I've been with the underground now for ten months. Doesn't that count for anything?'

'I'm afraid not. Not when we have our orders from General Eisenhower.'

It was my turn to bang the table. 'I don't give a damn about General Eisenhower's orders! You're going to ship me over to England to sit in a cage with a thousand German prisoners. Can't you see what they'll do to me?'

'Look, Mr Nütt, all of that's none of my business. My orders are to check that you are really Hans Nütt. Beyond that, it's none of my business.'

Next morning, a military police guard and a driver took me to Dieppe, where I was escorted aboard a British destroyer. The military policeman led me below decks where he locked me in the ship's brig. I could hear British soldiers crowd on to the ship, but I was not permitted to talk with them. At Newhaven, my guard led me ashore into a compartment reserved for us on a train bound for London.

'You're not going to handcuff me?' I asked the huge policeman.

'It's not necessary,' he rumbled. After the train picked up speed, he asked, 'What was it like in the Resistance?' He pointed a thick finger at my FFI armband.

We were still talking when the train stopped at a station on the outskirts of London and we got off. An army officer was waiting on the platform. My guard handed me over, saluted, and got back on board the train. For the first time, I felt a glimmer of hope. They would not send an officer to collect one man if they merely intended to hold him as a prisoner-of-war. The British might have something else in mind.

'Nearly there, sir,' the WAC driver called out half an hour after we left the station. A few minutes later, we stopped at high wrought-iron gates, where our papers were checked by a military policeman, who waved us on. We drove slowly along a gravel drive that swept among the trees in wide curves. Finally we pulled up in front of a huge old English country mansion.

I was quickly ushered in through the hall and into the office of a British major.

'Sit down, won't you. I'm Major Wilkinson. You're Hans Nütt, right?'

'That's right.'

He pulled out a questionnaire. 'Just one or two details. You don't mind?'

I shrugged. 'No, go ahead.'

He continued, in perfect German, 'Date of birth? . . . Name of father? . . . Name of mother? . . . brothers? . . . sisters? . . . Schools attended? . . .'

I answered mechanically. When I told him about the boarding school near Lübeck he looked up. 'Oh, that's where Jäger-regiment No. 24 is stationed,' he commented.

'How do you, an Englishman, know that?'

He smiled but didn't answer my question. His assumption of superiority irked as well as impressed me.

'What's going to happen to me?' I demanded.

'We haven't made a decision about you yet. But, for the time being, don't worry. Enjoy your stay here.' He pushed the questionnaire into a file folder and sat back to chat. His German was so faultless that I assumed he had spent a great deal of time in Germany before the war. Moreover, his knowledge of the country was extensive and detailed. He seemed to be quite familiar with several places associated with my boyhood, and I received the impression that he even knew some of the people whose names I mentioned.

'Well, I think that's about all for today, Herr Nütt. I'll get someone to show you to your room.' He stood up.

'Just a second,' I interrupted. 'I'm not clear what is going to happen to me. Do I stay here until the end of the war, or do I go to a prisoner-of-war camp, or what? I'd like to know.'

He sat down again and looked at me searchingly before answering. 'What would you like to do?'

'I'd like to go back and rejoin the French.'

'Hmmm.' A pause. 'Why?'

'Because I want to help them win the war.'

'You want to see Germany defeated?'

'I want to see . . . the Nazis defeated, thrown out, but for that to happen Germany must be defeated and start again as a new nation.'

'I see. Well, I don't want you to feel under any pressure, Herr Nütt. Just take life easy for a while. I think you probably could do with a rest. Tell Major Duff if there's anything you need. He's the chap with the Tank Corps badge.' He accompanied me towards the door. 'And I wouldn't worry about going to a POW camp if I were you.'

I calculated that the mansion and its grounds were some fifty miles southwest of London and that we were in a holding centre of some sort, while the British decided what they wanted to do with us. There were men aged from twenty to forty-five, from Germany, France, Belgium, Holland, and Luxembourg, but German was the only language spoken. Every one of the inmates was tight-lipped about himself. I was no exception; I felt little desire to talk about my past. We each had our own room and were free to wander through the gardens and the grounds as far as the high barbed-wire-topped fence, outside which soldiers patrolled. All the British officers we met were fluent German-speakers.

After a few days of strolling in the grounds, eating well, and listening to recorded music, I found that I was, in fact, relaxing. Even the Irish sergeant who led us in phys. ed. every morning contributed to my feeling of well-being. I was not conscious of any pressure at the manor; in fact I gained the impression that I could spend the rest of the war there and nobody would mind. Yet, when I stopped to think, I knew the war was still going on, and that my homeland would soon be occupied. I wondered if the Nazis would surrender or if they would fight to the last man as they promised. I wondered too how Alfred and my mother were faring. It was two and a half years since our last meeting. Each day I tried to tire myself out, so that in the evening I could sit drowsily by the imposing stone fireplace in the common room before retiring. That way I would tumble into my comfortable bed and fall asleep immediately, rather than stare at the high ceiling and think of my family, my fatherland, and my own future.

Five days after my arrival at the centre, I was called in for a medical examination. Nagging doubts about my heart still remained after my ruse in Copenhagen, but the

Scottish doctor pronounced it perfect. I started to feel very optimistic.

Major Wilkinson sent for me a couple of days later. In his small office, with its war-office-issue desk in stark contrast to the opulent decoration of the walls and ceiling, we talked casually about Germany and the war. He took notes.

'Would you be willing to work for us?' he asked finally.

I hesitated. 'As long as it's as useful as what I did with the French.'

'That's good. By the way, do you have the courage to jump by parachute into enemy territory?'

'I think I could do it. Who's "us"?'

'Us? Oh, British Intelligence.'

British Intelligence? That was it then. I should have realized earlier. It had been a long time since I had thought of joining the British against the Nazis; perhaps the time was right now.

That was the first of several conversations we had in the next ten days. Each time, Major Wilkinson listened intently and made brief notes as we talked. At first I thought our conversations were casual, a pleasant means of passing time, until I became aware that this slightly built man with a pleasant face was making absolutely certain of my identity. There were times when he seemed to know things about me that I had forgotten long ago.

'. . .then there was old Herr Beckmeister in Hamburg,' he 'reminisced' one afternoon. 'You'll remember him, an old gentleman with white hair. He always slapped his left hand on his chin to emphasize what he was saying.'

I looked at him in amazement. The Beckmeisters were old friends of our family, but they were far from being well known in a large city such as Hamburg. 'How do you know the Beckmeisters?' I asked finally.

'Oh, we have our ways,' he grinned, pouring himself another cup of tea and politely refusing to answer any further questions.

Later as I strolled alone round the grounds of the manor house, I thought about how thorough British Intelligence was, and this fact gave me a tremendous amount of confidence. I felt sure that Major Wilkinson was making plans for my future, so I was not surprised when he asked me to appear before what he termed a 'commission board'.

Seven high-ranking officers sat behind a long table in what had formerly been a drawing room. They questioned me thoroughly about my past, especially about my activities in the French Resistance and why I would act against my own countrymen.

'What do you think will happen to Germany after the war is finished?' the officer in the middle asked me.

'Well, I realize Germany will be occupied by the Allies.'

'How do you feel about Soviet occupation of part of Germany?'

I hesitated. 'Well, yes, I guess they too will occupy Germany.'

'What made you hesitate before you answered the last question?'

'I don't like the idea of Russian occupation of any part of Germany.'

'Oh, why not?'

'I know what will happen there.'

'What?'

'The secret police, the lack of freedom, the fear. It would be no better than the Gestapo. Only the uniforms would be different.'

'Thank you.' The white-haired officer in the centre of the group looked around. 'Any more questions?'

An officer on my far left signalled, and the chairman nodded his permission. 'Are you willing to work for British Intelligence?'

'Yes.'

'Why? Do you think we'll pay you well?' His voice sounded sarcastic, challenging.

I grew angry. 'No, if I help you, it won't be for your English pounds! I'm willing to work for you because I understand, no, I know, that the war is lost as far as Germany is concerned. I believe it's better to finish the war today rather than tomorrow. I want to help finish the war as soon as possible.'

'Thank you, Herr Nütt.' The man who had angered me smiled broadly, and I recognized that these men were adopting various roles in order to gain a complete picture of my political opinions.

The chairman looked around again. 'Any further questions?'

'No, Brigadier, I think not,' said an officer on my left. 'I've heard enough; I'm quite satisfied, thank you.'

The chairman dismissed me, telling me I would hear from the board soon. I thanked them and left.

It irritated me that I had come so close to losing my temper, but I could not accept the suggestion that I might become a British spy for the sake of making money. My stay at the manor had given me time to think, and I realized that freedom had become the single most important issue in my life. I was proud to have been a part of the French Resistance's fight for liberty. When I thought of my homeland now, I was determined to do whatever I could to save German as well as Allied lives.

The officers left me alone for at least four days, and I wondered whether British Intelligence had lost interest in me. But one afternoon, while I was playing table tennis with a Belgian of about my own age, a soldier came up to us with orders for me to accompany him. I followed him to a brick building behind the main house, where I was measured, and within five minutes I found myself dressed in the uniform of a member of the Royal Signals. They handed me a canvas holdall in which to put the clothing I had been wearing; my other personal effects were already neatly packed in the bottom.

'You're in, Nütt,' Major Duff told me, grinning.

I was too surprised to ask questions. In the two weeks since my arrival I had sat around with time on my hands, waiting for a decision to be made. Yet, when they decided, they did not give me any time to pack or say farewell. Perhaps that was deliberate; the British seemed to have a good reason for everything they did. It might have been that they preferred transfers to take place quietly and unnoticed.

'All ready? Let's go, then.' Major Duff picked up my canvas holdall and steered me outside, where a large black civilian Vauxhall was waiting. The chauffeur set the car in motion as soon as we were seated. Before long, we were on a main highway, and Major Duff was highly amused that I found the 'cat's eyes' road markers so intriguing.

Within an hour, we arrived at 10, Kew Gardens on the outskirts of London. Duff handed me over immediately to the house-officer, Mr Peters, and left.

'Welcome, Nütt. I hope you'll be happy here.' Mr Peters spoke fluent German as he handed me my holdall. 'You'd better change back into your civvies as soon as you get to your room. And, by the way, your house-name will be Nordmann.'

'House-name?' I was puzzled.

'Yes, that's the name you'll be known by in this house.

Everybody you meet here will have a house-name; you'll soon come to accept that. House-names always begin with the same initial as your real name.'

'I see. Thank you.'

In my small, comfortable room I changed back into the clothes I had been wearing when the British picked me up, then went downstairs for supper. There were ten or so others in the dining room. Like me, they were all dressed in civvies, and everybody spoke German. Conversation was general, and nobody referred to his past. We were all future British agents, and it seemed to me that our origins varied greatly. I guessed there were German Jews, Belgians, Dutch, and possibly Scandinavians.

Next morning, my training began.

At nine-fifteen a Mr Young called for me. In fluent German he told me we were going for a tour of London. We must have appeared a strange pair, because I was wearing my now somewhat shabby French clothes, while he was beautifully clad in an expensive suit.

'Pay close attention, Herr Nordmann. If London is to be your base, you must get to know the city well. Keep your eyes open so you can find your way around.'

Mr Young knew how to make the day interesting, and he regaled me with snippets of history as we passed by the Houses of Parliament, Fleet Street, and St Paul's cathedral, as well as making detours into some of the suburbs. As a public relations officer he was superb. My respect for the British grew; Germans were supposedly noted for their thoroughness, but the British left nothing to chance. Even the suits and overcoat made up for me were cut from cloth made pre-war in Germany or Czechoslovakia. This was the first step in preparing to send me behind enemy lines.

That evening, I sat in the lounge at our house in Kew

Gardens, leafing through the *Völkischer Beobachter*, the Nazi daily newspaper. We were kept supplied with German newspapers and magazines, never more than a week old, which presumably were brought into the country via Sweden or Switzerland. It was a strange feeling to sit in freedom in England and read the vicious lies and nonsense the Nazis were putting out. The German newspapers were there to keep us up to date on life in Germany, but I found they served another purpose. Each time I read on, I felt more determined than ever to do whatever I could to rid my country of Nazi tyranny.

Although my basic training as a British agent was crammed into a very short period, it was nevertheless exceedingly thorough. Early the next day, a group of us began espionage training. A series of officers drilled us in military identification; we had to learn how to recognize every type of vehicle and armament. Another officer explained the significance of all the military insignia: division, brigade, infantry, tanks, etc. My head reeled with the amount of information I had to memorize, but there was no respite until we all knew every detail perfectly. At intervals during our further training, one of the officers would test us without warning on material from a previous course.

'I'm sorry. I know I got some of that wrong.'

'Yes, I'm afraid you did, Herr Nordmann. Don't worry, you'll get it next time. Everyone forgets sometimes you know.'

It was only a short exchange and I doubt if that officer realized the effect his words had on me. All my life at school and in the forces, I had grown accustomed to sharp, harsh criticism whenever I made a mistake. Now this British officer regarded mistakes and forgetfulness as normal, and spoke encouragingly to help me learn my material. As a teacher he was tough and demanding, but he was also brave enough to be human.

Other officers trained us to recognize significant details that should be reported. They would give us masses of information which we had to skim through rapidly, sifting out the key data. We were also shown ways of finding out secret information by unsuspicious methods.

'It's not very cloak-and-dagger, I'm afraid,' Captain Jackson explained, grinning, 'but, you know, it works. It really does, and there's little or no danger in it. I don't know what you expected when you volunteered for this, but, believe me, a lot of espionage work is sheer drudgery.'

Captain Jackson and the other instructors soon convinced us that vital information was obtainable without heroic deeds. 'You'll be behind enemy lines with a cover story and documents we provide, and you'd better not slip up. Don't throw your life away. Think of your security. Be careful, and watch yourself at all times. Remember, we don't want heroes, we want information. None of you will ever get a medal anyhow.'

The British Service constantly stressed that our job was gathering and transmitting intelligence, and not sabotage. 'There'll be times you'll see some place, a power station or something like that, and you'll say to yourself, "That place should be blown up!" Don't do it! Get the information out to London, and leave the rest to us. Don't go around blowing things up, however much you feel tempted to do so.' Captain Jackson's words echoed closely the instructions we had received from London in the French underground.

British thoroughness even extended to giving us all a course in current German military slang. We were all, of course, thoroughly fluent in German – for some of us

German was our mother tongue – but for those who had not been in the German Armed Forces the course was invaluable. I was surprised how many new expressions had become current since I was in the German Navy.

Just when I thought my head would burst from all the knowledge being crammed into it, I received orders to put on my military uniform and report to Manchester for a parachute course. For the next ten days I jumped from towers, balloons, and finally from a Dakota airplane, until I had acquired a skill that, in fact, I never had to use.

Immediately after my return, I began my radio training. For eight hours a day, six days a week, I slaved to learn Morse code in an eight-week course at a radio school near Hyde Park. Every student at the school wore civilian clothes, and I was given the school-name of Neville. This meant I lived with two names: Nordmann at the house and Neville at the school, where I spent my days practising until I could handle 120 letters a minute.

'Congratulations, Mr Neville, you've done quite well.' Mr Robinson my teacher, had never been noted for excessive praise. 'Well now, the way you transmit C and F makes me blush. There'd be no doubt it's you on the key to anyone listening.' The old Scotsman grinned and shook my hand. 'Best o'luck,' he said as he handed me on to the recording section, which would record my 'handwriting' – the peculiarities and individual features which are possessed by each operator and which cannot be imitated. Then he turned away, giving no sign that he knew what I would use my radio ability for.

The most tiring part of my training was now over, but the skills that remained to be learned were still important, and there was no lowering of the high standards the British officers required. A nervous, emaciated-looking civilian in his early thirties taught me how to encode or decode a message. He told me that I was to carry out all my radio work in German, as my English was still far from satisfactory. Each agent had his own individual code based on a song or a poem that he knew by heart. An encoded message was divided into 'groups', each group containing five letters. Mr Coates kept reminding me, 'Never send more than fifteen or sixteen groups in one transmission. That way you're only on the air for forty seconds or so, and the enemy hasn't enough time to use direction-finders to locate you.'

Now I understood the significance of Mr Robinson's insistence of 120 letters, or 24 groups, a minute. 'What do I do if I have a great deal of data to send?' I asked.

'Send it next day from a different location. But remember, never be on the air for more than forty seconds. Now, here's something else I want to show you.' He sketched a grille on the back of a cigarette package. 'Assume that each square is an area of a city. What the Abwehr (German Counter-Intelligence) often do is switch off the power supply to each area in turn. If a transmission which they are tracking down goes off the air when they cut off the electric power, then they know which part of the city to surround and search.' He looked at me. 'Now, how do you avoid being caught like that?'

'Always use my batteries instead of mains power?'

Coates laughed. 'That would work on a short mission. No, here's what you do. See this?' He pointed at the transmitter-receiver. 'You keep one hand on this switch all the time you're transmitting. If the power goes off, you switch immediately – that very second – to batteries and finish your transmission. That way they can't find you with the power-cut trick.'

He laughed again. 'Now, here's something else. Pick

two German words of five letters each and write them down.'

I wrote down FISCH and HUNDE.

'Good. If the message you send is genuine you will always include "Fisch" in it somewhere. If you are being forced to transmit by the enemy you must include the word "Hunde". That way we can tell if you're in trouble or not. Got it?'

'It happens, then? The enemy tries to make agents send back false material?'

'Oh, yes, of course. If they catch you and try to turn you around, don't refuse. Agree, and include "Hunde" in your message. Then we'll know it's false information. Strangely enough, the false information often lets us know what the enemy is trying to conceal, so it's useful to us in the end anyway. Not much use to you, though. Best not to get caught.'

Coates made me go over the safety and coding procedures repeatedly until I was perfect at it. It was vital to be absolutely accurate in all coding, as a mistake in only one letter could make nonsense of a whole message. The end of the war might be drawing closer rapidly, but the British Service was taking no chances. I began to wonder if I would ever get the chance to put all of this training into practice before the war ended, but Coates and his colleagues did not share my impatience.

Then a Mr Osborne trained a group of us in the use of special inks, pens, and chemicals so that we could use secret writing. He also showed us how to store vast amounts of information on very thin sheets of paper which we could hide inside ordinary, everyday objects with concealed cavities.

Throughout our training, we had to take part in night-time exercises. Equipped with flashlight, map and compass, a pair of us would be dropped by car somewhere in the countryside at night and given an objective which we had to reach by a certain time. Our first task was to establish our position by reference to landmarks. Then, having laid down a route to the rendezvous, we could use map and compass to keep us on course. My knowledge of navigation and the stars gained on the *Wega* came in very useful.

I revelled in these outdoor activities. They were an excuse to enjoy fresh air and physical exertion after countless days of memory work and drill in radio. Quite by accident, these orientation exercises also taught me how vital it was to think of security at all times, even in a friendly country.

From three different directions, police cars converged on my partner, Simon, and me, their tyres squealing in the evening stillness. English bobbies surrounded us and pinned our arms to our sides, while their colleagues quickly frisked us for weapons.

'All right. Who are you? What's your nationality?'

Without thinking I replied, 'German.'

'You admit it then?' I could see the sergeant was surprised.

'Yes.'

'And what do you think you're doing here?'

'We're on a night exercise.' Then it struck me how this must sound to the policemen. I had admitted we were German and mentioned a night exercise; they could only conclude we were enemy agents bent on some nefarious task in the peaceful Surrey countryside.

Before I could even attempt an explanation, strong arms grabbed us and bundled us into one of the squad cars. A couple of heavyweight policemen crushed into the back with us.

'Get 'em to the station right away. Jenkins, radio

ahead. We'll escort you in the other cars.' Turning to us, the sergeant said, 'I suggest you gentlemen don't try to escape.' He closed the door, and we set off.

PC Jenkins's radio message must have caused bedlam at the local police station. When we were escorted through the door under the blue lamp, I could see uniformed policemen everywhere, plus a handful of civilians who were probably off-duty policemen or detectives. As we were marched past the counter, an old lady dressed in heavy tweeds nodded vehemently to the inspector, 'Yes, those are them.'

'Thank you, madam,' he replied. 'It's a good thing you keep your eyes and ears open. One of the officers will . . .'

I heard no more. We were pushed into a cell and the door clanged shut behind us.

'Was ist los? Was ist denn los?' Simon exclaimed repeatedly throughout the incident. Simon was a German Jew who had only recently escaped to England, and his English was almost non-existent.

I explained to him what I had been able to piece together. 'That old lady must have heard us speaking German and reported us to the police. They probably think we're German spies.'

I was still laughing when the police inspector came into our cell with a constable, who held his notebook ready.

'What's so funny?'

'You think we're German spies!' And I doubled up again with laughter.

'Well aren't you? You admitted as much.'

'No, of course not, you see we're . . .' I stopped. A little late in the day, I became security-conscious. 'We're not spies, sir. I can assure you of that.'

'What are you?' The inspector was becoming impatient. 'Your names?'

The constable waited, pencil poised.

'I'm sorry. I can't tell you.'

'Why not? Come on, your names.'

'Sorry. Look, will you please call Gardens 4583 and ask for Mr Peters.' I saw the constable making rapid notations of all my answers. 'Mr Peters,' I repeated; 'he can explain everything.'

'Don't waste my time with this Mr Peters. What were you doing?'

'Sorry. I can't answer. Please contact Mr Peters at . . .'

'Enough! How many others were there in your group? How did you get here? Were you dropped by parachute?'

I refused to answer all these questions. Sooner or later he would pass us on to his superiors, or else get tired and call Mr Peters our instructor.

Simon and I sat in the cell for an hour, waiting and talking quietly to each other in German. Then the door was opened.

'You idiots!' Peters's voice was scornful. 'Yes, they're two of mine,' he said over his shoulder to the inspector. 'I'll look after them.'

In the car back to Kew Gardens he said nothing, but, once in his office, he launched into a comprehensive tongue-lashing, in German, so that neither Simon nor I could miss the slightest particular.

'It's the fact that you were not security-conscious that is so annoying. The first and last thing we stress is security, preserving your cover. You forgot that. You spoke German where you could be overheard, and then you blurted out that you are indeed German. You're both lucky you didn't slip up like that on a mission or you would both be dead.'

We couldn't argue with him, and the experience taught me very vividly that I must always be on my guard. From that day on, I took no unnecessary risks but concentrated on what I needed to learn. Further night exercises followed, in which each of the agents-in-training had to penetrate a line of soldiers spaced only a few yards apart. It might have appeared ridiculous to crawl through the undergrowth at night, squirming on my belly over wet leaves, but I had learned the British slogan: 'Leave nothing to chance.' No detail was too trivial for my instructors. We had to practise over and over how to bury a parachute in woodland, until the senior officer in charge of our squad could not detect where we had disturbed the ground.

'Details, details,' Mr Peters stressed repeatedly. 'Details will convince the enemy you are who you claim to be, or just one small wrong detail will cause you to be suspected. Always remember details.'

Again and again our instructors reminded us that we would be given documents that would stand up to practically any test the enemy might apply. 'But the crucial factor is how you behave. You must always act in accordance with the character in your cover.' He told us true stories to illustrate his point.

The first was about an Allied agent who was smuggled into occupied Belgium. Disguised as a Roman Catholic priest, he was able to move around fairly easily, but identification checks caused him great tension and also occasionally resulted in his being late for a rendezvous or a radio transmission. One day, he needed to visit a fellow agent some twenty miles away, travelling on his old bicycle. With great imagination, he bought a large funeral wreath and wired it to the handlebars of his bicycle. He was waved through every check stop. 'A minor detail, that wreath,' Mr Peters commented, 'but it worked. Think about it.'

The other story he told us revealed the importance of acting in character. A British agent was dropped by parachute during an air-raid over Germany. Dressed as a German pilot, he was carried off course by a strong wind and come down on a farm far from his destination. A wedding was being celebrated at the farm, and, as the family was wealthy and influential, the local Gauleiter was in attendance. This high Nazi official not only convinced our 'hero of the Luftwaffe' to join the wedding party and toast the health of the happy couple in champagne, but also insisted that he take his car in order to rejoin his squadron and continue his defence of the Reich. The agent swaggered just enough to convince the Gauleiter he was a bona fide member of the Luftwaffe.

'Your cover is your defence,' all our tutors said. 'Preserve that cover and you will never need your pill.' The 'suicide pill' was our last resort. We were given no orders about committing suicide. 'It's up to you,' Mr Hawkes, another of our instructors, told us. 'If it comes to the point where your life is in danger, then it's up to you to decide what you should do.' He produced a glass capsule from his pocket. 'That's what your pill looks like. Bite on it and you're dead in three seconds.'

'Where should we keep it?' one of the class asked.

'Again, that's up to you. Most people tape it in their armpit.' He noticed our worried looks. 'It's tougher than you might think. We had one fellow who slipped his pill into his mouth just before being interrogated by the Gestapo. He believed he was on the verge of being unmasked and was determined to avoid torture.

'Fortunately for him the interrogation left his cover intact, and the Gestapo released him. In his relief he swallowed involuntarily as he left their headquarters, and down went the pill. You can imagine what a terrible couple of days he spent, waiting for the glass to break at any second and kill him.' Hawkes laughed.

'Well, did the pill break?' one of us asked.

'No, of course not,' Hawkes replied. 'You have to *bite* it. Eventually he crapped it out. I think you could say he was very relieved.'

Our training was intensive and serious, but life had its lighter side too. Many of our evenings were unoccupied by courses, and I revelled in the freedom I had never really experienced before. I soon became aware that Londoners didn't bother about my foreign accent, as there were refugees and allies in the city from all parts of Europe. So with the ample pocket money given us by our officers, I began to enjoy the frantic gaiety which still existed in England's capital in spite of the dozen or so 'flying bombs' or V1s which we heard explode each day.

Lotte Hallstein felt the same sense of romance. Her family had fled from Germany in 1938, realizing that, as Jews, they had no future in their homeland. Their clothing business in England was thriving in spite of wartime rationing.

We never talked much about the past, lost as we were in our growing affection for each other. Our affair was intense and progressed at a rate that in other times would have been regarded as scandalous. Whenever possible, I spent the night at her flat in Willesden Green. One evening, as I was making love to Lotte, I burst out laughing.

'Was ist los? Warum lachst du? (What's the matter? Why are you laughing?)' she cried out.

'If only the Führer could see me now. A good Aryan boy like me making love to a Jewish girl!'

I never told Lotte I was a British agent, but I think she suspected something of the sort. Many of my fellow agents were Jews, determined to fight back against their oppressors.

Without even a chance to say farewell to Lotte, I was transferred to Brussels at the beginning of February 1945, to stay in another 'safe' house. Our organization was kept very busy with counter-intelligence in the Belgian capital, as the Germans had left many agents behind when they abandoned the city, and the British had to find out who and where they were. However, because I had no training in counter-espionage, I was given futher radio training. The British seemed to have a mania for training; anything rather than have an agent idle.

My house-name was Nordmann again; I shared a room with 'Sanders'. At first I thought Sanders was German, but later he told me he was an English Jew who had spent some years at university in Germany before the war. Certainly his German was perfect. I understood that he was due to go on a mission behind the German lines and I had the feeling I too might be offered a mission soon, but it seemed that nothing definite had yet been decided. For two weeks I enjoyed all the pleasures of the recently liberated city. Had it not been for the tight security in and around our apartment block, it would have been easy to forget why I was in Brussels.

In the middle of February, I was sitting in our apartment with Sanders one evening, trying to persuade him to come out on the town with me, when the bell rang. The porter informed us that a Major MacPherson was on his way up. Sanders waited at the door and let him in.

'Evening, Sanders, Nordmann.' He sat down.

Sanders looked in my direction, then spoke to the major. 'Soon?'

'Yes, tomorrow.'

I got up to leave, but Major MacPherson signalled me to sit down again. 'No, I'm afraid this concerns you too, Nordmann.'

'Oh?' Sanders was surprised.

'Petersen's in hospital,' the major explained. 'Walked out in front of a car. Broken leg and injuries to his back.'

'It's off then?' Sanders asked.

'Maybe. That depends on Nordmann here.' He turned to me. 'I'm offering you a mission, Nordmann. It's very short notice, and it's up to you to accept it or refuse. You know how we work.'

I knew. Early in our training Captain Jackson told us that we would never be ordered on a mission. An assignment would be offered and we could choose whether or not to take it.

Even before Major MacPherson began to outline the mission I decided to accept. Better this way than spending days or weeks waiting.

PART FIVE
Behind Enemy Lines

16

Icy black, the Rhine tugged at our small skiff as we steered towards the eastern bank, where German forces awaited General Montgomery's onslaught. The Rhine is wide between Rees and Wesel and the current strong. Beside me Sanders crouched in the bottom of the boat. We both wore German army uniforms and carried Wehrmacht identification. I peered ahead but all I saw was darkness. It was only thirty hours since Major MacPherson had offered me the mission.

'Well, that's it, Nordmann. If you say yes, you'll leave tomorrow with Sanders.'

'Yes, I'm willing. I'll take it.'

'You're sure? It's very short notice. How about it?'

'I want to go.'

Major MacPherson nodded and made a brief telephone call. A few minutes later, the doorbell rang. 'It's for me,' he said. He returned with a suitcase. 'Put this uniform on, please. We need a photograph.'

I changed quickly into the uniform of a Wehrmacht corporal. It fitted me perfectly and had obviously been prepared earlier for my first mission. The major called in a photographer, who took a couple of photographs for the army pay-book, and I changed back into my own clothes.

'Your cover.' Major MacPherson handed me a file folder. I flicked through the pages. 'You'll be up all night learning the background. Sorry about that.'

'It's all right,' I told him, eager to assume my new identity as Corporal Friedmann.

For the rest of the night, I sat at the table studying my cover until I knew Werner Friedmann's life history almost better than my own. The typed sheets gave his date of birth, his family background, the schools he attended, and the progress he made in his various subjects. To help me visualize and assimilate this mass of detail I found maps, plans, diagrams, even photographs, in the dossier. Fortunately for me, Werner Friedmann was a native of Pomerania in North Germany, an area I knew quite well from my boyhood.

A second dossier provided the details of our mission in Germany. I experienced a strange feeling to think I would soon return to my homeland – a confused sense of great excitement and anticipation – which I forced myself to suppress as I began the task of memorizing our transmission times and radio frequencies.

Sanders was an intelligence officer, but as he had absolutely no ability with radio, I was assigned to be his radio operator. I practised using the new type of code which employed one-off sheets in a tear-off pad. This new type of code was a great advance; it was more efficient than the one I had learned during training because, as each sheet was used only once, it did not give the counter-espionage forces enough material to be useful in code-breaking. I would carry our transmitter-receiver, but Sanders would carry the code pads, which measured about nine inches by four. This arrangement was made for security reasons, as neither of us would be much use to the Germans without the other. Sanders would keep the code pads concealed on his body in a bag containing a vial of chemical. If the vial was broken, the chemical would completely destroy the codes in a matter of seconds.

I checked several times to make sure I understood these new arrangements, then returned to studying details of our mission. Our cover story seemed very plausible. Sergeant Dietrich Holzer (Sanders) and Corporal Friedmann (myself) were supposedly en route from Xanten to Essen, where we were to inspect anti-aircraft-gun establishments. Suitable documents to support this story were provided, including travel warrants and ration vouchers.

The real purpose of our mission, however, was to discover the rate of production of certain anti-tank weapons in Essen, and to assess the effect of Allied air-raids on their production and delivery. We would be behind enemy lines for several weeks and were to radio back as much military intelligence as we could pick up on our wanderings.

Early next morning, before I had had a chance to grab more than an hour's sleep, Major MacPherson and a driver called for us. We left Brussels and joined the mass of army traffic on the road towards Holland and Germany.

I had hoped to sleep during the journey, but MacPherson had not completed his briefing. 'Here are your documents,' he said, handing each of us a large buff envelope. 'Study them carefully.'

I opened the envelope. Inside was an ordinary leather wallet. I also found a genuine army pay-book with my photograph – already suitably aged and wrinkled – genuine travel warrants and orders, and photographs of Werner Friedmann's family. I studied them carefully. The elderly couple must be his parents, the young woman standing by a beech tree would be his sister, Hilde. There were even letters from home to Corporal Friedmann.

Beside me, Sanders was finding similar thorough documentation in his envelope.

'Everything satisfactory?' Major MacPherson asked, turning and leaning over the back of the front seat to talk to us.

'My God!' I exclaimed. 'This is fantastic.'

'Not really. Just hard work. You can trust those documents. The pay-book, photographs, and letters are all genuine. Corporal Werner Friedmann does exist. In fact, at this moment he is a prisoner in England. The same goes for Sergeant Holzer. All we've changed are the photographs, but the descriptions, etc, are all as they were originally entered in the pay-book. These men are the same height as you, same colour hair, eyes, etc. You can rely absolutely on those documents passing inspection.'

I was astounded again at their thoroughness. How many hundreds of pay-books had they examined before finding the one that fitted me so perfectly it might originally have been issued to me?

'What about these?' Sanders asked, tapping the travel warrants and ration vouchers.

'They're genuine too. What I mean is, the paper is genuine; they are the real forms. Some of the details are forged, but it wold take a real expert to detect that. The signatures are forgeries of an actual officer's handwriting. He can't be contacted by the enemy to confirm or deny these documents because he was captured a couple of days ago.'

There was nothing more to say. I slept all the way to Nijmegen, where the bumping of the car on the patched approaches to the great bridge over the River Waal wakened me. A few miles further on we crossed into the Allied-occupied section of Germany.

My emotions were mixed and very intense. I was deeply moved to return to my homeland, and yet anxious for the mission to succeed and for the Nazis to lose the war as soon as possible. My loyalty was to Germany, but not to its rulers.

Military traffic was heavier and our progress slower now, so that it was already night when we arrived near the front close to the Rhine. We were received by members of the First Canadian Army. Major MacPherson had arranged a fabulous dinner, accompanied by the finest Moselle wines. Both Sanders and I ate and drank with great enjoyment. and then as we finished, Sanders glanced over at me and grinned. 'The condemned men ate a hearty last meal,' he said.

An adjutant showed us to a room, where Sanders and I changed into our German uniforms and packed our equipment into German valises. We checked our submachine-guns and concealed automatic pistols.

Major MacPherson gave us each a money-belt with Swedish krone, Swiss francs, a small pouch of cut diamonds, and several gold coins. 'You probably won't need any of that,' he told us, 'but if you do, be careful not to draw attention to yourselves.'

As we left the building, he stopped Sanders. 'You've got the letter for Fräulein Klapper?'

Sanders nodded. 'Yes, it's in my pack.'

'Good. Here, you'd better take this. It's going to be cold on the water.' He pressed a small flask of rum into my hand. 'All ready, then?' He didn't wait for any answer, just shook our hands and left.

'This way, sir,' a voice whispered out of the darkness. 'You know to be very quiet. It's a couple of miles or so to the river, but our orders are there's to be dead silence.'

'Right,' we agreed.

As our eyes grew accustomed to the darkness, we saw eight soldiers in Canadian uniforms lift a small but heavy wooden skiff on to their shoulders. They set off into the darkness and we followed.

The journey to the river seemed endless, the silence and the darkness weighing heavy on my nerves. At last we saw the dull sheen of the river ahead of us. The Canadian soldiers set the skiff down at the water's edge, unshipped the oars, and helped us on board with our luggage and arms.

'Ready?'

'Yes, thank you.'

They pushed us off, and we started to row the small boat out into the middle. Major MacPherson was right; it was bitingly cold on the river. By the time we had fought through the current and reached the other bank, we were more than thankful for the rum. All the way across we heard no sounds of any human activity, yet we knew there must be German sentries stationed on their side of the river. We could only hope that we had gone undetected as we unloaded our gear and pushed the skiff back out into the current to drift away.

We listened intently for a while, but there was no sound. Cautiously, moving very slowly, we crept away from the river, expecting to be challenged at any second. It seemed incredible to me that anybody could come ashore here undetected. Within an hour we were a couple of miles from the river, hiding in an abandoned barn. But we found it impossible to sleep. In the distance, the sounds of an artillery bombardment crept uncomfortably close.

'Be a fine mess if our own side gets us,' Sanders remarked as we finished off the last of the rum and ate some of our sandwiches.

Early next morning, soon after dawn, we set off towards Essen. We soon reached the town of Wesel on the way. Even from a distance we could see the terrible effects of air-raids and artillery bombardment. Smoke was still rising from the ruins, and buildings were still burning as we picked our way through the rubble. We noted down much useful information about troop and equipment movements, and hid the slips of paper in our belongings as we had been taught.

'Keep your wits about you,' I whispered to Sanders as we approached what had been the centre of Wesel. 'Checkpoint ahead.'

We joined the group of soldiers waiting patiently at the check stop. The other soldiers in line seemed no different from us; we weren't the only unshaven military men that morning. Even the military policeman on duty showed a black growth of stubble on his chin. The soldiers' faces were all weary; some men limped or were bandaged, some had parts of their uniform torn or missing, but the military policeman checked all papers thoroughly.

When our turn came, he subjected our sets of papers to a minute scrutiny before handing them back with a curt 'Alles in Ordnung.'

Everything in order! I found it difficult not to reveal my delight as we walked through. Suddenly, 'Halt! Zurück!' the military policeman shouted. He was calling us both back.

My exultation evaporated. I glanced at Sanders. He appeared cool and unhurried, but I could guess the turmoil his mind was in. We did not need to look around;

there were soldiers everywhere. We could neither fight for it nor run for it. We would have to bluff it out.

'Ja, was ist denn los?' Sanders inquired as we returned to the checkpoint, an edge of irritation to his voice.

'I meant to tell you. It's useless even hoping to get a train. This last raid's buggered everything up. Set off along there until you come to Dinslaken.' He gave us directions out of town and suggested we walk until we could get a lift.

We walked three or four blocks before we even looked at each other. Then we each released a tremendous sigh.

'I thought we'd had it then,' I said to Sanders.

'Me too, me too. Shows we shouldn't be too hasty to act, doesn't it?'

I agreed, starting to feel more confidence now in our papers and other documents. In fact, we were stopped several times by the Feldgendarmerie, and each time our papers were handed back without comment except for 'Alles in Ordnung'.

We made no effort to hitch a lift, fearing we might be separated or foolishly give ourselves away. Moreover, we observed more as we walked, and could take the opportunity to make surreptitious notes far more easily when we were on our own. Many troops were moving toward the front, and the roads were jammed with men and vehicles. The Rhine had temporarily halted General Montgomery's advance and there was now a lull in the fighting as both sides prepared for what all knew would be a momentous and decisive battle.

It horrified me to see how many older or obviously disabled men were in uniform. Together with young boys, some only about fourteen, they made up the bulk of several units. Of course, we had heard about the Volkssturm (People's Army), set up by Heinrich Himmler of the SS in October 1944, but to see the reality of this last-ditch force, and compare it with the lean and fit soldiers of Canada, Britain, and the United States, made my stomach turn with pity for what had to happen soon.

In all the apparent confusion of the troop movements, we felt quite safe walking along the highway, at least as far as detection by the Germans was concerned. We soon discovered that the main threat we faced came from the frequent air attacks by Allied fighters and bombers, which flew over almost with impunity. Many times we had to take cover, and by the time we reached the address we had been given just outside Essen two days later, we felt like seasoned front-line soldiers.

'You sure this is the right place?' I asked Sanders.

'Yes. Anyway, we just ask for Fräulein Klapper, and if there's any mistake, if she doesn't live here, then we just ask where we can find her.'

'I suppose so. I guess I'd be happier if nobody saw us arrive.'

The house was in a quiet suburb, Essen-Kupferdreh, across the river from Essen's smoky factories and mines. In contrast to the devastation we saw in the town centre, there were few signs of war damage in this peaceful residential area and its surrounding woodland.

After nightfall we walked up the path and Sanders knocked on the door.

'Fräulein Klapper?'

'Ja.'

'Fräulein Franziska Klapper?'

'Yes, that's me. What can I do for you?' She was in her late thirties, and her eyes betrayed the strain of five and a half years of war.

'Your brother is Father Josef Klapper?'

She hesitated a second. A wary look came into her

eyes. 'Yes, I'm Father Klapper's sister.' She looked at Sanders inquiringly.

Sanders pulled the letter from her brother out of his boot. He had hidden it there when he took it from his valise, while we waited in the woodland for evening. 'Here. It's a letter from your brother. We were asked to deliver it.'

She gave a little panic-stricken gasp. Her hand quivered as she reached out to take the letter. She glanced at her name and address on it, then past us at the street. There was nobody about. 'Please, come in,' she asked us, fighting to appear calm. We stepped inside and gratefully set down our luggage. 'In here, please,' she said, opening a door off the hallway.

We all went in and sat down.

'I don't understand,' she said, making jerky little motions with the hand that held the still-unopened letter.

'It's from your brother, Father Josef Klapper,' Sanders repeated gently, trying to help her overcome her shock and suspicions. 'Please read it.'

She hesitated.

'Please read it and you'll understand.'

We watched her open the envelope, take out the letter, and read it.

'It's Josef's handwriting,' she called out excitedly. Sanders and I remained silent.

Finally she looked up. 'It says here my brother is in England, that he's safe.'

'That's correct.'

'In England! But how?'

'Surely he explained in the letter.'

'Yes, but in England!'

'When he left here, he knew the Gestapo were after him. He managed to escape into Holland. Luckily, he got into contact with the Dutch underground, and they took him out into the North Sea on a fishing boat. He was transferred at night to an English submarine and taken to England.'

'Why did the English take all that trouble for one German?'

Sanders explained. 'Your brother came into possession of some information about new types of anti-tank weapons being developed in Essen. This knowledge was very important to the British, and they wanted to talk to your brother personally and get every detail they could from him.'

'My brother is working for the British?'

'Yes.'

'He says in this letter that I'm to help the two of you in any way I can: food, lodging, anything.'

'We'd be very grateful if you could, Fräulein Klapper. This is Corporal Werner Friedmann, and I'm Dietrich Holzer.'

She looked at us again, closely, her expression a mixture of fear, hope, consternation, and amazement. 'Where's my brother?'

'He's in England.'

She stared at us, then at the letter, then back at us in our German uniforms. Her confusion grew. 'Where are you two from?'

'We're from England.'

I could see she couldn't believe it. 'How did you get here?'

'We were dropped by parachute last night.'

'Why?'

'To deliver the letter to you and to ask you to help us. We have a mission to perform here in Essen. Your brother knows about it. We're British agents.'

She stood up, shaking. 'How do I know you are not Gestapo men out to trap me? How do I know my brother is really in England? Maybe he didn't get clean away when he left. What if the Gestapo got him and tortured him and made him write this letter? How do I know you are not both Gestapo agents? My God, what am I to think?'

'Please believe us, Fräulein Klapper. We really are British agents, and you brother is safe in England. You must trust us. All we need is a room where we can sleep. We won't bother you at all, and we have plenty of money for food.'

'I don't know what to do.'

Sanders and I took turns trying to persuade her. She agreed to let us stay in the house, but I am sure she did not believe our story fully.

'Please don't disturb my mother. She's seventy-four and very sick. I'll tell her you've both been billeted here.'

'Is there anybody else living here?' I asked.

'My married sister, Else, that's all.'

'Please tell her the same story – that we've been billeted here, will you?'

'Of course. What sort of a room do you want?'

'It doesn't matter. Somewhere we won't be in your way.'

She led us upstairs. Sanders and I hauled our luggage and weapons up to a room on the third floor. Fräulein Klapper showed us where to find mattresses and bedding, and we settled in.

'How close to panic do you think she is?' Sanders asked when we had removed our boots and stretched out on the mattresses.

'You mean, giving us away?'

'Yes. Do you think she will?'

'I doubt it very much,' I replied. 'In fact I'm sure she won't. Did you see how she shook when the Gestapo were mentioned? I think she's scared stiff that we are Gestapo men sent to trap her, but I'd guess she hates the Gestapo so much that she couldn't play a role and persuade us all is in order while she reports us. She just would never go to the Gestapo on her own accord.'

'I hope you're right.' Then Sanders and I got back to work assembling the military information we had gathered on our way to Essen.

'There's a hell of a lot of it here,' I remarked after a while.

'That's what I was thinking. We've enough here for two, maybe three transmissions. I'll work out the first message.'

Sanders checked and rechecked his code work until he was sure that it was accurate. This was the real thing; the data we were preparing could be vital in shortening the war. At last he was satisfied all was in order and gave me the encoded message, which I stuffed in my pocket for transmission later that night.

There was a soft knock on our door and Fräulein Klapper asked timidly if we wanted supper. 'Only some bread and cheese or sausage,' we replied, knowing that otherwise her fear might cause her to give us the food meant for her family. When she brought the snack for us, we gave her money and told her to buy extra food on the black market while we stayed with her.

I could see she was still uncertain whether the note from her brother was genuine. She wanted to talk about it but was scared to open the conversation. 'Please believe us, Fräulein Klapper. We are who we say we are. Your brother fled because the Gestapo were after him. If they wanted, they could have arrested you then.'

She nodded, but I don't think I convinced her. We returned to our work.

'What about this transmission? Are you going to send from here?' Sanders asked.

'No, we daren't transmit even one message from here; it's too dangerous. We'll use a different place in the woods each time. We daren't give the Abwehr a chance to locate us by using the same place more than once.'

'Okay. Let's go then. Keep a sharp look-out for any sign that the house is being watched or we are being followed.'

We saw no suspicious signs as we left. In fact, the streets were deserted as we headed out into the nearby woodland where we had waited earlier that day. It was dark among the trees, but we did not want to risk using a flashlight, so our progress was slow as we held our arms in front of us to turn aside branches. When we had gone far enough, I set down the valise containing the radio, unrolled the aerial wire, and attached it to the branch of a tree.

Thankful that we had been taught how to use a radio in the dark, I felt around the knobs and switches until I was ready to switch on.

'You stand guard,' I whispered to Sanders. 'I'll have to switch my flashlight on to read by.'

'Okay. Go ahead.'

I took out the crumpled paper with our coded message and smoothed it out. Then I switched on the set and waited for the reassuring hum in my earphones. A glance at my watch told me it was time to transmit. It was cold and damp in the forest, but I felt sweat running down my finger as I worked the Morse key. Sixteen groups, about forty seconds. I turned off my flashlight and switched the set to receive. I heard the brief signal from London confirming that they had received my message.

'All okay,' I hissed at Sanders as I shut the set down and rolled up the antenna wire. We set off back to the house immediately, hurrying, fearing that soldiers and police might be looking for us.

All was quiet. We slipped into the house and tried to relax. I had hardly slept for three nights, but I was too excited to fall asleep immediately. At last I had achieved something, had used my training, and, I hoped, helped bring the end of the war a little closer. I curled up on my mattress, contented, and even the heavy air-raid on the factories in nearby Essen hardly disturbed me when I finally slept.

'We should take it easy today, I think,' Sanders suggested after breakfast, which we ate in our room, alone, 'We can prowl around the restaurants and bars and see what information can be picked up there.'

As we walked toward the centre of Essen, I was appalled by the extent of damage done by the previous night's air-raid. Fires were still burning, rubble was strewn over the roads, and it seemed as if few people could have survived the bombing; yet, amazingly, most of the factories were still in production and evidence of continued war production was everywhere. Transportation seemed to be the main problem; so many roads, bridges, and rail lines were destroyed that it seemed almost impossible that armaments could be delivered where they were needed.

'Let's go in here,' I suggested as we came to a restaurant. 'I think I need a drink.'

'Okay. It's got to me too,' Sanders replied.

We went in, sat down, and ordered coffee. The landlord, a one-armed cripple, brought us each a cup of what passed for coffee at that time. Except for one or two middle-aged women, we were the only customers. Sanders and I looked at each other; this place was no use to us. We drank our 'coffee', paid, and left. For a couple of hours we wandered around Essen, noting the exact location of factories that looked relatively unharmed and still capable of production. This was useful information that we could radio back, so that future bombing waves would know where to drop their bombs.

Towards five o'clock in the afternoon, we sought out a suitable-looking café near the factory reputed to be manufacturing the new anti-tank weapons. All was quiet when we entered and bought drinks, but within half an hour it began to fill up with workers from the nearby factory, among them a number of women and girls. Many of the girls were pretty, and it was no hardship to get into conversation with a couple of them.

We had to be careful how we handled our questions about their secret war work, but in the end it was surprisingly easy to ferret out crucial pieces of information when everybody had drunk enough.

'Have another drink, Magda.'

'Oh, no I don't think I should.'

'I'd like to buy you a drink. You must be the prettiest of all the fifty girls at the factory.'

'Fifty!' she laughed. 'There are more than two hundred and fifty of us.'

'Well, I bet you're still the prettiest.' If not the smartest, I added to myself. We now knew how many girls worked on the assembly line at the factory.

I took Magda's hand and pretended to study it. 'And these beautiful hands work in a factory all day. It must take ages, hours of toil, for you put one of those weapons together.' I assumed an expression of infinite sadness at the cruelty of war's demands.

Magda giggled. 'Oh, you are funny, Werner. The work's not that difficult.'

'No? How long does it take you to put a weapon together then?'

'Not more than fifteen minutes.'

'All on your own you can do it in fifteen minutes?'

'That's right.' The drink made her slur her words a little.

'Incredible! I can hardly believe it. These pretty, delicate hands too.' I made as if to brush them with my lips. Amid the general hilarity at my assumed gallantry, nobody seemed to notice what key facts Magda had given away. Two hundred and fifty girls working an eight-hour day assembling the anti-tank weapons would produce eight thousand units a day if it only took them a quarter of an hour to complete each.

Eight thousand a day! The figure staggered us when Sanders and I discussed it later that evening, after taking our new girl friends home. The weapon was a new and potentially terribly effective defence against tanks. The original 'Panzerfaust' anti-tank weapon was far lighter and less powerful than this new advance, which needed two men to operate it, somewhat like a bazooka. When the weapon was fired, the missile would attach itself to the enemy tank, melt through the steel armour plate in seconds, and finally explode inside.

'Hell, if it's only half as good as they told us in our briefing, then . . .' Sanders did not need to finish the sentence.

'We've got to find out everything we can as quickly as we can. My God, this weapon, produced at that rate, could just about wipe out Allied armour!' I looked at my watch. 'It's one of my scheduled transmission times in just over two hours. Let's get a message ready.'

Together we composed the message, encoded it, checked it, and set out into the forest. The sky above reverberated with the sound of bombers approaching Essen for the nightly air-raid. With any luck, the factory producing the anti-tank weapons would shortly be on its list. By the time we had the radio ready to operate, we could hear the bombs exploding across the river. I switched on the set and glanced at my watch. Right on the second, I began my transmission and London confirmed reception immediately. We hurriedly packed away the set and made our way back to Kupferdreh, while nearby Essen rocked and burned.

We felt it best not to delay our visit to the factory any longer. Next morning found us in the office of Direktor Stammler, where Sanders showed him our papers. Herr Stammler was very willing to talk.

'Yes, indeed, a miracle weapon,' he enthused, when we asked him about the new missile. 'Fantastic! It goes through armour plate like a hot knife through butter. Yes, like a hot knife through butter.' He laughed at his comparison.

'Marvellous,' I replied. 'God knows, we need something like that at the front. What we have now is none too good; sometimes I think we would do as well firing pea-shooters. Not that I'm defeatist, you understand, but we could make good use of these weapons.'

'You will, you will, believe me.'

'When will our division get hold of them?' Sanders asked.

'Within a month at the latest. I'd like it to be sooner, but it's difficult sometimes to get raw materials. The air-raids, you understand?' He shrugged at the nuisances that slowed down production of the new weapon.

The potential destruction chilled us, but Sanders and I both smiled. 'Excellent,' we chorused. 'With the new missile we'll show those Tommies yet. By the way, how many can we expect?'

'You're from Wesel way, eh?' The director looked serious. 'Well it all depends, you know. From what I've heard – and mind you it's only a rumour – preference will be given to divisions on the Eastern Front.' He pursed his lips. 'Those Russian T-34s they're using on the Eastern Front are superior to anything of ours, and our troops need these new missiles there.'

We nodded solemnly in commiseration.

'But, my friends,' he said, brightening visibly, 'this new weapon will wipe out even a T-34. You'll see.'

'You promise we'll get some within a month on the Western Front?'

'I'm pretty sure of it. You see, we're going to run an extra shift and raise production to at least fifteen thousand warheads a day!'

We tried to look surprised and delighted as we prepared to leave.

'Have a cigar each, boys,' Direktor Stammler ordered, pulling a box of Havanas from his desk. He noted our surprised expressions. 'For special occasions only, you understand. I've had this box since 1940.'

He handed each of us a cigar which we stowed in our uniform pockets, and after further protestations of how his new brain-child would turn the tide, we left.

'In here,' I said to Sanders, grabbing him by the arm as we came to the first bar. 'C'mon, I think we both need a drink.'

We did no further investigating that day. Instead, we waited as patiently as we could in our room at Fräulein Klapper's. The priest's sister was the only member of the family we saw during our stay. She bought extra food on the black market with the money we gave her, and she cooked us some good meals while we were there. She was probably very relieved that we insisted on eating in our room and not with the family. The strain of talking to us, even for a minute at a time, made Fräulein Klapper tremble with fear and agitation.

Once we had the message about the factory and the new weapon encoded, we had nothing to do except sit around and smoke. Because of our training, which emphasized secretiveness, Sanders and I talked little of matters of a personal nature. Consequently we restricted ourselves to business, and, when we had exhausted that topic, we were quite content to remain silent.

'This might be our last transmission,' I remarked later that night to Sanders as I strung up the aerial wire in a tree. 'We've got all the data we had to get and we should be able to set off back tomorrow.'

It was not to be. That night London gave the split-second signal that not only confirmed they had received my message, but also signified that they had a message for me at the next pre-arranged time and frequency. Sanders and I discussed this softly as we made our way out of the forest.

'I wonder what it is now,' he muttered. His impatient tone told me I was not the only one to feel the strain and tension. 'When is the message coming through?'

'In just under two hours. We'll set up in our room.'

'But I thought you . . . Is that safe?'

'Oh yes. It's just receiving, really. I don't have to send a long message back – just the letter "C" to confirm I heard them.'

The message from London gave us further orders to remain in the Essen area, gathering more information about damage to factories and communications and the exact location of factories that were still producing.

'God Almighty,' I cursed as I decoded the message.

Sanders looked over my shoulder and swore softly. 'Jesus! I was hoping to get out of here soon. Look at that! We have to stay here another two weeks. We'll be here until the end of the war!'

'Why do you think they want us to stay?' I asked him.

'I don't know. I can only guess.' He handed me a cigarette, and we smoked in silence for a while. 'I guess we may be the only British agents left in the Essen area now,' he suggested. 'There must have been others once in such an important industrial city, with all those Krupp factories.'

'But why only us now?'

'As I say, I'm guessing, but I would think the air-raids may have killed off all the other British agents.'

Our whispered conversation turned to what it must be like to be a 'sleeper', an agent who establishes a cover as an ordinary citizen and carries out no espionage work until activated. We tried to picture British agents among the men working in Krupp factories, accepted by their workmates and friends of many years as ordinary work-men like themselves. Neither Sanders nor I could imagine ourselves able to live that double life for so long. After only a few days undercover we felt under severe strain and were worried about surviving for two more weeks.

The next day we went back to work. It amazed me how much useful, indeed vital, information we collected simply through apparently idle gossip. We talked to girls, foreign labourers, and older workers, and from each one we learned something to add to the picture we were assembling. And we kept our eyes open as we walked around, noting where bombs had done the most damage and which factories looked ready to be hit again.

Most nights I set up my radio at different spots in the woods. At the pre-arranged time, I made my brief forty-second transmission in code, while Sanders stood guard, sub-machine-gun at the ready. Either the Germans had given up trying to track down clandestine broadcasts, or the security precautions I had learned in my training were sound. Whatever the reason, we never experienced any threat while transmitting, and our confidence grew.

As we went about Essen, talking to people and collecting information, we found almost everybody in a depressed mood. It was clear to anyone but a fool that the war was lost. The Allies were advancing on all fronts and bombing Germany at will. The nightly air-raids, with their appalling loss of life and constant assaults on the nervous system, sapped the will of the population of Essen. Countless days and nights in the air-raid shelters broke down the normal pattern of family relationships, and, although most people turned up for work each day at their normal hour, the spirit of victory had long ago disappeared.

'Bloody nonsense!' a girl shrieked at the radio on the wall of the snack-bar not far from Krupp's main offices. Every head in the place turned to stare at her, not because of disagreement with her sentiment, but out of horrified surprise that she dared to break down and express publicly what nearly everyone thought privately. Many of the customers cast anxious glances around. Who was the Gestapo informer here? Everybody in the place felt endangered now; it was an offence to fail to report defeatist talk. Nobody could doubt that it was defeatist to label as 'bloody nonsense' Dr Goebbels's radio appeal for more volunteers for the Volkssturm, that tattered, under-equipped, badly trained group of youths and pensioners we had seen on our way down to Essen.

Dr Goebbels brayed on. 'Let us fight to the last drop of blood for our Fatherland. Sacrifice! Sacrifice for the Führer and the Reich! Join the Volkssturm to preserve our sacred German heritage! Fight to . . .'

It gave me no joy to observe Goebbels's failure. The listeners in the snack-bar rejected his passionate words and persuasion now that the war was lost. If only these same people had labelled his broadcasts 'bloody nonsense' twelve or thirteen years ago, and laughed at him and the Führer, Germany would not now be facing defeat and humiliation. My country was being crushed. Nothing could disguise the bitter taste of defeat that was evident everywhere.

I longed to be a thousand miles away, far from these scenes of destruction, far from the smell of defeat and decay, far from Fräulein Klapper's terror that Sanders and I were Gestapo agents. I had known for a long while now that Germany would lose the war, and it angered me to hear Goebbels's pleas to 'fight to the last drop of blood'. Everything I saw added fuel to my rage against Adolf Hitler. He was the traitor to Germany, and now, in his desperation, he was dragging the country down to destruction with him.

I wondered what the Russians would do to Germany. They were unknown, and I feared them. Who could blame them if they took revenge for all their people the Germans had so callously murdered, for their dead children gunned down by the SS, for the thousands of poor and destitute villages we Germans had burned to the ground? Mercy was too much to hope for.

Only God was capable of forgiving Germany.

I wondered frequently how my own family were faring.

I knew the Hamburg area was being bombed as heavily as Essen. When I prayed for Alfred and my mother each night, I wondered if they were still alive, and I had to fight down the temptation to write to them or to get Sanders to write and tell them I was still alive. I wrestled with my desire to risk a telephone call to my home village to find out their fate. I would call a friend of the family and pretend I was some official, from the post office perhaps, checking on the arrival of an official form. But I stopped myself in time. It was foolhardy; I would risk their lives as well as Sanders's and my own.

Finally, after almost three weeks in Essen-Kupferdreh, we received orders to make our way back and to collect as much military intelligence as possible en route. Fräulein Klapper was as relieved to see us go as we were anxious to leave. 'I've never slept all the time you've been here,' she told us. A glance at the puffiness around her eyes told me she was telling the truth. 'I can't sleep. How can I when I'm not sure you are what you say you are?'

'We are British agents,' I reassured her. 'You have nothing to fear.'

'But you speak perfect German. How can you be British agents? You are both German, aren't you?'

'We're from England and we're working for the British,' Sanders replied.

'If only I could believe that. But . . . the uniforms, the arms.'

'Please believe us. And remember, your brother is safe in England. We'll see he hears you're all right when we get back.'

'Tell him we love him and miss him.' Her face suddenly softened, her mouth quivering.

'We will. The war won't last much longer now. Then

you'll be together again. Thank you for looking after us. We'll leave early in the morning.'

Next morning, after a sleepless night, we said farewell to Fräulein Klapper.

'May God be with you,' she whispered.

Sanders pulled an envelope out of his pocket and handed it to her. But, shaking her head, she refused to take it, thinking it was money.

'No, please take it,' he insisted. 'It's a letter. I want you to keep it somewhere safe – hide it behind a picture. It's a letter to the Allied forces. It won't be long before they occupy Essen. The letter states that you helped us and that the Allies are to protect you and help you.'

We made our way through what was left of Essen. Several of the factories we had mentioned in our radio messages were now smoking ruins. I felt no joy when I saw them but I knew that what I had done was right.

To our surprise, the railwaymen were still attempting to run the trains on schedule. We presented our travel warrants made out for Wesel and, strangely, nobody checked our other papers. We settled down in a compartment with our guns and luggage to rest and think how we might get back across the Rhine.

We'd hardly finished our first cigarettes when the train halted.

'Alle'raus, bitte. Alle'raus!'

I got up and looked out the window. 'What's the trouble?' I called out to a man in railroad uniform on the platform.

'Out please,' he replied. 'The train cannot go any further. This is the end of the line. Sorry. Air-raid last night.'

We gathered our gear and got out.

'Oberhausen,' I cursed, 'not even a quarter of the way!'

Sanders said nothing. The look on his face was enough.

We left the station and headed north, looking for the highway. Less than a mile from the station we came up to two men, one in civilian clothes, the other in the uniform of an SS captain.

'Soldiers, halt!' the captain ordered.

We snapped our arms out. 'Heil Hitler!'

'Secret Field Police,' the civilian said, displaying his identification. 'Show us your papers, please.'

'Of course.'

I was not worried. Our papers had proved good before. This was just routine.

The civilian took our pay-book and marching papers, glanced at them, and then handed them to the captain, who studied them while the civilian asked the routine questions.

'Where are you going?'

'Back to join our unit north of Xanten.'

'Why are you here?'

'We've been inspecting some facilities in Essen. It's in our papers.'

'So it is.' The civilian turned to the SS captain to retrieve our papers.

'One moment, please,' the SS captain said. He indicated some details on our papers. I looked straight ahead, trying to act like a soldier tired of all the bureaucracy. Inwardly I was shaking.

The captain put the papers in his uniform pocket. 'You don't mind coming with us to HQ to answer a few questions?'

17

My heart thumped, creating a tight physical pain under my ribs. Next to me, I sensed Sanders stiffen. We must not show concern.

'No, of course not,' I replied for both of us, as I tried desperately to guess what he could have found to arouse his suspicions. 'We're quite willing to go with you. I hope it won't take long. We have to rejoin our unit as soon as possible.'

'Of course. This way, please.' They positioned themselves on either side of us, but the captain held his submachine-gun quite casually and they did not ask us to hand over our weapons. They can't be too suspicious, I kept telling myself, I hope we can talk our way out of this. The two officers were very relaxed, almost friendly, and I suspected that they had to bring in a certain quota of men for interrogation each day, whether they had a good reason or not. However, I could not ignore the way the captain had pointed at our papers. There was something wrong, but how serious was it?

We stopped on our way at a private home and were joined by four Wehrmacht soldiers, one of whom was limping. They still had their rifles, but I gained the impression that they too were due for interrogation. We marched along a road on the outskirts of town, with houses on our right. On our left were flat fields that reminded me uncomfortably in the damp mist of the area around Börgermoor-Emsland concentration camp.

My mind raced. Do they know already who we are?

Have we been betrayed? Why don't they disarm us? In my valise was our radio transmitter; we were both carrying foreign currency and gold coins; under our uniforms we each had a Lama 9mm Spanish-made pistol that was not standard issue for a Wehrmacht corporal or sergeant. If they searched us, we were finished.

We began to see arrow-shaped markers with the sign 'Secret Field Police HQ' on them, arousing my old fear of the SS. Sanders glanced at me, then at his submachine-gun, and I read the question clearly in his eyes: should we pull the trigger and make a run for it? I thought rapidly. We would have to kill six men – four soldiers and two SS Secret Field Policemen. I shook my head, warning Sanders: don't do it! With our automatic weapons and the element of surprise, there would be no difficulty killing the six men. The problem would be escaping out of Oberhausen. The authorities would seal off the whole area and search until they found us. Even in the confusion of the approaching battlefront, the authorities could not let a six-fold murder pass. Sanders nodded back. We would have to try and talk our way out of this one.

During the tense twenty-minute walk to the SS Head-quarters, I tried to anticipate the questions I would face. Mentally I reviewed my cover until I became Corporal Werner Friedmann. But at the back of my mind floated frightening memories: Franz Ziemat's flight, the Kapitän-Leutnant in Kiel, the marine interrogators, the Schar-führer at Börgermoor-Emsland, my unmasking by the French Resistance.

The sign on the big, dark brick building read 'Kaserne (Barracks)'. We had arrived.

'Please wait here. We'll call you in,' the SS captain ordered.

I looked around. The room was large, furnished with

tables and benches. Some fifty or so off-duty SS soldiers sat around relaxing, playing cards, smoking, talking. They ignored us, unconscious of our presence. Sanders and I set down our guns and luggage in a corner and waited, trying to appear unconcerned. I forced myself not to look at our valise with the transmitter in it.

After about twenty minutes, the SS captain reappeared and called us into a large office. He closed the door and positioned himself behind us.

'Heil Hitler!' We saluted the SS colonel seated behind a large desk on which lay all our papers. He looked very strict, a military man about forty years old, his brown hair short and immaculately groomed. We were left standing at attention while he continued to study our papers. Then he looked up and started interrogating Sanders.

'Name? Rank? Number?' It was a searching but standard interrogation, and Sanders answered each question promptly. The colonel gave us no clue to what had roused the captain's suspicions, nor did he show whether he was satisfied with Sanders's answers.

Next he turned to me. 'Name? Rank? Number?' If it went on like this, we were safe; everything we told them fitted in with what our papers said.

Suddenly, 'Where did you sleep during the last three weeks? There are no entries in your papers to show where you stayed. You could not have been with a military unit.'

So that was it. The captain had spotted the weak point among the details in our papers. We could be in serious trouble for a breach of military discipline. If it was suspected that we had deserted, then changed our minds, we would certainly be arrested, and it would only be a matter of time before one piece of evidence led to another and our cover was destroyed.

I tried to look contrite. 'Well, Colonel, er . . . hmm . . . you see . . . we had some girl friends . . . and we . . . er . . . stayed with them.' I assumed a shamefaced air and shuffled my feet at this admission.

The colonel smiled, but only briefly. 'And where did you eat during those three weeks?'

The same stumbling, shamefaced manner of replying. 'Oh, sometimes here, sometimes there.'

My ploy failed. The colonel reddened, leaned forward angrily, and slammed his fist down hard on the table. 'Listen, Corporal, are you mad? Don't answer me like that. I asked you a specific question and I want a specific answer. Now, answer me!'

We were in real trouble. Somehow I had to lead the colonel away from this potentially fatal line of questioning. Skimming rapidly through my options, I gambled that he had read our papers carefully while we waited outside. If so, he must have seen the entry in my military pay-book that recorded a head injury from two years ago, and the medical officer's notation that subsequently I occasionally suffered from amnesia. It hadn't occurred to me when I studied my cover that this could work to my advantage, but there was a chance that my spontaneous idea might succeed.

'Answer me, Corporal.'

'Oh Colonel, I'm very mixed up. I'm so confused now that my mind is a blank. I'm sorry.' Did I detect a hint of sympathy, a softening of his expression? I hurried on, 'You asked us about food. We haven't eaten anything for the last two days. Can you let us have some food?'

If ever time stood still for me, it was then. It seemed an age before the colonel replied, an age when I took in every detail of the scene. The colonel's face, both ruddy and pale, the place under his left nostril where he had missed a couple of whiskers when shaving, the redness on the side of his neck where his collar rubbed. There was a circular mark on the desk where a cup or glass had rested; a fly buzzed somewhere out of sight to my left near the street map of Oberhausen pinned to the wall. I could smell the pomade of the captain behind us over the odour of tension from Sanders and me.

Mr Peters and Mr Hawkes had mentioned several times in our training that the military mind is often susceptible to suggestion. They had subjected us to mock interrogations and demonstrated the use of the counter-question in changing the subject.

The colonel shook his head. 'What did you say?'

'Colonel, we haven't eaten for the last two days – not a thing. Could you arrange for us to have some food?'

'I can't give you any food right now, but I'll make sure you get your food ration for the next few days.'

My attempt appeared to be working. Gratefully, I began, 'Thank you, Colonel. It's very . . .'

Suddenly the captain behind me broke in.

'Excuse me, Colonel. May I interrupt your questioning about those papers?'

I stiffened. The captain, who had noticed the omission in our papers immediately, was much cleverer than the colonel. He recognized what was happening and saw through my attempt to lead the colonel away from the question of papers into the innocuous area of food. I heard Sanders' sharp intake of breath beside me. We both wondered briefly if it would have been better to gun down the captain, his assistant, and the four soldiers when we had the chance.

But the colonel was furious. He lifted his hand high

above his shoulder, and for an insane moment I nearly burst out laughing because he seemed to be giving a caricature of Hitler's salute. Then his hand slammed down on the table. His face was purple as he shouted, 'Listen, Captain, who is conducting this interrogation, you or me?'

I realized immediately that there must be some personal animosity between the two to provoke such a reaction from the colonel, and I rejoiced at our luck and at the captain's discomfiture. He was the one to fear; we were fortunate that the colonel and not he was interrogating us.

The captain snapped to attention. 'You, sir, of course. But I . . .'

'Shut up, Captain! Get out of my office! Leave it all to me.'

Behind me, the captain's heels clicked as he gave the Hitler-gruss.

'Heil Hitler,' the colonel responded, fighting for self-control as the captain left, closing the door quietly.

I studied the colonel carefully. Timing was everything. His face was now a mass of red spots, almost like measles, as he fought down his anger. I dared not wait too long to speak for fear he would find some way of returning to our papers and the inexplicable three-week gap. I had to take the initiative. 'Colonel, sir, when will we get our food?' Sounding as weak and starved as I could, I presented no threat to his authority.

He eagerly seized the opportunity to be magnanimous, to prove that his anger extended only to his subordinate, the captain, not to us or the world in general. 'Your food? Of course. I'm sorry I can't feed you boys here, but that's quite impossible, I'm afraid.' He placed his hands on his desk and pushed himself wearily upright, then laid a finger on the street map on his wall. 'Here's our HQ here.' Sanders and I pressed closer, both to see and, I realize now, in an instinctive desire to make him feel close to us emotionally so that he would not lash out at us in anger and suspicion.

The colonel cleared his throat. 'Now, when you leave this Kaserne, go down this street until you reach this depot. It's a big grey building made of stone. That's where you'll be issued your food ration.'

'Thank you, Colonel, thank you indeed.'

He sat on the corner of his desk, relaxed now. 'But understand one thing very clearly! I don't want you two gallivanting around the country. You are soldiers.' He snapped the words out as he stood up from the desk and addressed us as he would speak to a thousand men on parade, his voice rising. 'You are soldiers of the Reich. You realize how much the Führer needs every soldier at the front. Our enemies are strong, and they are pressing us hard. We must fight, to the last man if necessary, to the last drop of German blood. We must defend our Fatherland, the holy soil of Germany. We need every man, and that means you' – he pointed at Sanders – 'and you,' pointing at me. 'I order you to go back immediately to your unit.'

Then suddenly he frowned. 'You've spent three weeks here already. Where have you been all the time? These are days of crisis for the Fatherland. Where have you been?'

He was on the dangerous topic again and he was demanding an answer.

Sanders spoke up clearly, his voice edged with surprise that our intentions as good soldiers of the Reich should be questioned. Ignoring the subject of accommodation or food, he said, 'We went to Factory E, Number 11, in

Essen, sir. It was part of our assigned duty, Colonel. It's all there in our papers. We did what we were ordered to. Factory E; you may telephone Direktor Stammler if you wish. He will confirm what we say.'

The colonel looked ready to slam his hand down on the desk again, but he restrained himself. 'That's all well and good, Sergeant. Telephone Direktor So-and-so you say. But I can't telephone. The connections are all out of order.'

The news relieved me. There was no reason for us to fear his telephoning Direktor Stammler, for we had been to his factory, just as we had said, but, if the SS colonel once started telephoning, he might just decide to place a call to our supposed unit, as shown in our papers. Then we would be in trouble.

'Colonel,' I began, 'we want to get back to our unit. We are ready to defend the Reich. But we've lost time already today. We've been here all morning.' I gestured at the clock on the wall. 'All morning, and when we leave here we'll be stopped again. We're always being stopped, all over the place, for document checks. It takes time, and we want to get back to the Front.'

I spoke as passionately as I could, hoping only to stop him asking questions about those missing three weeks. But his reaction astounded me.

'You're right. You've wasted too much time already. It won't happen any more.' He picked up our orders and military pay-books with a brisk, determined air. 'I'll make sure you won't lose any more time. This will ensure that you both get straight through to your unit without delay.' He picked up his pen and scribbled furiously for a while, sat back and silently read what he had written, then reached over to the rack on his right and took a rubber stamp. 'This will do the trick. The SS still counts for something, you'll see.'

He breathed on the stamp and endorsed our papers. With a proud smile he handed them back to us. 'Read that!'

I could hardly believe my eyes. 'The bearer, Cpl W. Friedmann, has been interrogated by Col. Walthers of the SS Secret Field Police. Any military unit is hereby ordered to give said Cpl Friedmann every assistance in transportation back to his unit.'

'Thank you, Colonel,' we stuttered, really meaning it. Then, without thinking, I stuck out my hand instead of saluting. Too late I saw the expression of horror on Sanders's face.

The Colonel never noticed. He grabbed my hand and shook it, then Sanders's. His expression was very friendly and warm. 'Good luck, boys.'

'Thank you, Colonel, so much.'

'It's nothing.'

'We hope to see you after the war to thank you, Colonel.'

He gave us both a fatherly look. 'Remember, the Führer needs you both. Fight for the Fatherland and our Führer. No sacrifice is too great.'

'Jawohl, Colonel.'

'Heil Hitler!' His face gleamed with patriotic fervour.

'Heil Hitler!'

He ushered us to the door. Back in the large rest area where we had left our luggage, I felt my knees begin to shake. My guts knotted, and I thought I was about to vomit.

'You okay?' Sanders whispered.

'Yes, I'll be all right.'

None of the off-duty SS seemed to notice my faltering

step. Perhaps most people tottered out of the colonel's office in a feeble condition. I would have enjoyed sitting down to rest at one of the tables, but knew I had to get moving. The captain might reappear at any time and I didn't want to see him again. He was too smart and would ferret away until he uncovered the truth.

I shouldered my pack, lifted the valise with the radio set in it, and picked up my submachine-gun. Then we stepped out into the street and followed the colonel's initial directions as if we were going to the kitchens he had indicated. There was probably nobody observing us, but we took no risks. After a few turns, we cut across town until we reached the highway heading north towards Wesel.

The cold mist still hung over the fields, and the air was biting and raw. Neither Sanders nor I spoke a word for half an hour. We were too relieved to speak. What was there to say?

At first I thought a horse was neighing and snickering, then I realized the sounds were coming from Sanders. 'Hold on a minute,' he giggled. 'Oh my God, my God!' He burst into an infectious bout of giggling and laughing, and I found myself joining in until we leaned helplessly on each other.

'Remember, boys, the Führer needs you at the Front,' Sanders mimicked the colonel.

'Make every sacrifice for Führer and Fatherland,' I admonished.

The tension had broken like a log-jam on a mountain river, and for several minutes we were immobilized by laughter, our sides heaving and aching. Finally we regained our composure and set out once more along the road. I began to feel confident again, sure that we would return safely to our allies, whatever the difficulties in our

way. As we strode along happily, I kept thinking of my
hike across Holland and Belgium into France, remembering how lucky I had been then, and convinced that
Providence was looking after me.

Sanders, in his sergeant's uniform, was the senior rank.
When we flagged down an army truck, he presented our
papers and pointed at the SS colonel's endorsement. The
driver treated us like senior officers as he invited us into
the cab.

'I'm only going about thirty kilometres north,' he told
us.

'All right, that's fine,' Sanders replied.

We began to meet more military traffic. I would have
liked to make notes but could not in the presence of the
driver. However, I recognized divisional insignia I had
learned in London and tried to memorize key pieces of
information.

As soon as the driver had set us down from his truck,
we found a sheltered spot and made notes which we
concealed in the ways London had instructed us. Then,
in a mood of great optimism, we continued our hike
north, back toward the spot where we had originally
crossed into enemy territory, passing through several
check stops without incident.

Both Sanders and I were anxious to return 'home', but
there was so much military information to collect that we
decided to move more slowly than we could have. London
had supplied us with several normal items that had been
converted into hiding places for the many notes we made
on thin paper. We kept our eyes open and made notes of
every military unit that we saw, as well as its armament.
There were tanks and artillery everywhere, camouflaged
ammunition dumps, and innumerable 8.8 guns mounted

for anti-tank use. The battle for the Rhine would be bitter, costly, and bloody.

Two days later, we were in the same area between Rees and Wesel where we had first crossed the Rhine. Now our task was much more difficult, as we had no boat provided for us and were forced to spy out the Rhine bank for ourselves.

We turned left off the highway and hid until nightfall. We seemed to have left all signs of the German army behind us, and were puzzled not to see any sentries or military outposts guarding the Rhine. Perhaps the sentries were pulled back at night out of fear of bombardment, but, if so, who would give warning of an attempted night crossing? It was incomprehensible that we saw no sentry in the mile down to the water.

Mist rose from the river and hung over the low ground as the night grew darker and colder. It was pitch black when we left our hiding place in a wrecked shed and made our way down to the water's edge. We crouched down and looked around, listèning intently for sentries. All was quiet; there was no 'Wacht am Rhein' ('Watch on the Rhine') in this sector.

It would be suicidal to attempt to swim across. The current was deadly, the water was high from snow melting further upstream, and the icy cold would chill a man in only a couple of minutes. We crept cautiously along the bank, our nerves taut, knowing we would be lucky if we found something to serve as a raft.

But, to our amazement, after only half an hour we stumbled upon a fishing boat moored to a stout post with a thin chain and a padlock. We could not believe our luck. The boat was some twenty-five or thirty feet long, open but sturdy. It would easily take us across, if we could only unchain it. We tugged at the chain, trying to pull it loose from the post, but it would not budge at all.

I pulled out my wire-cutters. 'It's the only way,' I whispered to Sanders.

'Yes, go ahead. But be as quiet as you can.'

The chain was thicker than any wire the cutters were designed for, but I had to try. I set my gun and luggage down and looked at Sanders. He nodded and turned away, sub-machine-gun at the ready.

I leaned on the wire-cutters with as much force as I could muster. With a crack like a rifle firing, the link broke and I wrested the chain free.

We waited anxiously, our hearts thudding, but nobody had heard us. The silence seemed ominous. It was hard to believe this was not a trap, and that at any minute armed men would not spring up all around us and take us prisoners.

'You hold the boat while I get in and find the oars,' I whispered to Sanders.

I threw a leg over the gunwale and crept around inside the boat. I felt over every inch of it but found no oars.

'Any luck?' Sanders's whisper sounded like a shout.

'No, I can't find any oars. Hold on.' I felt around, testing the boards covering the bilges. One of them was loose. I gripped it with both hands, ready for a struggle, but it lifted out easily. 'I'll have to break it,' I told Sanders.

When the board broke, it sounded like thunder, and both Sanders and I were gleaming with sweat. But now I had a piece of wood some eight feet long that we could use as a steering oar.

Not waiting to see if anybody had heard the wood breaking, we threw our guns and equipment into the boat and pushed off. Immediately, the current caught us and swung the boat round in several complete circles before I controlled our progress with the board. Once I had the boat under control, I started to steer it across the current, edging it little by little toward the far bank.

'Keep your head down!' I hissed at Sanders. To present the smallest possible silhouette, I knelt at the stern of the boat with only my head and shoulders showing.

After about ten minutes I calculated that we were more than halfway across, with the west bank now showing more clearly that the east. A few more minutes to safety, I thought. I'm pretty certain there are no German troops on this side.

Suddenly, the silence was rent by the roar of a powerful engine. From upstream the din came closer and closer.

'What the hell?' Sanders yelled.

'I don't know. Get down!'

Out of the darkness, an amphibian tank roared past close to us at tremendous speed. I couldn't tell whether it was British or German. Then the wash from it caught us, and I fought in vain to prevent our boat veering around. As I struggled with the board, I tried to make sense of what I had seen and concluded it was just coincidence that the noisy monster had loomed out of the darkness and nearly run us down. There had been no hesitation in its speed to indicate that we had even been seen.

My brief attempt to bring our boat back on course came to an abrupt end. Artillery fire broke out from the British side, whether in response to the amphibian tank's noisy progress or not I couldn't say, and I flung myself down beside Sanders as our world went mad. The boat, with no one to steer it, spun in wide circles in the powerful Rhine current and the wash of the amphibian. The air was filled with the flash and explosion of bursting shells all around us.

For what was probably only half a minute but seemed much longer, I lay terrified on the bottom of the boat, my arms around my head, praying for the shelling to stop. The irony of having come this far, only to be bombarded by our allies, failed to amuse me.

As suddenly as the bombardment had started, every gun fell silent. The night was deadly quiet. I lifted my head slowly and risked a cautious glance over the gunwale, half expecting the firing to start up again at any second.

But there were no more shots. I could make out nothing because of the boat's spinning. I grabbed the board and slowly brought the craft under control, until I saw with relief the west bank of the Rhine growing closer and closer.

'Just a few more minutes,' I whispered to Sanders, at the same time saying a silent prayer that the British or Canadians would not be so trigger-happy that they would fire on sight.

With a jarring crunch, the boat stopped dead a hundred yards or so from the bank.

'What's the matter?' Sanders asked.

'We've run aground, hit a sandbank probably.'

'How do we get the boat off?' His voice was shaky.

'We can't. It's stuck fast.'

'What now, then?'

'There's only one way. We can't back off, because the boat's stuck fast. But the water is shallow here; we'll have to get out and wade ashore.'

'Okay. I guess we've no choice.' He sounded close to panic.

The water was chest-deep but chillingly cold, and the current tugged threateningly at us. One slip and we would be carried away. Holding our guns and the bags containing the precious information above our heads, we set off for the shore. The icy water penetrated our clothes in seconds, but we had to move warily, feeling for each foothold and praying that there were no holes or channels between us and the bank.

At last we made it to shore, and I sat down gratefully beside our equipment. I glanced at my watch. The whole crossing had taken slightly over twenty minutes. Sanders flopped down on the ground beside me. At first I thought he was exhausted, until I heard him sobbing and crying to himself.

'What's the matter?' I asked, puzzled. 'Come on, we've just about made it home.'

'I can't go any further.'

'Why not?'

'What about the minefields?'

'What minefields?'

'There are minefields here, I know it.'

I don't know if he really knew about any minefields, or whether the stress of the past three weeks had finally caught up with him. I felt close to breaking myself. 'I don't care about any effing minefields. We don't have any choice. We can't just stay here. There's only one way, and that's to keep on going.'

'I can't go any further.'

Too tense myself to argue further, I grabbed him by the arm and pulled him to his feet. 'We're going,' I said, pushing his equipment into his hands. 'Come on.'

For a mile or so I dragged him along with me across the fields by the river. Then, as we walked, Sanders began to regain his nerve. 'Sorry about that,' he apologized.

'It's nothing,' I whispered back. 'Sshh! Quiet!' I had just noticed a figure ahead of us, silhouetted against the sky.

He saw us too. 'Halt!' he screamed.

We were in a dilemma. The way he pronounced the word could be either German or English. He has to be English, I told myself. There can't be any Germans left west of the Rhine. The shadow pointed a rifle at us.

'Corporal! Corporal! Hey, Corporal!' he yelled.

With great relief, Sanders and I dropped our guns and raised our hands high in the air. Shivering in my wet uniform, I still felt a great sense of relief. We were among friends again. Within seconds some fifteen or twenty soldiers rushed up and surrounded us, pointing their rifles at us threateningly. We said nothing.

When the corporal arrived, Sanders addressed him formally. 'Corporal, would you please call your commanding officer?'

'Why? Why should we do that?'

'Please, will you do as I ask you?'

At this the corporal grew very confused. It was not difficult to guess what was passing through his mind. Before him he saw two captured German soldiers in everyday German uniforms, yet one of them spoke to him in perfect English with a tone of authority, giving him orders.

Being a sensible soldier, he passed the responsibility higher up. He ordered us to be taken to a tent and guarded by two armed soldiers, while he went in search of an officer.

A few minutes later, a lieutenant came into the tent, 'Now, what's the trouble?' he inquired.

Sanders replied, 'Please, will you contact your intelligence officer?'

'Why?'

'Please will you do so, because I'm asking you and it's very important.' Sanders's voice showed an edge of impatience. We were both shivering and cold, with no prospect of getting dry and warm. I thought of the mass of military intelligence we had accumulated and felt like Sanders; the sooner we could pass it on, the more use it would prove to be.

The lieutenant went out of the tent looking very dubious, but within half an hour an intelligence captain came in to see us.

Sanders quickly told him that we were working for the British. 'Please contact London,' he requested, giving the address and our code word to include in his message.

'Okay, I'll give it a shot, just as you ask,' the intelligence officer replied. 'But, until I hear otherwise, you are still a couple of German soldiers.'

'That's fine. As long as you get the message off as quickly as possible. It's very urgent.'

We spent the next hour shivering as we waited. One of the soldiers guarding us gave us cigarettes – our own were ruined when we waded ashore – and we sat on the ground smoking, saying nothing while steam rose from our uniforms.

'Well, this is a surprise! A real surprise!' The intelligence officer was very friendly now. 'You chaps can go now,' he told the guards. 'Put them down here,' he commanded a soldier who was carrying a pile of clothing.

Thankfully Sanders and I stripped off our sodden clothing and towelled ourselves dry, while the captain chatted away amiably. It was a delight to get into dry clothes again, even if the uniforms did not fit too well. We made arrangements to have our luggage taken to our billet, but hung on to the notes of military intelligence.

Led by the captain, we went over to the large farmhouse used as a headquarters by this unit. There, we each took a hot bath and ate a delicious meal. All the while, the captain chatted away, clearly delighted with an aspect of his work that was out of the ordinary. 'I'm to send you up to Divisional HQ first thing in the morning,' he informed us. 'But we have a room for you here tonight. I suppose it's a great relief to be back.'

We agreed, sleepy from the warm bath and the good meal. But when the captain showed us to our room and we lay down, neither of us could sleep. Instead, we talked for hours about our mission, how lucky we had been, how we never expected to survive, how we had been shaken by the interrogation at Oberhausen. Gradually we felt the strain of living a lie falling away from us. When a soldier brought us breakfast on a tray in the morning, we both burst out into uproarious laughter at the sheer luxuriousness after our recent experiences. The soldier glanced at us suspiciously and fled, no doubt believing we were either shell-shock victims or madmen.

Shortly before eight o'clock, a Canadian driver called for us in a greenish-grey Dodge car. He drove us to Divisional HQ and ushered us into Major Smith's office. We shook hands with this officer, whom neither of us had met before, and our debriefing began.

At first, the stout little major grilled us thoroughly about the anti-tank weapons and made extensive notes. He knew his job and dredged every last piece of information from our memories. He kept on until he was satisfied we knew no more on that topic.

When we moved on to the details of troop strengths and movements we had observed beween Oberhausen and Wesel, he grew even more interested. Sanders and I produced the notes we had made and hidden, and laid them on his desk.

'I say! Have you chaps been writing a book or something?' Delighted, he worked with us to arrange the notes in order and transcribe them. That done, he insisted on going through every one of our entries again in order to add any details we remembered but had not written down. The pile of papers in front of him grew as did his excitement.

Every few minutes he would comment, 'These details of troop movements you have given me are very, very valuable,' or, 'So useful to have one of our men on the spot.' Then, 'You'll never know or guess how useful this information is.'

When we showed him our papers stamped by the SS colonel, his eyes bulged in amazement. 'Incredible, simply incredible!' he murmured.

Our debriefing finished, the same Canadian driver drove us at breakneck speed across Holland into Belgium, and within a few days we were flown back to England and sent by car to a large white stone country-house near St Albans. This estate was mainly a rest centre for agents, and the atmosphere was very relaxed. Although we never spoke of our background before joining the British Service, we were quite free to talk about our missions. Among the other agents I discovered the same feeling of confidence in British security. Many told how their papers had been checked several times without arousing comment. Everybody laughed uproariously when Sanders and I re-enacted the scene at Oberhausen where the SS colonel interviewed us.

Other agents, too, had survived tight situations. A Dutchman was parachuted into Holland as a radio operator. Stopped by a German patrol as he made his way to his area, he was ordered to open up his luggage.

'What's that?' the soldier asked, pointing at the radio set.

'It's an electonic device, a bit like a voltmeter. We use it for checking circuits and things. As you see from my papers, I'm an electrician.'

'That's okay. You may pass,' the sentry replied, waving him through.

One agent had parachuted into Germany, landing in a tree and cutting his leg badly. He hobbled to the nearest farmhouse and asked for help, but the farmer immediately reported him and he was tried and found guilty of espionage. On the morning he was to be shot, the Allies rolled into the city and he was saved.

Another agent was reputed to be very nervous, indeed terrified, of jumping by parachute. He smuggled a bottle of Scotch onto the plane and drank it to settle his nerves before jumping. He jumped all right, but passed out immediately on landing, waking up in the morning to find a cow licking his overalls. He buried his parachute, picked up his equipment, and set off, very confused by his mistakes and with a terrific hangover.

As he lurched along he met a German gendarme and forgetting himself, greeted him with 'Good morning!' In English!

'Guten Morgen, mein Herr,' the policeman replied, never even recognizing the mistake our agent had made. Perhaps he too was hung over.

But my thoughts kept turning sombre. About halfway through our stay in St Albans, we heard the news that General Montgomery's troops had forced a crossing of the Rhine at almost the exact spot where we crossed on our return from Essen. Each day brought news of further Allied advances. Progress towards the eventual defeat of Germany was rapid, and I prayed for Germany to surrender so that peacetime reconstruction could begin. Events were moving so quickly now that I doubted if I would go on any more missions during the war. What would my post-war role be? There was talk among the agents of a massive search beginning for war criminals. I would be happy to work in that field, especially against the Gestapo and the SS, as well as against many local Nazi politicians.

I felt more than a sense of revenge. Germans had to learn of the evils that had taken place in their country; the diabolical acts of her leaders must be exposed and Nazism rooted out. Only then, when Germany was cleansed of dictatorship and Hitler-worship, might she eventually be allowed back into the community of nations with her honour restored.

One morning, after breakfast, while Sanders and I were debating whether to take a walk or use the shooting range, we received a summons to the office.

When we saw Major MacPherson waiting to see us, we guessed at once what he had in mind.

18

'Go to it, boys!' was all the CO said as he saw us off after a few days in Brussels. Beside me, Sanders grunted, 'Go to it be damned! I'd like to see him go on this one.' But we were both exhilarated by the challenge and the danger. 'They must let us sit around like that a while,' I laughed, 'so that we get good and bored, and are willing to do anything to see some action again. How else would we be so damned foolish?'

We went over our new identities, practising who we were now as the chauffeur drove us through Arnhem and Nijmegen to Kleve in Germany. From there, an armoured car with our bicycles tied to its sides took us into no-man's-land. We were to cycle through to the German lines.

The driver stopped in a quiet, heavily treed area that must have been carefully chosen. It was hard to believe we were about fifty miles south of Bremen. The trees stood about us, thick and unspoiled. It might have been an ordinary day in an ordinary year, except for the unearthly quiet. There wasn't a sound. Not even a bird stirred or sang.

'Eerie, isn't it?' It was Sanders beside me. 'What do you make of it?' He spoke softly.

'I don't know.' I was almost whispering. We stirred uneasily, looking about for some sign of life.

'Well, chaps,' the driver called down, making us jump, 'goodbye and good luck. You fellows sure look the part; you're enough to make my trigger-finger itch.' He laughed

at his own joke, but I found it hard to say a polite
goodbye. My German uniform fitted me well, but I felt
odd being in it again.

We cycled down a narrow path to the east, Sanders
leading the way. The physical activity helped dispel the
unsettling foreboding which the quietness aroused in us,
but the brief peace proved to be the calm before the
storm.

We emerged from the forest into deserted farmland,
criss-crossed with minor roads; then, as we pushed on, we
came to a secondary road and saw signs of disorganized
German troop movement. Soldiers came and went hastily
on all kinds of vehicles.

Eventually we reached the main highway which would
take us to the point of greatest German military activity
and concentration. As we kept on our way, dodging
convoys and armoured vehicles, no one paid the slightest
attention to us. When night fell, we camped in shrubbery
a short way off the road, made a hasty radio transmission
to London, and turned in early.

Lying under rhododendrons on the rough damp
ground, I wondered again why I'd let myself in for this,
especially after the good times we'd just enjoyed in
Brussels. The city was heady with a sense of victory, but
against a background of hideous memories and
still frightful possibilities. Prostitutes and wild parties
abounded, and every man lived life desperately, extract-
ing what he could. Now Sanders and I were back in
Germany, knowing that death might be waiting for us on
this mission.

We were up in the dawn chill and ate sandwiches as we
pedalled. But before we'd ridden half an hour, hell broke
loose. Suddenly, heavy artillery fire opened up behind
us, and German tanks ahead fired back as they retreated.

We were in the midst of the battle. The British were overrunning us! Heads down, we scurried off on a side road, cycling as fast as we could to get away. Shells whistled overhead until we had gone a couple of miles, and I was panting heavily when we finally stopped. We didn't know where to go next. Then I noticed British tanks already rushing ahead of us to the east.

'We've been completely overrun by our own,' I called to Sanders over the din of the battle that filled the air. My voice rasped, 'What the hell do we do now? We're surrounded by British tanks!'

'Not bloody much we can do, is there?' he replied between shell bursts.

'Let's go east on smaller roads. We may still be able to get back through to the German side and see what they're doing,' I shouted in his ear.

'Yeah, okay. But for God's sake, let's throw down our guns and stick our hands up quick if any of ours see us, or we'll be dead on the spot.'

'Lord, yes!' I yelled as we set out east again, pausing now and then to wait for tanks to pass, flinging ourselves off our bikes into ditches.

I don't think either of us thought we'd succeed. The 'front' was receding into the distance faster than we could ride and British tanks were roaring up the highway in large numbers. A big push was on. I found I was shivering with excitement and tension. We were too small a target for tank fire. If they did see us, they ignored us as they roared eastward; or so we thought.

A shell exploded in a bare field beside us. We both leaped from our bikes without stopping, and dropped into the ditch. My bike lay in front of me, its back wheel still spinning fast. A second shell exploded into the road just behind us, sending up a spray of gravel, and I heard a pebble ping off Sanders' helmet.

Silence followed.

'They weren't meant for us,' I said finally, but in spite of myself, my voice shook. Slowly we stood up and peered through the settling dust at the crater in the road.

'A bloody big one!' Sanders exclaimed. 'We'd have been mincemeat if that one had got us.'

Silently, trembling, half deaf, we picked up our bikes and set out again. Trees lined the road here and we got only infrequent, hazy glimpses of vehicles in the distance. We could hardly make sense of their movements, but apparently the British were still pushing ahead.

I put down my field-glasses. 'Seems they're starting to mop up. I doubt we'll get through.'

I had just spoken when a British jeep bounced toward us down a side road. Hastily we dropped our bikes and shed our guns on the road, making no attempt to hide. Our arms shot into the air as the jeep skidded to a stop beside us in a cloud of dust. A British captain sat in the front passenger seat beside the driver, his pistol pointed at Sanders's chest. Two soldiers in the back also trained their rifles on us.

'Don't shoot!' Sanders called out quickly.

'We're with you,' I said loudly, 'on a special mission for the Allies.'

'What the hell?' the captain said, startled at hearing us speak English. 'Who in hell are you?' His gun remained steady.

'We're British agents. We must ask you to take us to your CO,' Sanders replied. His voice quavered unexpectedly.

'We've given up, as you can see. Just take us in to your

CO. You'll find out we're telling the truth,' I explained, unnecessarily loudly.

We both stood perfectly still. Tension filled the air.

'Okay. Put 'em in the back. And keep a gun on them till we see what this is. We'll run them in to Division Headquarters.'

They pushed us in, back to back, and the captain barked at us, 'Hands out front.' But already we were breathing easier. We knew we were safe, even though our captors kept us under close guard all the way back. I remembered our last capture by the Allies. 'At least it wasn't dark this time,' I said over my shoulder to Sanders.

'Yeah,' he replied, 'it could have been a lot worse. No rivers or minefields either.' He laughed at himself, and I greatly admired his honesty.

After a poor night's sleep and a lot of exercise and tension, we were exhausted. Our guards looked at us quizzically as we dozed on the way back and I woke when I heard one of them, a very young blond boy, exclaim, 'Well, if that don't beat everything! These blokes are sleeping at a time like this.'

At the field headquarters, we explained our situation to the CO, who reacted very calmly. 'I'll put in a call to Intelligence, and they can send someone here for you.'

That evening, the CO of the nearest Intelligence unit arrived. 'Well, men,' he said, 'I guess you got short-circuited. Can't be helped, and I don't see any way to get you back in. Doesn't matter just now though, with our forces rolling right along. They're going so damned fast, and they're so excited, that they're not worried about food even, only petrol and ammo. They've really got the Boche on the run.

'How would you like to do some interrogation work

here for a while? Ever done any? We can't get you back to Blighty for a while.'

I burst out laughing, remembering my weeks of interrogation in France. I reflected that I'd still be doing it, probably, if the British hadn't come for me. 'I've done a fair bit,' I said, 'but I guess I could do a little more. There's not much else to do, is there?'

'Great,' he said. 'There are some local Gestapo types we'd like you to have a go at, including the alleged Gestapo chief of Münster up the road here. You could work on his case, Smith.'

Smith was the name he gave me to use there, together with a new ID. I wondered what Major MacPherson would say when we got back to him. Probably something about holidaying in Germany. Anyway, I reflected, we may as well relax and help out where we can. MacPherson would have to wait until we could be sent back to England.

'You will contact our unit?' Sanders asked, obviously thinking of Major MacPherson too.

'It's being done, chaps. You'll likely be back in a week or two anyway.'

That evening, we were driven to Münster, where we were to start interrogations. The Gestapo chief of Münster, Schlegel, was brought to me the following morning.

Before his appearance, I was briefed on his case so far. 'Refuses to admit he's the Gestapo chief, but here's his record book with all of the orders signed by him. It checks with his signature elsewhere,' the adjutant told me.

Before me lay a grisly ledger of executions, imprisonments, deportations, and forced sterilizations. Schlegel's viciousness was directed equally against German and alien, any who opposed the Nazis or who, by their genes, might have prevented the purification of the master race. Each page I turned infuriated me more. His record book was a microcosm of all the atrocities the Gestapo and the Nazis had perpetrated on my countrymen.

When the man was brought in, I could scarcely contain myself. His appearance matched the atrocities perfectly. He was a short, fat, balding man of about fifty, his features dominated by a pugnacious jaw that jutted out defiantly, even in captivity. Piggy eyes glared from between rolls of pink flesh. I'm going to enjoy bringing this one down, I decided, and I didn't bother to address him by rank when I began.

'Schlegel, I have here the record of all your crimes against humanity. There is no use denying them; your efficiency is your undoing. Every one of these murders and other crimes has your signature authorizing it, and your handwriting has been absolutely verified.'

I was really overstepping my role, but I was determined to make sure there wasn't the least doubt that this was the guilty man. It would be a terrible injustice for such a monster to go free because of an identification problem.

He was clearly shaken by my forceful opening, and his face paled a shade.

'You are identified beyond doubt,' I repeated. 'Schlegel, this is your record book, isn't it?' He nodded, giving in more quickly than many of his victims must have done.

'Say yes!' He nodded but refused to speak. 'We can use your own methods to make you talk, you know,' I said instinctively.

I'd touched some well-spring of memory. His face went many shades lighter, and he stirred uneasily in his chair. He looked at me fearfully. 'Yes,' he whispered.

'Yes, what?'

'Yes, I am Schlegel, sir.'

I felt a twinge of pity for him then and a little distaste for myself. The man had lost all dignity, but I felt I had demeaned him even farther. The full horror of his life stood between us, unmasked and shared, and I could see why he didn't want to admit to his identity. As Schlegel seemed to shrink, I almost vomited. Hastily I rang the desk bell and asked for him to be taken away to sign a confession. I couldn't bear to be with him again to finish the interrogation.

I wished fervently I wouldn't have to meet any more like him, but the next day wasn't much better. A woman in her early thirties was brought to me. Her name was Helga Sturm; she was very ordinary-looking, but quite tall, with blonde hair. She sat down opposite me, resigned but casual. I was shaken that she could be so cool.

'Your name is Helga Sturm.'

'Yes.'

'Your profession?'

'I am a nurse.'

'What have you done during the war?' I wondered how long this would take.

'I am in the Werewolf organization, but I can see now that it is all over. Since I left my nursing over a year ago I have been chief organizer in this area to train women of all ages to attack you after the invasion. This was an idea of Dr Goebbels. It's hopeless. It doesn't matter now.' Suddenly she began to cry and I felt a little pity for her until I realized that her tears sprang from anger and frustration not remorse. I took the rest of her testimony with tight lips. It shocked me that she still wished to be out there with her gang of harpies, enticing Allied soldiers, then murdering them in their sleep. She reminded me of Janine, the young French exterminator in Isbergues whose calmness had so appalled me. How could people debase themselves so?

After another week, I had only two more interrogations to do and I wanted them over with. My own intense feelings were wearing me down; I wasn't able to distance myself mentally.

I slept badly that night, dreaming of our old neighbour Krüger being castrated because his family's history of epilepsy was discovered; and then, in my dream, a laughing, dark-haired, muscular young American soldier was lured to bed with the blonde nurse, Helga Sturm. She pulled a kitchen knife from her mattress, and plunged it into his smooth muscled back above her. I woke sweating and choking. The war is getting to me, I thought as I sat at the window, longing for the sunrise.

My first session that day was with a crippled Wehrmacht captain. His story reflected another aspect of the demented Nazis. Captain Steinert had been an intelligence officer on the Eastern Front, helping to calculate the strength of the Russian forces. Repeatedly, his sobering estimates were sent to Berlin and shown to Hitler, who had a fit and tore them up. The estimates had to be redone and redone to present a more optimistic picture to Hitler, the result being disastrous sacrifice of many soldiers.

'I began to despise Hitler's megalomania,' Steinert said. 'He should have realized that he was Commander-in-Chief in name only. He was no general.'

Injured in the back by Russian shrapnel, Steinert was taken to the nearest field hospital for an operation, where, in his delirium, he was overheard cursing Hitler. After the operation, Steinert was given truth serum and spilled out his true feelings.

They threw him into a concentration camp before his wound healed, and he was put into hospital there.

'I thought at least they were treating me decently by putting me in a hospital. But I soon found out differently, I'll tell you.'

Camp doctors began experimental surgery on him without any explanation; he was simply wheeled out of his room and anaesthetized. When he regained consciousness, one of his feet was bandaged and extremely painful. Nobody told him what had been done or why; he was treated as a common criminal rather than an officer.

A nightmare of operations followed, performed in rapid succession on his other foot and on both his hands. Soon he was crippled for life. 'And I fought for the Fatherland like any other man. I did my duty, and I was wounded in battle for my country too.'

I hated having to drag out of him information for war-crimes trials. There were tears in my eyes as this poor, bitter man hobbled from the room a mere shell. Still in his early thirties, he had to face a long life of disillusioned bewilderment.

I didn't have long to reflect before the guard came in with a tall, slim woman in her late twenties. As she sat down she studied me with calculating eyes and I hoped she wouldn't use her obvious intelligence to be difficult. I wanted to be finished and gone.

'Name?'

'Lisbeth Fettermann.'

'Fräulein Fettermann, this can be long, difficult, and tedious for both of us, but the end result will be the same. You are well enough known that we will learn the whole truth. I can see that you are an intelligent woman. Will you not agree that it is best to tell the whole truth now? It will certainly help you later if you do, particularly if you show remorse for what you've done.'

It was a ploy, but it was also the truth. We sat silent a moment, looking at each other, while she considered. Perhaps she expected much harsher treatment or torture.

'I have worked for fools,' she began. 'I believed the myth of Aryan superiority because I could see my own intellectual superiority. Now I don't know what I feel – let down, certainly.'

I lit a cigarette and passed it to her. She inhaled deeply.

'Yes, I feel remorse. You can write that.'

I wondered if it was merely remorse for having worked for fools. There was another long pause.

'All right. Here it is in brief. I started out in a bank in the provinces and then went to the Reichsbank, where I learned a lot more about people and their money. After we began invading the territory around us, a special branch was set up to confiscate wealth from the rich. I was head of a division that located the valuables of rich women. They were ingenious at hiding them, but we soon learned all their tricks. They had diamonds and other gems in every opening of their clothes and bodies. We had to strip them to find it all. I think they cared more about those jewels than about their children. We searched rooms, houses, sheds, and banks, and we found billions of marks. Efficiency was our byword; to be better than any other unit.'

'And what did you keep for yourself?'

Her dark eyes flashed in anger.

'Nothing! It was all for the Reich. We found gold, silver, money, jewels. Enough to fill this room and more. Worth billions of marks.'

It staggered my imagination. If this woman and her band of twenty women did that well, then the total confiscated by the Germans must have been stupendous. As I wondered where all of this wealth was, and who would get it after the war, it suddenly occurred to me that the top Nazis might try to escape and take it with them. I fervently hoped they'd all be caught along with Hitler.

I took down endless details from Lisbeth Fettermann, and finally emerged from our offices in the early evening. I leaned against the portico and lit a cigarette. Exhausted, I hoped never to do another cross-examination, never to have to probe again into the sordid details of lives which had gone criminal.

Mid-April. I wanted so badly to be part of the spring and buoyed up by it.

I met Sanders in the mess, and we discussed the situation. 'Let's put in for leave,' he suggested. I hadn't thought of that. We'd had slack periods, but never leave.

'Where could we go?'

'Just away from here would help.'

'Out into the country!' I said quickly.

Two days later, we were driven to the small town of Diepholz, where Intelligence provided a comfortable house. We were the only occupants.

Sanders and I acted like children. Dumping our packs in the entrance hall, we found food and some German wine, and a bath-tub on each floor. We stripped off and soaked and drank and ate, roaring insults and jests at each other through the house.

What a glorious release! Suddenly we hated uniforms, and for the rest of the evening wore only towels around our waists. We sat before a cheery fire, swapping tales and getting tipsy on fine Moselle wine.

Early next morning, I went for a walk before Sanders woke. I was careful to slide my pistol into my belt. There could be Nazis still in hiding, and I was alone. Diepholz was a pretty town, softened by a cool spring mist, shot through with the first rays of morning sun. I walked through to the edge of town, and out into the fresh countryside. Apple blossoms glowed in a farmyard, and a rooster crowed in the morning calm. Balm for my soul, I thought; I wished I was back on our own land. Sadly, I wondered if it could ever be, as I pictured my mother with me in our own small orchard. I broke off a small cluster of apple blossom from a branch that reached over the fence and turned back to walk toward our house.

I took a different route back, and in a poorer part of town the familiar sight of barbed-wire electric fences stopped me in my tracks. I edged my pistol loose in my belt. What could it be? There seemed to be no one about. Inside the compound, the dingy barrack building was still. Probably empty, I guessed, as I walked over to investigate.

No guards, no movement, but as I drew nearer I became convinced there were people in that barracks. I stopped to listen, and heard someone coughing inside. Then the grey, weather-beaten door began to open slowly. A thin, humpbacked man in a shabby grey uniform stepped out clumsily and shuffled off to the latrine building by the wire fence. I walked along the wire to the guardhouse, my hand on my pistol. The building was empty, stripped bare. I found the electrical panel; the power was still on, as I suspected. I shut it off and went outside. How long have they been left like this? I wondered.

The old man had left the latrine and was crossing to the barracks again. He saw me as I stepped out of the guardhouse and threw up his hands in alarm, staggering back, his eyes wide with fear.

'Who are you?' I called gently. But he shook his head, uncomprehending. The gate was locked. I went back inside and searched for keys. The bastards must have taken them too. I went out again and looked at the fence. It was too tight to unwind; I needed tools.

The man had disappeared inside, and I glimpsed a line of haggard faces watching me through the small, dirty windows. I tried to smile, and waved at them to come out. After a couple of minutes a younger man finally emerged. He stood uncertainly by the door, barefoot in his grey, rumpled prisoner's uniform.

'Who are you?' I called again.

'Poles. Slave labour,' he answered uncertainly, but in fairly good German.

'Why are you here?'

'They simply arrested us and brought us from Poland.'

'Where are the guards?'

'We haven't seen them for days. We haven't eaten either, and we can't get out,' he added, sounding a little hopeful now.

'I'll get you out, but there are no keys here. I am from the Allied forces. If you can just wait a bit more, I'll get you out.'

He stumbled toward me, tears starting from eyes that were sunk into his bony face, emphasizing his Slavic features.

'Are you? Will you? Oh, thank God!' He reached out to clutch the fence but jerked his hands back. I wanted to tell him the power was off, but didn't for fear they'd cut themselves badly trying to climb out.

Tears stung my eyes as I hurried away, looking for tools. Fury welling up inside me, I was determined to make some small restitution to those poor people. I thought of the mayor of Diepholz. He'd be a Nazi. A man stepped into the street in front of me, and I rushed up to him, waving my gun.

'Where is the mayor's house?'

He turned as though to flee, but I grabbed him. He began to give directions, looking frightened and sullen.

'You will show me,' I interrupted him.

When we arrived at the mayor's imposing house, I made my guide knock and ask to see the mayor. We stepped inside, and the mayor waddled toward us dressed in his bathrobe. He jumped when he saw me with my gun out, his tiny eyes blinking in fear.

'There is a slave labour camp in your town, and the people are starving. Why aren't they fed?'

'What can I do? I did not bring them here, and I have no food for them.'

'No?' I said and poked my gun in his fat belly. His robe came open, revealing roll upon roll of hairy fat.

'You look starved,' I sneered. 'Let's see what you've got to eat.' I marched him to his larder, which was crammed with hams and sausages, then to his kitchen, which was loaded with other food, and finally to his wine cellar, well stocked with bottles.

'We'll take it all, Mr Mayor, and you'll prepare a feast with the aid of your wife and family. Then, with that fine wagon I see in your yard, you will pull it through the street to feed those poor starving Poles.'

'Jene Untermenschen! No!'

I wanted to hit him for calling the Poles sub-humans. I raised my gun as though to strike and he shrank back, before scurrying off to the larder to fetch the hams.

What a spectacle as we rolled through the streets, the mayor pulling the wagon, his wife and two daughters following tearfully while I brandished my gun like a cattle prod. Lace curtains parted in the houses as we passed, and astonished faces peered out.

As I cut the barbed wire with the mayor's pliers, I explained to the Poles that they were now free and could go where they wished. 'The good mayor of this fair town has personally prepared and brought a feast to you, by way of restitution and atonement. His charming wife and daughters have agreed to serve it.' I indicated our ménage in the street.

The Poles stood huddled in a group, some weeping silently. I had opened the mayor's cash-box, and now, feeling like Robin Hood, I distributed among the thirty prisoners several thousand marks. The Poles shook my hand repeatedly, praying softly over it, and several embraced me too. I couldn't hold back my tears as they made the sign of the cross.

I led them all through the fence, and the mayor's family waited on them in the street. The food and wine vanished in minutes. As I left the scene, they proudly began to sing the Polish national anthem, while the mayor and his family edged away, abandoning his wagon.

On the way back to our house, I stopped at another rich Nazi's house that my morning guide had identified for me. 'I want to see your wine cellar,' I demanded. Seething, he led me downstairs, where I selected several bottles of fine wine, schnapps, and cognac. 'Put these in a sack for me,' I said, laughing in his face. 'Don't try to hide the rest, and give me the cellar key while you're at it.'

Sanders was still sleeping when I got back to the house. I smiled, thinking of a way to wake him quickly. Quietly, I thrust a cold bottle of wine under the covers against his belly. He leaped from the bed, howling like a wild man, then stared disbelievingly at me and the row of bottles on the table, while I sank into a chair laughing. He looked so funny in the nude with his bristly hair all askew.

'You son of a bitch! Where'd you get that?' he asked, suddenly calm, as he took a bottle of wine, opened it, and sank languidly on the bed. He up-ended the bottle and drained it, scarcely pausing. 'Let's forget the bloody war,' he said, reaching for another.

'Precisely my sentiments,' I answered, and we proceeded to get very drunk until well into the evening, when we tottered off to our beds.

It was the catharsis I needed. The morning sun throbbed through my window, my head swam, and my stomach was near revolt. But I felt cleansed by fire. I had been more deeply depressed by recent events than I would admit, and I could see that Sanders was too. We had been foolish to risk leaving ourselves undefended overnight and I didn't like to drink so much. But it was worth it this time.

In the afternoon, we went for a walk. The day was beautiful, and I felt young again. As we strolled, an old woman approaching saw us, and crossed over to the other side. I called to her, 'Lady! Why did you cross over?'

'Because I was afraid of you.'

'Come back,' I told her. When she did, I said, 'You don't need to be afraid of us. Decent law and order is returning to this country.' She looked at me uncertainly for a moment, then nodded, as if confirming something in her mind, and continued down the street.

Sanders surveyed me calmly as I watched the woman go. Then, putting his hand on my shoulder, he said, 'Let's hope it's over soon, chum.'

That afternoon, Sanders went out alone and came back with an American Studebaker. 'Where in the world did you get that?' I exclaimed.

'Requisitioned it. Jump in and we'll go for a spin in the country.'

The fresh country air was wonderfully exhilarating as we sped along with all the windows open. We stopped for beer, bread, and cheese at a cosy inn by the road. Untouched by the war, it was a marvellous haven of peace. We sat in the cool twilight, revelling in the quietness of the parlour.

A little later, we came to a clean, placid river down a country lane. There was no one about so we stripped off and swam, diving deep in the cool green water. The wonderfully sensuous feeling made me glad to be young and alive again, rediscovering feelings that had lain dormant so long. We swam and swam, until we flopped exhausted in the grass to dry, not caring if anyone saw us.

Brussels was as frenetic as ever when we were taken back there the next day. I wondered what our next mission would be, and whether Sanders and I would go together again. We never discussed who we really were or what we'd do after the war. It was forbidden, and we could see the wisdom of that. I doubted his name was Sanders; certainly he never heard my real name. But, despite that, we were friends, had been through a lot together. And we worked well as a team. A friend, however briefly met, was worth holding onto at a time like this, especially if you knew you could trust your life to him.

One night, Sanders and I began chatting with two attractive girls at a table beside ours in a bar. They'd looked us over when we arrived, and now were quite receptive to our advances. We sat with them, laughing and joking, until they invited 'Come to our place for a snack,' and we left in keen anticipation.

Their apartment was in an ordinary building, but was well furnished. They didn't seem to be prostitutes, and they were Belgian, so I wondered how they were doing so well. But we were quite happy with our prospects for the night as the girls poured us drinks and left us while they prepared the food.

I finished my drink and went to the bathroom, but as I passed the kitchen, I overheard the girls talking together in low voices. Suddenly I realized they were speaking German. I froze for a moment, then tiptoed back to Sanders.

'They're speaking German,' I whispered.

'German!' He leaped to his feet. 'Gestapo agents!'

'Probably. We've either got to be very careful or get the hell out of here. You can see how it is they're doing so well. German money.'

'Okay. Let's go. We could be overheard right now,' he whispered. 'Damn! We don't have our guns!'

The door clicked softly behind us, and we hurried down the stairs. Back at our apartment, we reported the girls to the house-officer. Apparently the Germans had left behind a complete network.

Three weeks later, we came out of a crowded cabaret to find ourselves in the midst of a cacophony of blaring horns, and shouting, cheering crowds.

'Hitler's dead! Hitler's dead!'

'Did you hear that?' I shouted at Sanders over the noise.

'Did I? It's the greatest news in years!' he shouted, throwing his hat in the air and thumping me on the back.

All around us people danced and cheered, but I felt a sense of disappointment. 'It's too bad we've lost the chance to take him alive. I'd like to send him all over the world in a glass cage, playing his bloody speeches back at him.'

Within a few days, Sanders and I left for Antwerp in an army car. We knew the war was about to end; word was out around headquarters that German envoys were suing for peace. As we headed for the coast, I speculated how long the British Service would need us.

'God only knows,' Sanders replied. 'As long as there are people who stop thinking for themselves and listen to people like Hitler, there'll be more bloody wars.'

Halfway across the North Sea, we heard that this war was over.

PART SIX
Home

19

'She's not there. She went to visit old Frau Kirstens.'

'Oh, thank you.'

'It's Hans, isn't it? I'm sure I recognized your voice.'

'Yes, it's me, Frau Hartmann.'

She was still uttering surprised exclamations as I headed down the street to Frau Kirstens'. It was June 1945 but the war hardly seemed to have touched my home village, the buildings at least. Rosenberg's store was boarded up, and the paint was peeling from the woodwork, but otherwise all was as I had last seen it four years ago. When I caught my first glimpse of our home, I had known at once that my mother still lived there, as if her presence was stamped into the very fabric of the building.

Frau Kirstens' niece didn't recognize me, but she called my mother to the door. Now, after all the joy with which I had looked forward to this moment, I felt nervous and awkward.

'Hans! Hans, my son!' My mother flung herself into my arms. She seemed smaller, as if the last years had shrunk her.

'Mutti, Mutti,' was all I could say as I held her to me.

'Oh Hans! I was beginning to think I'd never see you again,' she said jerkily. 'When the Gestapo came asking questions, after you escaped from that camp, I didn't know whether to laugh or to cry. And your hair, Hans, it's turned grey.'

It was true. I was only twenty-two years old, but my

fair hair was almost completely grey. 'Don't worry, Mutti, I'm back. How's Alfred?' I asked through my tears.

She slumped in my arms. 'Nobody knows. I haven't heard from him for months. He was called up again into a parachute regiment and sent west. That was the last news I had of him.'

'He's probably safe, Mother,' I replied as soothingly as I could. 'Everything's broken down, and he just can't let you know.' I hoped I was right.

Attracted by the commotion at her front door, Frau Kirstens hobbled up, attended by her anxious niece. Mother and I made our farewell and hurried home. There, Mother fired a barrage of questions at me.

'Why didn't you write?'

'Mutti! The mail is not working. The only things that get through are some military and government business.'

'Was it bad in the camp they sent you to?'

'It wasn't very good.'

'Then I'm glad you escaped.' With that simple statement she dismissed the camp.

'Mutti,' I asked, 'did the Gestapo make it tough for Alfred and you?'

'Oh, they kept coming and coming. And always the same questions. They couldn't believe we knew nothing about it. They followed Alfred everywhere and questioned his friends and the people he worked with.'

'Did they threaten you?'

'Not really.'

'What d'you mean, Mother, "not really"?'

'They repeated several times that we could be shot if we helped you escape or concealed you instead of turning you in. But that was all.'

'I'm sorry I couldn't let you know I was safe, but that would have been dangerous for everybody.'

'I know, Hans, I know. It's a strange thing, though. About a year ago Hauptmann Wenten – you know, he's with the Gendarmerie – well, he said to me one day, "Don't worry about your son. He's safe. He's in England. But never mention this to anybody." Is that where you were, Hans? Tell me, where were you?'

At first, I was too astonished to reply to her question. How had any German known I was in England? How did a country police officer know that? My head whirled at the possibilities. Fortunately, before I was forced to answer, Mother came back in with a bowl of soup.

'Here, eat this. Then you can tell me where you've been and what happened to you.'

As I drank my soup, I took the chance to recover my thoughts. The words of Major Duff, who had brought me almost to my home town, came back to me. 'Don't forget what we told you, Nütt, Nobody must know about your work with us.'

'That was good,' I said appreciatively, setting down my spoon.

'Ah, thin stuff. Just you wait until I can get good ingredients; then we'll have soup like in the old days.' She cleared away bowl and spoon, then returned to her previous questions. 'Where were you? Where did you come from?'

'I was in Holland.'

'In Holland!'

'Yes. I stayed there all through the war. As soon as I could, I set off to walk home.'

'What were you doing in Holland?'

'I was with the Dutch Resistance. Here, look.' I pulled out a false certificate of service with the Dutch underground, given to me by British Intelligence. They had insisted on this cover story, and I went along with it.

We talked far into the night, laughing and crying.

For some weeks I stayed with my mother, letting her think I was looking for a job. In fact I was weighing British Intelligence's offer of post-war work with them. But I wanted to stay at home, to forget about fighting, espionage, deceit, and killing. We had some land and I wanted to farm it.

At the end of July, a parcel arrived from the burgomaster of a small town near Bremen, very close to the scene of my last mission. My mother's cry of anguish brought me running into the kitchen. On the table lay Alfred's military passport and some personal belongings – I noticed a snapshot of us three brothers taken just before the war. I snatched the piece of paper from my mother.

'The grave of your son, Alfred Wilhelm Nütt, is located at . . .'

We held each other and sobbed.

First my father; then Willy in Russia; now, when everything was supposed to be finished, Alfred near Bremen. At least I was at home to comfort my mother. That was the only consolation. I recalled the time we had blacked the SS man's face with shoe polish. The memory wasn't much to replace a brother with.

After a couple of weeks, life had returned to what passed for normal when an official postcard arrived. My mother and I read it in incredulous silence, then sank down onto the kitchen chairs, staring at each other. The card was from Alfred! He was alive and safe, held in a British POW camp. The card said nothing else, but it was more than enough.

The least I could do for my mother now was to ensure Alfred's early release; the British owed me some favours. I went into Hamburg the same day, telling my mother I was hoping to find work there. Using the identification British Intelligence had given me for such an emergency, I got the machinery set in motion to free Alfred. A few days later, he was released to work on a farm south-west of Hamburg, and we travelled there to visit him. His story unfolded between hugs and tears.

His unit was in a concrete bunker near Bremen in the last, hopeless days of the fighting. Some of the men swore to fight to the end, even though they had practically nothing to fight with, but Alfred and several others fled for their lives, leaving their coats and other belongings behind. The bunker took a severe artillery hit, and the soldiers remaining there were all killed. From the personal belongings in the bunker, the crew cleaning up the bunker assumed one of the corpses was Alfred and accordingly registered him as dead. But he was alive, if rather thin and tired, and later was allowed to return home to us.

The war was now over, although its effects would endure for many years. To many of my countrymen I was – and still am – a traitor because I chose to fight for the other side.

I have no regrets. Whatever I did in those days I did from my own sense of what was right and moral. I left the war with many emotional scars. Too many good people, of all nationalities, were killed in the upheaval. But it makes me hopeful for the future of mankind to recall the numerous very ordinary people who, because of their love of freedom and regard for human dignity, rose above themselves to perform exceptional deeds. They chose the path of honour.

I love Germany, my homeland. At the end of the war which had so shattered my country, I wanted nothing more than to settle down at home, find a job, till the few acres we owned, and, perhaps, return to my first love, the sea.

It was not to be. But that, as they say, is another story.